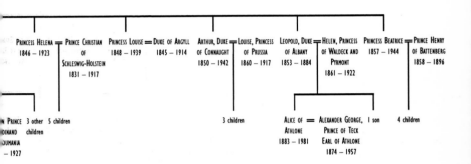

PRINCE ALBERT OF SAXE-COBURG-GOTHA
1819 — 1861

PRINCESS HELENA ══ **PRINCE CHRISTIAN**
1846 — 1923   OF
                    SCHLESWIG-HOLSTEIN
                    1831 — 1917

PRINCESS LOUISE ══ **DUKE OF ARGYLL**
1848 — 1939   1845 — 1914

ARTHUR, DUKE ══ **LOUISE, PRINCESS**
OF CONNAUGHT   OF PRUSSIA
1850 — 1942   1860 — 1917

LEOPOLD, DUKE ══ **HELEN, PRINCESS**
OF ALBANY   OF WALDECK AND
1853 — 1884   PYRMONT
                   1861 — 1922

PRINCESS BEATRICE ══ **PRINCE HENRY**
1857 — 1944   OF BATTENBERG
                      1858 — 1896

N PRINCE   3 other   5 children
DINAND   children
OUMANIA
— 1927

3 children

ALICE OF ══ **ALEXANDER GEORGE,**   1 son   4 children
ATHLONE   **PRINCE OF TECK**
1883 — 1981   **EARL OF ATHLONE**
                 1874 — 1957

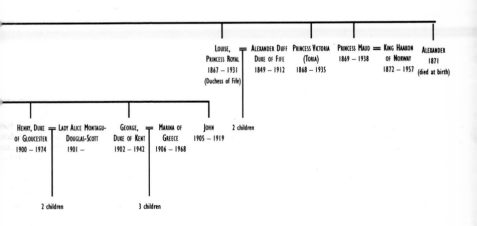

LOUISE, ══ **ALEXANDER DUFF**   **PRINCESS VICTORIA**   **PRINCESS MAUD** ══ **KING HAAKON**   **ALEXANDER**
PRINCESS ROYAL   **DUKE OF FIFE**   **(TORIA)**   1869 — 1938   OF NORWAY   1871
1867 — 1931   1849 — 1912   1868 — 1935   1872 — 1957   (died at birth)
(Duchess of Fife)

HENRY, DUKE ══ **LADY ALICE MONTAGU-**
OF GLOUCESTER   **DOUGLAS-SCOTT**
1900 — 1974   1901 —

GEORGE, ══ **MARINA OF**
DUKE OF KENT   **GREECE**
1902 — 1942   1906 — 1968

JOHN   2 children
1905 — 1919

2 children   3 children

See inside back cover for family trees of Queen Alexandra and Queen Mary

Darling Georgie

Darling Georgie

THE ENIGMA OF KING GEORGE V

Dennis Friedman

PETER OWEN PUBLISHERS

LONDON & CHESTER SPRINGS

PETER OWEN PUBLISHERS
73 Kenway Road, London SW5 0RE
Peter Owen books are distributed in the USA by
Dufour Editions Inc., Chester Springs, PA 19425-0007

First published in Great Britain 1998
© Dennis Friedman 1998

A catalogue record for this book is available from the British Library

ISBN 0 7206 1071 0

Printed in Great Britain by Redwood Books, Trowbridge, Wiltshire

Author's Note and Acknowledgements

M UCH HAS BEEN written about the political and social background to
the reign of King George V. It was not my intention when research-
ing this book to reproduce biographical material already well known to
social historians and their readers but to concentrate as far as possible on
coming to some understanding of King George the man. Some of those to
whom I mentioned the project objected to it on the grounds that what
little was known (to them) of the King suggested that he was dull
and uninteresting – and why had I not chosen to write about some more
charismatic monarch? To my surprise, the more I read about King George V
the more familiar he seemed to me to be. I felt that I knew him. I recognized his mannerisms, his style, his hopes and aspirations for himself and
his family, his morality and his view of the world, in the adults with whom I
had grown up. He ceased to be a stranger to me and metamorphosed into
my old headmaster – whose views on discipline and good behaviour
(respect for elders) were firmly expressed every morning in assembly –
and reminded me of my father. His was a world with which I was familiar.
From then on I had only to think of my childhood to understand and
empathize with the views of the Sailor King. That he was a 'product of his
time' confirms rather than belittles all that he stood for.

I am grateful to my publisher Peter Owen who suggested the work to
me and to the librarians at the London Library and the British Library who
were unstinting in their professional help. Among the many books con-
sulted for the historical background I am particularly indebted to, among
others, Sir Harold Nicolson for his official biography of King George V,
Kenneth Rose for *King George V*, Dennis Judd for *George V*, John Gore for
the official biography of King George V which was commissioned by

Queen Mary soon after her husband's death, James Pope-Hennessy's *Queen Mary* and Georgina Battiscombe's *Queen Alexandra*. The official biographers provided access to letters and diary entries that would otherwise be unavailable to an 'unofficial' biographer. I am grateful to my wife Rosemary for her overall supervision of the project and for her final editing.

Thanks are also due to Shirley Conran, Margaret Kaltinnick, Countess Ledochowska, Bruce Robinson, Cecily Engel, Lady Verity Ravensdale, Roy Shuttleworth, Pauline Neville, Lady Odette Dowding, John Spencer, Mette de Hamel, Lady Christine Cholmondeley, Graham Cornish, Father Thomas Bruun, pastor of the Danish Church in London, Ilse Yardley and Professor Hugh Freeman, all of whom contributed either anecdotes, personal reminiscences or constructive help in other ways. I am also grateful for the diligence and attention to detail of my researchers Dr Athena Syriatou of University College London and Maggie Millman.

Every effort has been made to ensure that there has been no infringement of copyright. I am grateful to John Murray for permission to quote from John Gore's memoirs, to A.P. Watt (on behalf of the National Trust) for permission to quote extracts from three poems by Rudyard Kipling in *The Sayings of Rudyard Kipling* published by Duckworth, to Oliver Everett, Keeper of the Royal Archives at Windsor Castle, for permission to quote from letters between members of the Royal Family which are in the public domain and to the Al Fayed Archive for permission to reproduce photographs from the Duke of Windsor's private collection and also to The Times Picture Library.

Contents

Illustrations between pages 128 and 129

The infant Prince George photographed in 1867

Prince Edward and Princess Alexandra with their baby son Prince George and his older brother Prince Eddy, the Duke of Clarence, 1867

Prince George aged fourteen with his mother Princess Alexandra

Prince George with his brother Prince Eddy, Duke of Clarence, learning to tie knots on the training ship HMS *Britannia*

Prince George aged nineteen in naval uniform, 1884

The Princes Eddy (left) and George while in the Navy

Prince George and Princess May of Teck, taken on their wedding day, 6 July 1893

Framed portrait of King George V's wife, Queen Mary, 1911

Prince George in naval uniform, signed 'Papa, 1896'

King George V's children, clockwise from top left: Prince Bertie (the future George VI), Edward, Prince of Wales, Prince Henry, Prince George, Princess May and Prince John, 1916

King George with Major-General H. Hudson cheered by men of the 25th Infantry Brigade, Fouquereuil, France, 11 August 1916

King George visiting war graves in Belgium with Rudyard Kipling, c. 1925

King George and Queen Mary during a shooting party at Sandringham, c. 1934

King George making the first ever Christmas broadcast in 1934

King George's last journey; his subjects pay their respects at Littleport, near Ely, as the royal train bearing the late King's body passes by on its way from Sandringham to London, January 1936

The Man Behind the Monarch

PRINCE GEORGE FREDERICK Ernest Albert, born 3 June 1865, was the second son of Princess Alexandra and Prince Edward and the grandson of Queen Victoria. Had greatness not been thrust upon him by the tragic death of his older brother, Prince Albert (Eddy), at the age of twenty-eight, King George V, a much loved monarch believed by many of his subjects to have been appointed by God, would not have acceded to the throne.

Prince George's mother, the society beauty and fashionplate Alexandra, Princess of Wales, held a place in the public affection similar to that of Princess Diana who, more than a century later, was to be granted the same title. Unlike Princess Diana, however, Princess Alexandra was not pursued by the press in order to satisfy the insatiable demands of the public, and her private life remained her own. While Princess Diana turned to those victimized by society to fulfil her needs, Princess Alexandra looked to her two sons to compensate her for the love that her husband, the philandering Prince Edward, was unable to give her. Her younger son, Prince George, was her blue-eyed 'Georgie dearest' and she was his 'Motherdear'. She remained so until her death in 1925, when King George was fifty-eight.

The stifling demands of his smothering mother, and the lacuna left by the frequent absences of his father, were profoundly to influence the life of King George V of the House of Saxe-Coburg-Gotha (later Windsor). Despite the fact that his Empire 'on which the sun never set' encompassed a quarter of the world's surface – an area greater than that ruled over by any other British monarch before or since – he remained a remote figure and the very model of a national patriarch, known intimately only to a privileged few.

Five foot seven inches tall, spare, kindly-eyed, rosy-cheeked, neatly bearded and inadequately educated, King George V was a man of few social graces, mediocre intellect (his artistic aspirations rose no higher than his favourite musical *Rose Marie*) and few words. His image is captured in formal portraits, dressed in naval uniform, in the field with a cocked gun in his hands or by the side of the only other woman in his life, the firmly corseted, statuesque, bejewelled, coifed and toqued Queen Mary (Princess May of Teck), the intended bride of his deceased brother Eddy. Always immaculately dressed (when not in uniform) with a white gardenia in his buttonhole, and having used the same collar-stud and hairbrushes for half a century, his creed, according to Edward VIII, the oldest of his six children, was a belief 'in God, in the invincibility of the Royal Navy, and the essential rightness of whatever was British'. While revered by many, and the epitome of 'British' virtues such as courage, dignity, honesty, common sense and devotion to duty, the pious King is usually remembered as an uninspiring monarch, a pale footnote to history, or for his acid comments such as on going abroad, 'I've been there and I don't like it,' and his apocryphal last words 'Bugger Bognor'.

Brought up by surrogates, the King was separated from his mother at the age of twelve, neglected by his unfaithful father and bullied as a cadet in the Royal Navy, an institution rife, according to Winston Churchill, with 'rum, buggery and the lash'. It is hardly surprising that he withdrew into himself, was unable to relate to women, loathed socializing, was terrified of public speaking (he declared the State Opening of Parliament 'the most terrible ordeal I have ever gone through'), communicated both with his beloved mother and his adored wife mainly by letter and communed silently with his unique collection of postage stamps, the majority of which bore his own head. Neat, precise and orderly, he was obsessed with time (he kept the clocks in Buckingham Palace half an hour fast) and when at home followed a ritual that never varied.

The King was passionate about horses and field sports and was a countryman at heart. He was never more relaxed than when killing birds and animals in the woods and meadows of the Sandringham estate or deerstalking on the Scottish moors with a flask of whisky for warmth. Having spent most of his life in ships' cabins, he preferred the tiny, cramped over-crowded rooms of York Cottage, his first marital home, to the splendour of Buckingham Palace.

At the beginning of King George V's reign, peace and prosperity were taken for granted, although the democratically elected government repre-sented the interests of the landowners and the wealthy industrialists, rather than those of the lumpenproletariat whose voice was yet to be heard. Twenty-six years later, by the end of his reign, the King had witnessed the bungled handling and futile losses of the Great War in which a generation of young men had been exhorted – both by himself and his cousin, Kaiser Wilhelm II (now his enemy) – to lay down their lives for 'King and Country', had interfered impotently in the debate over Irish Home Rule, seen the gradual move towards Independence in India and watched, appalled, as women struggled for emancipation at home. In the face of these reversals of the established order with which he was unable to cope, the King, heavily dependent on his mother, his beloved brother Eddy, his tutors, his valet and his dominant wife, clung to his unhappy past. He became immobilized in a time warp, and was, anachronistically, perhaps the last of the eminent Victorians.

So traumatized was he by his unhappy childhood that the basically kind, faithful, good-natured King George unwittingly passed on to his older son David (Duke of Windsor) and his younger son Bertie (King George VI) the crippling axiom of 'duty before love' which had been so rigorously instilled into him. He was inclined to suppress his sons' emotions and was unable to express his own warm feelings until, old and sick, he played nursery games with his granddaughter, Princess Elizabeth, whom he used to allow to ride upon his back. David was so terrified of his father that he had been known to faint when summoned to the King's study, and Bertie was not only a lifelong sufferer from chronic indigestion but, as a result of his rigid upbringing, was afflicted with a stammer.

Naïve yet grandiose, timid yet aggressive, weighed down by his oppressive sense of duty, King George V was a pivotal figure between the hypocrisy and repression of the Victorian era and the damaging 'kiss and tell' of today's liberated royals. Is the real King George V the tormented man – who concealed his true self first behind his mother's skirts and later beneath the robes of state and the braids and epaulettes of his naval uniform – or the right-minded monarch whose misguided attempts to make 'men' of his sons David (King Edward VIII, later Duke of Windsor) and Bertie (King George VI) sowed the seeds not only of their unhappiness but of the catastrophic misalliance of Prince Charles and Princess Diana?

· 1 ·

They are such ill bred, ill trained children,
I don't fancy them at all

O N 3 JUNE 1865 the birth of Prince George, the second son of Princess
Alexandra and Prince Edward the heir apparent, was welcomed
unreservedly by the people of Great Britain. He was christened George
Frederick Ernest Albert at St George's Chapel, Windsor, on 7 July 1865
and was henceforward known as 'Georgie' within the family. In the year
of the Prince's birth, the Prime Minister Lord Palmerston died – to be
eventually succeeded by William Ewart Gladstone – and Karl Marx published *Das Kapital,* which was destined to alter the fundamental percep-
tions of the individual and the state. A few years earlier (1859) Darwin had
sown the seeds of radical change with *The Origin of Species* which laid the
foundation of modern evolutionary theory. During the course of King
George V's life, industrialization and new technology, the decline of the
British Empire and an unprecedented war contributed to the transformation not only of the material world but also to the transformation of the
old moral order.

There seemed no more stable symbol of the old world than the British
Crown. Queen Victoria, Prince George's grandmother, was both the
world's mightiest sovereign and the incarnation of the Anglo-Saxon
Protestant values to which she believed she owed her enormous prosperity. For Queen Victoria, however, the year 1865 and the birth of Prince
George did little to relieve her deep mourning for her husband Prince
Albert, who had died four years earlier. For the young Princess Alexandra
and Prince Edward, however, Prince George's arrival enhanced what was
thought to be a felicitous marriage. Their influence on the personality of a
monarch who was to see Britain through radical social changes and world
upheavals cannot be in any doubt. They passed on the well-intentioned, if

not always well-thought-out, parenting they had themselves experienced.

In the early nineteenth century Britain's Royal Family (the precursor of the present House of Windsor) was, in common with other upper-class families, concerned more with instilling the virtues of correctness and discipline into their children and with suppressing their spontaneous feelings than with allowing them to develop at their own pace in a secure and loving environment. The system of child-rearing to which King George V and his parents were exposed was less impressed with the psychological welfare of children, about which little was then known, than with preserving the image of the Royal Family, that inflexible monolith currently known as the 'Firm'. The 'Firm's' members are expected to carry out functions such as attendance at ceremonial and social occasions and to behave in such a way as not to bring other (particularly more senior) members of it into disrepute.

The rigid and often sadistic upbringing to which King George V's father, Edward Prince of Wales, was exposed throws light on the behaviour of his son. As a child, the Prince of Wales rebelled helplessly against 'blind' authority. As an adult, he contested the morality thrust upon him before he was ready for it. As a parent, he was destined to dump his rage, his lack of self-assurance and the unresolved anxieties of his childhood on to his second son, the future King George V. King Edward VII's eldest son, the Duke of Clarence, died at the age of twenty-six, leaving the stage to his younger brother Prince George. It was to be several generations before the bewildering, exploitive, overdisciplined and intimidating upbringing to which both father and son were subjected would be regarded as anything other than normal.

Edward Prince of Wales, who was the second of Queen Victoria's nine children, was born to a fanfare of trumpets. Much was expected of him, not only by his mother but also by her subjects. The Queen, whose first baby was Victoria the Princess Royal, was overjoyed when she gave birth to a son. Prince Edward was the first male heir to be born to a reigning sovereign for seventy-nine years. He was also Queen Victoria's only male blood relative, since her father, the Duke of Kent, had died from pneumonia when Princess Victoria was only eight months old.

If Queen Victoria was expecting the infant, Prince Albert Edward, named after her father the Duke of Kent, to compensate her for his loss, she was disappointed. Prince Edward was unaware that his mother's approval was dependent upon his being a replica either of her father or of her husband Prince Albert, and he behaved like any other child. He soon discovered, however, that this was not what was expected of him. As a child and, later, as an adult, Queen Victoria had been dependent on elderly, wise and worldly men for advice and support. Prince Edward hardly came into this category and it was not long before his mother transferred the resentment she felt towards her father for leaving her on to her infant son.

The novelty of motherhood soon passed for Queen Victoria, but despite finding pregnancy disagreeable she had nine children. She would not have realized that being pregnant represented more a need to convert Prince Albert into a father than to produce children. The demands of her infants (other than those of her daughter whom she regarded as an extension of herself) were largely ignored. Shortly after Prince Edward's birth Queen Victoria wrote to her Uncle Leopold, King of the Belgians: 'You will understand *how* fervent my prayers are and I am [sure] *everybody's* must be, to see him resemble his angelic dearest father in *every, every* respect, both in body and mind. Oh! My dearest Uncle, I am sure if you knew *how* happy, how blessed I feel, and how *proud* I feel in possessing *such* a perfect being as my husband, as he is, and if you think you have been instrumental in bringing about this union, it must gladden your heart! How happy I should be to see our child grow up *just* like him!' It was not long before Prince Edward found these expectations difficult, if not impossible, to live up to. Not having herself benefited from the presence of a father, Queen Victoria envied her children for possessing one.

In her later letters, many of them to her Uncle Leopold, the Queen rarely mentioned Prince Edward. When she did, she robbed him of his identity by merely referring to him as 'the boy'. She was more enthusiastic about her firstborn, Princess Victoria, her dearest 'Pussy' and on

10 January 1843 she wrote to her Uncle Leopold, her mother's brother: 'She is very well and such an amusement to us, that I can't bear to move without her; she is *so* funny and speaks so well, and in French also, she knows almost everything.' Seven months later, she commented admiringly: 'We find Pussette amazingly advanced in intellect, but alas! also in naughtiness.' Prince Albert made no secret of the fact that Pussy was also his favourite child and, despite the arrival on the scene of her brother Prince Edward, she remained so.

At the age of twenty Queen Victoria, who was insufficiently confident of her ability to cope with new situations on her own, depended heavily on the support and kindness of her uncle. She also leaned on the advice of a dogmatic and fashionable German doctor, Baron Stockmar, who had befriended her uncle Leopold after his wife had died in childbirth. Dr Stockmar made himself indispensable to Prince Albert (a nephew of King Leopold) and after his marriage to Queen Victoria managed little by little to extend his influence over the British monarchy.

Queen Victoria first met Baron Stockmar when she was eighteen years old. He commented that he found her 'unintelligent and unattractive'. When he discovered that he was able to influence the Queen and to dictate techniques of parenting that were to affect the British Royal Family for five generations he changed his tune. Like Rasputin he became the power behind the throne and, after Prince Albert's marriage to his cousin Queen Victoria, the mentor to the English Court itself. The Baron's aim was to restore the monarchy to the moral high ground it had lost as the result of the sexual promiscuity of some of Queen Victoria's uncles, the brothers of her late father the Duke of Kent. Focusing his efforts on moulding Prince Edward into a model of morality, Stockmar laid the foundations for the hypocrisy which became the *sine qua non* of the Victorian era. He persuaded Prince Edward's parents that it was important to suppress their son's spontaneity and to instil in him a fear of his father and his teachers. Stockmar's interference was responsible for Prince Edward's later rebellious attitude to the social mores of his mother's puritanical court.

In Prince Albert's own childhood there also had been no question of 'unconditional' love. He had been only four years old when his mother, Princess Saxe-Coburg-Altenburg, was banished from the Court of Coburg for having a liaison with the Court Chamberlain and was forbidden to see her son again. Prince Albert's adult life was presumably overshadowed by this 'disgraceful' affair, and he was clearly not disposed to tolerate similar behaviour in his son. To have lost his mother because of her love for a man – other than himself (or his father) – when his closeness to her was fundamental would have left him not only motherless but also with a permanent curiosity about the sexual activities of those closest to him.

The Baron's was not a lone voice. In nineteenth-century Germany Dr D.G.M. Schreber's book on child-rearing methods was the nursery bible. Schreber was a popular physician and pedagogue whose advice to parents was to crush the spirit of their children before they reached the age of four so that they would remain for ever compliant. One hundred and fifty years later such recommendations would have attracted the attention of the social services. Although extreme, Schreber's attitudes were not entirely alien to Victorian parents to whom four-hourly feeds for babies, discipline and control, obedience, respect for elders and the injunction to be seen and not heard were regarded as essential. This child-rearing pattern was far removed from that of the late twentieth century when feeding on demand, the minimum of rules and few restrictions have become, for many, synonymous with love.

As an infant Prince Edward was much admired by his mother's subjects. This was manifest in his travels around the British Isles with his governess Lady Lyttelton, the eldest daughter of the second Earl Spencer, whom the Queen had appointed to look after him. Prince Edward was growing up to be quiet and dreamy and often seemed lost in a fantasy world, possibly because the real world did not provide the love and attention to which every child is entitled. A nervous boy, he was unable to bond with a mother whose own views on child-rearing were overruled by those of the ever-present Baron Stockmar. The Prince found great comfort, however, in the hands-on mothering of Lady Lyttleton who loved and protected him and also, whenever the royal entourage toured the country, in the admiration of the people. The seeds of love and attention were sown not in the arms of a loving and attentive mother but in the arms of a surrogate. They were later to germinate when, as a young adult, Prince Edward demonstrated an insatiable need for stimulating input from women. This need forced him into a life-style that distracted him from attending to the needs of his wife and children.

By the age of six, when his formal education began, Prince Edward had grown up to be ever more distant from his mother. He was to become more directly under the influence of his father who thought nothing of beating him if he was 'noisy' and of Baron Stockmar. Having given responsibility to Lady Lyttleton for her son's care in the nursery, Queen Victoria now decided that the time had come for him 'to be given over *entirely* to the Tutors' and 'taken *entirely away* from the women'. Lady Beauvais, a sister-in-law of Lord Melbourne, the Prime Minister, is quoted in the diaries of Charles Greville on January 1848 as having overheard the Queen commenting that '[Edward] is a stupid boy'. Greville, clerk of the Privy Council from 1821 to 1859 and very much involved in the day-to-day events of the royal household, elaborated on this gossip by adding 'that the hereditary and unfailing antipathy of our Sovereign to their Heirs Apparent seems thus early to be taking root, and the Queen does not much like the child' (Cowles, 1956). Another entry in Greville's diary, five years later, on 4 April 1853, quotes the eleven-year-old Prince's governess, Lady Lyttleton, now the Queen's Lady-of-the-Bedchamber and well placed to know, reporting to Greville that the Queen was 'severe in her manner, and a strict disciplinarian in the family'. The Queen may have been 'ecstatic' when her son was born but her interest in him seemed steadily to be waning.

If Prince Edward felt unloved at home, this was reinforced by his fear of the highly critical Baron Stockmar. By the time Edward was seven, Stockmar advised his parents that Henry Birch, formerly an assistant master at Eton, be appointed as his tutor. Despite his unfortunate name, Mr Birch was a humane and just man. He and his pupil got on well with one another; too well perhaps, because after two years Stockmar persuaded

Prince Albert to replace him with the unsmiling and far more strict Frederick Gibbs, who remained responsible for the Prince's education for the next eight years. Prince Edward, sad at the loss of the man to whom he had grown close, did not take to his new tutor. Soon after his appointment Gibbs noted in his diaries (Cowles, 1956) that Edward was becoming prone to outbursts of uncontrolled rage and that the Queen had drawn his attention to his habit of spending much of his time staring gloomily at his feet.

The once happy infant was developing into a sad and angry child. His hangdog expression could well have been one of the first signs of a depressive mood that was later to cause him to seek inappropriate compensation, not only in his demands for approval from women but also for approval from his sons. While Stockmar's aim might well have been the restoration of the morals of the monarchy, he was in fact undermining them.

Frederick Waymouth Gibbs, Prince Edward's new tutor, was thoroughly approved of by Stockmar, not least because he kept the Baron informed on a daily basis as to the Prince of Wales's educational progress. Mr Gibbs's diaries, however, recorded the gradual deterioration of his pupil's mental state and, when frustrated, his worrying outbursts of anger which he could only take out on his tutor. Gibbs's hope was that in time the Prince would take to him, but he never did. The over-strict regime advised by Stockmar led to bottled-up rage in the Prince. Had this not been relieved from time to time by his outbursts of temper it would certainly have exacerbated his depression, some of the signs of which – apathy and lack of enthusiasm – were already beginning to become apparent. Mr Gibbs may well have been Prince Edward's tutor, but the 'headmaster' of the school for two (Prince Edward was educated with his younger brother Prince Alfred) was undoubtedly Baron Stockmar.

For the next eight years intense pressure was put upon Prince Edward. There was no let-up from the overwhelmingly dull and intensive teaching regime proposed by the Baron and faithfully carried out by his tutor. Although sympathetically commented upon by the courtiers, Prince Edward's ordeal was completely ignored by his parents, other than when his father expressed his dissatisfaction at his son's lack of progress.

Prince Edward was thirteen when he was taken on his first holiday. Accompanying his parents on a state visit to the Court of Napoleon III gave him a glimpse of the glamorous life that he later believed could be found only in France. His nose-to-the-grindstone education in England had prepared him neither for the comeliness of French ladies nor for the grandeur of the French capital. On a drive through the streets of Paris with the Emperor he whispered, in a damning indictment of his father: 'I should like to be your son.'

By the time Prince Edward was fifteen his mother was bored with his company. In a letter to the Queen of Prussia she admitted that 'only very occasionally do I find the rather intimate intercourse with them [the elder children] either agreeable or easy'. Her attitude to her son was one of total indifference. When she did refer to him it was often to complain of his poor intellect. One of many who disagreed with the Queen was the Prince's tutor at Oxford, who found that 'his powers of application were greatly underrated' (Lee, 1925–7).

When Prince Edward was seventeen his birthday present from his parents was a memorandum reminding (and also infuriating) him that 'life is composed of duties' and 'that you will have to be taught what to do and what not to do' (Magus, 1964). As a final insult to his psychological well-being, Mr Gibbs, to whom he had gradually become attached, was summarily dismissed. Because (according to Prince Edward's parents) of Gibb's apparent lack of success in furthering their son's education, he was replaced by the Honourable Robert Bruce, the brother of Lord Elgin, a dour Scot, a strict Presbyterian and a colonel in a Guards regiment. If Prince Edward thought that with the dismissal of his tutor he could at last put his childhood behind him he was mistaken. Colonel Bruce had been ordered 'to regulate all the Prince's movements, the distribution and employment of his time, and the occupation and details of his daily life' (Hibbert, 1976). Despite his parents' ongoing dislike of almost everything about their son – the Queen complained of 'his small head, his big Coburg nose, his protuberant Hanoverian eyes, his shortness, his receding hair, his tendency to fat, the effeminate and girlish way he wore his hair' – others such as Robert Browning and Edward Lear saw Prince Edward as 'gentle and refined', 'well mannered and nice'. In July 1860 Prince Edward embarked on a state visit to Canada and the United States. Not yet nineteen, he was representing his parents for whom the long sea journey would have been too exhausting. To his great delight and probably surprise, he was received enthusiastically, not only by diplomats but also by crowds of young women who clearly found him attractive. On his return to England, the Queen (as ever giving with one hand and taking away with the other), having thanked him for the success of his tour, told him that the credit for it was due to Colonel (now Major-General) Bruce. Having convinced herself of her son's unwillingness to 'settle down' to further study, the Queen and her Consort decided reluctantly that the time had come for a wife to be chosen for him.

Although willing to discuss this matter, the Prince had other ideas. He had recently met Nellie Clifden, an actress (prostitute), with whom he was having an affair. He would probably have been totally overwhelmed by this encounter, having hitherto had no experience with which to compare it. A selfish concern for one's own gratification, an essential ingredient of commercial sex, would have been an entirely new concept for him, since, like other members of his family, he had been trained to put the interests of others first, with duty taking precedence over pleasure.

The horror with which the news of the Prince's sexual dalliance was received was, in the moral climate of Victorian England, understandable, although many in the royal circle might secretly have envied him. The timing was not auspicious. The Prince's maternal grandmother, the Duchess of Kent, had recently died, and his mother was still in mourning, his father was ill with a fever and his parents were afraid that his untoward behaviour would put off any prospective bride. The fearful Prince Edward was forced to confess first to General Bruce, who had been appointed an intermediary by the palace, then told he must apologize to Prince Albert in writing. His father's response was that he was prepared to forgive his son, but he made it clear that forgiveness could not restore him to the state of 'innocence and purity' which he had 'lost for ever'. He also warned Prince

Edward that because of his 'sin' he should now 'hide himself from the sight of God'.

A few days after delivering this homily, and in the grip of a worsening fever, Prince Albert insisted on going up to Cambridge where, since the beginning of the year, Prince Edward had been enrolled as a student. Prince Albert's intention was to discuss his son's folly further. Father and son walked and talked for hours in the rain. Finally, when Prince Edward had expressed himself sufficiently contrite, Prince Albert returned to London. Within three weeks he was dead. The diagnosis was typhoid fever. His so-called 'chill' was misdiagnosed by Sir James Clarke, physician to the Royal Family, who, paranoid and grandiose, refused to allow a second opinion until it was too late. The Queen blamed Prince Edward for his father's death. In a letter to her married daughter two weeks later she wrote: 'I can never look at him without a shudder, as you may imagine. – Beloved Papa told him that I could not be told all the disgusting details.' Queen Victoria was never to forgive her son. This was hardly comforting to an adolescent who had been brought up to believe that his parents had never loved him and who was now accused of 'killing' one of them. He might also have wondered why it was a casual sexual liaison with a prostitute that had provoked his father for the first time into taking a personal interest not only in him but in the intimate details of his affair.

King George V's mother's family was as democratic as his father's was autocratic, as open as his father's was closed. When the renowned Danish beauty, Princess Alexandra, was informed soon after her seventeenth birthday that she was being considered for the role of Prince Edward's wife, she was thrilled at the idea of becoming an English Princess. She was told that provided the audition with Queen Victoria, her prospective mother-in-law, went well there was no obstacle between her and the throne of England. She met Queen Victoria six months after the death of Prince Albert. It was a difficult time for the monarch who was so affected by her husband's death that no smiling was permitted in the royal presence. Unable to show off her radiant happiness at being short-listed for the role of Prince Edward's wife, the most beautiful Princess in Europe felt herself at a serious disadvantage. Despite the gloomy atmosphere, however, and the natural tensions present, an obviously distressed Queen Victoria expressed conditional satisfaction with what she saw. She decided that she would give her full consent only after further in-house assessment of Princess Alexandra, scheduled to take place at Windsor and at Osborne, her home on the Isle of Wight.

Princess Alexandra survived her ordeal. Although at the time a Danish marriage was not politically expedient, after several weeks the Queen reluctantly professed herself satisfied. Prince Edward not only fell in love with Princess Alexandra but saw in the marriage a way out of the gilded cage of his childhood. He proposed to the Princess immediately and was immediately accepted. Because the bereaved Queen Victoria was unable to face the crowds of well-wishers, the nineteen-year-old Princess Alexandra, who had been looking forward to her new status, was denied both a state procession and a London wedding. The marriage ceremony took place on a cold March day in 1863 in a cold St George's Chapel, Windsor. The chilly atmosphere at the wedding was to be a foretaste of the marriage itself.

During the ceremony Queen Victoria, dressed in black, sat almost completely hidden from view. Her son's reaction to her behaviour is not recorded. The 22-year-old Prince Edward had to balance the gloomy send-off against the freedom from his mother for which he had wished for so long. Princess Alexandra's feelings while she was undergoing the weeks of positive vetting that her mother-in-law had insisted on are not recorded either, but her sense of self-worth can hardly have been enhanced. Had she known her husband better she might have wondered whether the 'great escape' from his family, in which she had played a part, would be replaced by a happy family life.

Princess Alexandra readily accepted the responsibilities of marriage. She could hardly have been a more attentive mother or a 'less attentive' wife. Despite the machinations with which she was surrounded at Court, she saw no evil in anyone and seemed to have made a conscious decision to ignore her husband's philandering. Like many other Victorian wives, she may indeed have regarded her husband's sexual indiscretions as proof of his virility. After his marriage, having survived the death of his father and the disapproval of his mother over the Nellie Clifden affair, Prince Edward continued to enjoy life amongst the *demi-mondaine* in London, Paris, on the French Riviera and in Germany.

Between 1864 and 1870 Princess Alexandra gave birth to six children. the last of whom died immediately after birth. While her husband dedicated himself to a life which sought to rectify the wrongs of his childhood, the popular Princess was never lonely. Prince Edward was not short of company either, but it was company that existed not only outside his home but outside his marriage. The envy of his peers and his rich friends for his sartorial elegance, for his fabulous parties and his success with women fulfilled his need for admiration. Even his vast gambling debts struck awe in his companions at the card table, the race track and the casino. Larger than life in every sense, Prince Edward's appetites were gargantuan and his need for sex and food insatiable. In the 1870s he insisted that the custom of leisurely eating and of polite conversation at his table should come to an end. He decreed that at the Marlborough House dinner parties no meal should last for more than one hour. Delayed pleasures did not appeal to him. His appetites had to be gratified immediately. The unseemly haste with which he fulfilled his need both for food and for sex pleased neither the chefs who provided him with lavish gastronomy, nor the women who, with equal attention to detail, attempted to satisfy his (possibly equally short-lived) sexual appetite. In indulging his needs in this peremptory manner, Prince Edward was repeating the pattern of his dysfunctional childhood, when moments of pleasure were few and had to be seized upon before they were spirited away.

When Princess Alexandra and Prince Edward returned from their one-week honeymoon to an enthusiastic society welcome, the Princess believed that a glittering life lay ahead of her. She and her husband were attracted to one another and shared a love of 'fun'. This often took the form of practical jokes. Such jokes were a cover for deep-seated feelings of hostility and were played at the expense of their house guests who were often humiliated by them. While the jokes may in fact have been 'fun' for the perpetrators, it was not always so for the victims of them who were forbidden by the social mores of the Court from retaliating in kind.

Prince Edward could hardly have been more pleased with the Princess his mother had chosen for him. He found her beautiful, charming, sympathetic and understanding. With few inner resources of his own he needed a great deal of input from those around him. Since his upbringing had failed to put him in touch with his own assets (it had in fact successfully suppressed them), he needed to draw upon the assets of others. His new wife, however, was able to provide him with neither stimulating conversation nor with wit, and after her first child was born could not rely upon her looks either to maintain her husband's attention. Prince Edward saw to it that he was always surrounded by beautiful women. His emotional deficits as a child, the vacuum left within him by his parents' lack of love and understanding, made it impossible for any one person to satisfy him, and as an adult it was only natural that he should turn to married women (other 'mothers') whom he often then rejected.

Within a year of her marriage Princess Alexandra had herself become a mother, but for Prince Edward even a live-in and loving mother could not compensate for the wrongs of his past. Although Princess Alexandra was loving towards her overly dependent husband, when he ceased to be her only 'child' he became disenchanted with her. He not only began to find fault with, among other things, his wife's lack of intellect but he envied the attention she was giving to their rapidly increasing family. A downward spiral developed. The more Princess Alexandra was involved with her children, the more Prince Edward felt justified in looking outside the marriage for comfort. The more he did so, the more the Princess relied upon her sons to make up for the love that her husband withheld from her. Their mother's smothering and their father's frequent absences began to sow the seeds of the dysfunctional background in which their sons and daughters were to grow up.

In the latter stages of her third pregnancy Princess Alexandra became seriously ill. She complained of severe joint pains and, after she had been diagnosed as having rheumatic fever, took to her bed. Prince Edward who had only just returned from St Petersburg, where he had attended the marriage of his sister-in law Princess Dagmar to Tsar Alexander III, had difficulty in putting aside thoughts of the Russian women he had left behind. Despite his wife's suffering, and the fact that her pregnancy was virtually at full term, he insisted on leaving London to attend a steeplechase in the country. Three telegrams later he returned anxious and irritated and acting like a dependent child whose mother is ill. Unreasonably, he resented the fact that his sick wife was unable to fulfil his needs and night after night left the marital home to seek comfort in the arms of others who were able, and sometimes paid, to do so. While protesting his love for Princess Alexandra, the Prince was none the less becoming increasingly addicted to the more immediate gratifications of illicit sex, lavish banquets and the excitement generated by gambling, all of which were allowed to take precedence over his family responsibilities.

After her illness Princess Alexandra was left with a swollen, stiff and painful knee. While still beautiful, she was temporarily unable to dance either with her husband or to his tune. Gradually she became aware of a second disorder, a form of deafness such as had afflicted her mother, Princess Louise. Increasingly isolated by her inability to hear what was going on, particularly at state and on other social occasions, the Princess withdrew into herself and devoted more and more time to her children and the simple pleasures of the country.

The effect on Princess Alexandra's and Prince Edward's children of their parents' behaviour towards them cannot be over-emphasized. As a child King George V was indoctrinated with the belief that his mother was in love with him. This later prevented him, out of misplaced loyalty, from making an absolute commitment to any other woman, including his wife.

Had Prince Edward and Princess Alexandra been able to look into the future, they might have realized that they had introduced into the Royal Family a pattern of behaviour which, four generations later, was to change its image for ever.

·2·

Darling Georgie

Q UEEN VICTORIA LIVED the life of a recluse at Windsor Castle and refused
to appear in public. The British people resented the fact that for four
years, since the death of her mother, the Duchess of Kent, and her
Consort Prince Albert, she had turned her back on the country which
nationally, politically, socially and economically was in turmoil. Princess
Alexandra had not expected much from the grieving Queen when her
first grandson, Prince Albert Victor Christian Edward, was born. When,
eighteen months later, a new royal baby arrived, it was hoped that his birth
would win back the devotion of Queen Victoria's subjects, restore her
popularity and have a stabilizing effect on the country.

The future King George V made his appearance on 3 June 1865 at
Marlborough House, London, only two hours after his mother Alexandra,
Princess of Wales had bade goodbye to the last of her dinner guests. Within
a few moments of birth Prince George experienced a second separation
from his mother. As was the custom, the midwife showed the young Prince
briefly to his mother then handed him over to one of the attendants who
was responsible for his physical (and, albeit unknowingly, for his emotional) well-being. This parting sowed the first seeds of the clinging dependency, first on his mother and later on his wife, Princess May of Teck,
which would persist throughout King George V's life.

Four weeks after Prince George's birth a fire broke out in the
Marlborough House nursery. Although the infant Prince was quickly
removed by his father to another part of the building, Prince Edward at
once returned to help the fire brigade cope with the fire. The noise and
disruption could hardly have been beneficial to a baby barely four weeks
old. Throughout his life Prince George's father derived almost as much

pleasure from 'big blazes' as he did from the smaller conflagrations of his extra-marital affairs.

Princess Alexandra was aware of her husband's distant treatment as a child at the hands of Queen Victoria, and she was anxious not to expose her own children to a similar experience. For this reason she was reluctant to allow their grandmother anything other than minimal involvement in their lives. Because of Princess Alexandra's desire to bring up her children according to her maternal intuition rather than according to royal protocol, Queen Victoria found it difficult to show unconditional approval of her daughter-in-law. In occasional letters of complaint to her daughter, Crown Princess Victoria, which were similar in tone to those she had written almost twenty-five years earlier about the behaviour of Prince Edward, she accused Princess Alexandra of being 'haughty and frivolous' and complained that 'Alix shows me no confidence whatsoever especially about the children.'

While the honeymoon period between Princess Alexandra and Queen Victoria seemed to be over, the honeymoon between the Queen's recalcitrant son and his wife had barely begun. The gradual onset of coldness which reflected Prince Edward's need to scapegoat Princess Alexandra after she had become a mother for his own mother's coldness had yet to show itself. Both of them, however, provoked angry reactions in Queen Victoria. Her hostility to her son and heir was never far from the surface and it was exacerbated by his flamboyant life-style of which she may have been jealous. Princess Alexandra appeared to have everything she herself might have had, had she not married the pathologically obsessional and moralistic Prince Albert.

Despite Queen Victoria's misgivings about Prince Edward and Princess Alexandra, both the general public and fashionable society had had enough of the austerity and the gloom cast by Queen Victoria's years of mourning, and they welcomed on the scene the arrival of the glamorous and charismatic young couple.

Princess Alexandra, 'the people's Princess', was encouraged by them in her giddy round of balls and banquets, in her obsession with lavish ballgowns and jewellery and in her vivacious sense of fun. They were yet to appreciate her love for the country and her pleasure in making homes for her family at Sandringham and Marlborough House, two cold and concrete symbols of her husband's inheritance. Prince Edward's insatiable appetites, his gambling and flamboyant extravagances also fascinated the 'royal watchers'.

A little over a year after her return from honeymoon Princess Alexandra became pregnant. The social whirl continued, however, much to the annoyance of Queen Victoria. Reticent perhaps about discussing the pregnancy, either with her daughter-in-law or her son, she found an alternative way to voice her dissatisfaction with the Princess. She complained to the Waleses about the continuing presence in Marlborough House of her youngest son Prince Alfred, who had become one of his sister-in-law's most ardent admirers. Sensitive to any hint of impropriety, the Queen focused her disapproval on the nineteen-year-old, although Prince Edward welcomed his brother's innocuous company.

When Princess Alexandra went into labour prematurely with her first-born son, Prince Albert Victor Christian Edward (subsequently known as Eddy), to her amusement (but to their mortification) all six of her medical consultants arrived too late for the birth. Eddy caused anxiety from the beginning. Small and delicate, his parents were concerned about him, not only because he was their first-born but because he was the heir apparent. His grandmother was always on the look-out for an opportunity to blame her son and daughter-in-law for perceived or imagined wrong-doing. She attributed the child's fragile health to the boisterous social life led by his mother during her pregnancy, although Prince Eddy's fragility was more likely due to his premature birth and – in the absence of the *accoucheurs* – to his precipitate delivery. In a letter to her daughter, Vicky, Queen Victoria described Eddy as 'fairy-like, placid and melancholy'. She also told Vicky that unlike her own children 'all with your fine chests', he is 'rather pigeon-breasted which is like Alix's build'.

Princess Alexandra's possessive style of mothering was probably exacerbated by the fact that Eddy closely resembled her. She felt a sense of familiarity which made her even more attached to him. Because of Eddy's prematurity, she was obliged to breast-feed him until a suitable wet nurse could be found. Since the close bond between an infant and his mother centres on his relationship to the breast, Eddy's later difficulties in committing himself to any one woman would have replicated his early struggle to bond with two women (one a wet nurse) rather than with just one, his mother.

When, eighteen month's later, Eddy's brother, Prince George was born he also attracted his grandmother's concern. Queen Victoria referred to the two boys as 'poor frail little *fairies*' and to one of them as being 'puny and pale'. If both were to survive their tenuous start in life they were going to need a considerable amount of maternal input which in fact they later received, if only intermittently. The birth of Prince George in no way reduced his mother's involvement with Prince Eddy. She made herself equally available to them both. Queen Victoria, however, made herself even more unpopular by insisting that she wanted a major say in the upbringing of her grandchildren. She had written to her Uncle Leopold that her son 'should understand what a strong right I have to interfere in the management of the child or children'. She complained, not to her daughter-in-law but to her son, that she had not been informed early enough to have been present at their birth. 'It seems that it is not to be that I am to be present at the birth of your children, which I am very sorry for.' It was some time before the Queen would acknowledge that her lack of intimacy with Princess Alexandra, to which the Princess could not help but react, was more political than personal. In view of the ongoing hostility between Denmark and Germany, she would have preferred her son to have married a nice German girl.

Princess Alexandra, unlike her mother-in-law, who had a hands-off relationship with her children, was totally involved with the day-to-day welfare of her two sons, although such involvement as there was must be understood in the context of mid-nineteenth-century nursery life as it applied to upper-class families. Whenever Princess Alexandra could be spared from the onerous duties incumbent upon a Royal Princess, the two boys had their mother's company. They took breakfast each morning with their parents, after which their 'training' was discussed with their attendants. This training emphasized the common courtesies, but attention was also paid to familiarizing the children with the French and German languages. Bi-lingual governesses were employed, virtually on a daily basis, solely for this purpose. Queen Victoria was in fact far less concerned with her grandchildren's education than were their parents. She had never forgotten Lord Melbourne's comment about her eldest son, that she should not be 'over solicitous about education as it may mould and direct the character but it rarely alters it'.

Prince Edward was not indifferent to his children. Like their mother, he also adored them and in the absence of more pressing engagements played boisterous games with them. While Prince George was in awe of Prince Edward whom, according to his father's mood, he either respected or feared, he remained passionately in love with his mother until the end of her life in 1925. He always addressed her in his many letters, both as a small child and as an adult, as 'Darling Motherdear'.

The Prince's upbringing was constantly disapproved of by their grandmother. Queen Victoria disliked in particular the freedom given to them by their mother to express their feelings. Being seen and not heard may have been a feature of her own son's childhood but it was certainly not a feature of her grandchildren's. She wrote: 'they are such ill bred, ill trained children. I don't fancy them at all. [The boys] are past all management.' They, however, appeared quite satisfied with the free and easy life-style their parents thought appropriate. There seemed to be little danger at the time that either Eddy or George would end up being both bullied and ignored like their father.

Until Eddy was eight years old, and George six, they were treated in much the same way as their father had been until he was their age. While Prince Edward had had his loving governess, Lady Lyttleton, to fuss over him, Eddy and George had their mother who fulfilled almost the same role. The only difference at this pre-tutoring stage, was that while Prince Edward had had uninterrupted 'mothering' from Lady Lyttleton, Eddy and George were to find that their mother's loving attention was, puzzlingly, intermittent.

Prince Edward and Princess Alexandra were tolerant in the extreme to their boys, but they behaved differently towards their three daughters, Princess Maude, Princess Louise and Princess Victoria. It was not that they did not love the girls; they simply ignored them. While the heir and the 'spare' were important, the girls were left to their own devices. It seemed that Prince Edward's ambivalent feelings for his mother were spilling over on to his daughters.

It might be asked why the Prince and Princess had so many children. Could it be that Prince Edward, presumably unconsciously, was determined to go one better than his father, Prince Albert? Had he seen the Prince Consort as a powerful rival for his mother's love? By attempting to become a father more often than his father was Prince Edward trying to demonstrate his superiority? If so, he was to be disappointed. Princess Alexandra produced six, not nine children and, following the death of Prince John, her last child, about twenty-four hours after his premature birth (attended only by the local doctor) she was left with two boys and three girls.

Having been snubbed by Queen Victoria throughout his childhood and attracted to his wife because she seemed to be the antithesis of his mother, Prince Edward now found that the frequently pregnant Princess Alexandra was becoming more and more like her mother-in-law. When she was advised by her gynaecologist not to have any more children, Prince Edward's hopes of successfully competing with his father were dashed, and it was at this moment that he turned away from his wife/mother not only physically but emotionally. Prince Edward saw little point in encouraging his daughters, who were not particularly attractive and were unkindly known as 'the Hags', to find husbands and to become mothers themselves. One of them, Princess Louise, did in fact marry at the age of twenty-two, possibly to escape from a home life that was becoming increasingly miserable. Princess Maude had to wait until she was twenty-eight and was then married off to her cousin, Prince

Charles of Denmark, later King Haakon VII, whom she disliked. Princess Victoria, the third daughter, was kept at home to look after her mother. Queen Victoria spoke to Prince Edward about this because she thought it unjust, but her son replied that he was 'powerless' to do anything about it. Perhaps it relieved him of the responsibility of having to look after Princess Alexandra himself. Women born into the Royal Family, like those of other upper-middle-class families in Britain, were yet to be emancipated. As the historian F.M.L. Thompson claims, they were the 'unrebellious believers in the dutiful and subordinate role to which their upbringing had conditioned them'. Despite the rumblings of the early feminist movement, despite the support of philosophers such as John Stuart Mill, marriage was still the only way for most women to gain some freedom from the authority of their parents, only to find themselves similarly fettered by the wills of their husbands.

The two young Princes, who were now approaching the age at which a formal education was becoming necessary, were inexorably being cast into a mould similar to the one their father had found so onerous. Prince George reacted to his carefree childhood as if he could not bear to leave it, and his attachment to his mother was so loving, and so refreshingly naïve, that all who knew him remarked upon his happy disposition. Princess Alexandra was anxious to keep her son that way. She saw the social excesses of the Marlborough House set as contaminating and disagreeable but, unlike most doting mothers, made no objection when the time came for Prince George to leave home at the age of twelve, with the educationally subnormal Eddy, for the rigours of the training ship *Britannia*. All this, however, was in the future.

When Prince George was six a tutor had to be found to initiate him and his brother into the disciplines of formal education. This time there was no Baron Stockmar to insist on the most humourless and authoritarian tutor possible, one who could be instantly dismissed if he did not live up to the Baron's sadistic expectations. A benevolent and kindly Reverend J.N. Dalton (father of Hugh Dalton, the Labour Chancellor of the Exchequer in 1945) took on the task of introducing the two boys to the 'joys of education'. Until the arrival of Mr Dalton the life-style of the two Princes was a relatively unstructured one. Their lives were carefree and happy and, apart from the routine of regular mealtimes, they were more or less free to do as they pleased. The vast estate of Sandringham was their home and their playground. The changes introduced by their tutor came as a shock to both boys. Their day started at 7 a.m., with English and Geography, continued with Bible Studies, History, Latin and Algebra and, after a short afternoon break for sporting activities, the day finally ended with homework followed by bedtime at 8 p.m. Such relentless pressure on two small boys would hardly have been likely to impress them with the 'joys of education'.

Despite Prince Edward's unhappy scholastic experiences, particularly with Mr Gibbs, he in no way discouraged the Reverend Dalton from pressurizing his two sons to strive for what he regarded, with undeniable cynicism, as 'moral excellence'. In the case of Eddy this was a forlorn hope. He was backward in learning, slow, apathetic and indifferent to what was being taught. Prince Edward was irritated with his older son's lack of progress, but his mother and sisters thought Eddy gentle and kind and compensated for his father's anger by loving him dearly. Prince George, although younger, was in fact the more lively and he was certainly easier to teach. Learning, however, had to proceed at his brother's pace and he was held back by his less intelligent sibling. If King George V's parents believed that in their concern for the well-being of their children they were righting the wrongs done by their parents to them as children, they were deluded. No matter how much Princess Alexandra might have wanted a 'liberal' rather than a rigid upbringing for Eddy and Georgie, in their unique circumstances it would not have been possible. Queen Victoria's claim that Princess Alexandra spoiled her children by being too indulgent was perhaps just. The Princess was so involved with trying to keep up with her husband socially that it would not have been possible for her to pay anything but spasmodic attention to her sons. She was either entertaining at Marlborough House or Sandringham or being entertained at the country houses belonging to the Waleses' many friends. She raced, hunted and sailed. At the times when she was with her children she smothered them with love, and when she was not with them she saw to it that their needs were gratified by 'sensible' nurses and nursery maids.

Prince George was no more than two years old when his mother began to experience the deafness that not only effectively destroyed her social life but was powerfully to influence her relationship with her children. While Prince George could see and hear his mother, his mother was unable to hear him. The frustration experienced by a young child would have been intense. It could not have been long before Georgie took the view that exchanging letters with his mother was the best form of communication. If his words could not be heard, at least they could be read. As a very young child he might have wondered whether his mother, rather than not hearing him, was in fact not listening to him. A 'mother' who was near, but too distant for the exchange of intimate confidences, became the prototype for the distant love of Prince George's adult life; the 'marriage of convenience' which was arranged between himself and Princess May of Teck.

3

Inclined to be lazy and silly this week

KING GEORGE V was six years old when his formal tutelage began, one year after the 1870 Education Act made school attendance compulsory for all British children up to the age of thirteen. Concern for education came to Britain later than to other European countries. It was to be another twenty-one years before schooling was to be made free for all. This was a far cry from the type of education that the royal children were about to receive. They would not be competing in overcrowded classes, nor would they be attending preparatory schools as did some children of the aristocracy. Like many others in their position they were to be privately taught.

Prince George's only classmate was his brother Eddy, and his tutor was the Reverend John Neale Dalton, the 32-year-old son of a vicar, a curate in Holy Orders and a Cambridge graduate. John Dalton was a deeply religious man and his powerful pastoral intonation particularly impressed their parents, who were as much concerned with his manner, his strength of character, his industriousness and his assertiveness as they were with his scholastic credentials, which in fact were excellent.

Bearing in mind his own childhood experience with the zealous Frederick Waymouth Gibbs, and later with the fearsome General Bruce, Prince Edward might have kept well away from the aristocratic and autocratic products of Eton and Cambridge, or from officers in Guards regiments, when it came to educating his children. That he chose to follow the example set by his own parents says more about the unconscious repetition of patterns of behaviour in families than it does for his prescience as a father. Nevertheless Prince Eddy and Prince George got on well with their new tutor, who stayed with his charges and supervised their education both at home and when they became naval cadets six years later.

The disadvantages of educating two children at the pace of the one less well endowed intellectually became immediately apparent. Despite the interest taken by Prince Edward in the education of his sons and the contentment felt by both boys with their tutor, every time Mr Dalton stopped to make a point clear to Prince Eddy Prince George's progress was delayed. Mr Dalton, officially *in loco parentis,* soon became not so much a father as a mother to Prince George, and the boy's feelings for his real – but frequently absent – mother gradually became transferred on to his tutor. Unable to express the anger that he felt towards his elusive mother, he let his feelings out on to his brother or on to Mr Dalton, both of whom became scapegoats for Princess Alexandra.

Mr Dalton kept a personal weekly journal in which he noted comments about his charges which might have offended Prince Edward. It was clear that he was concerned about his pupils. On 2 September 1876 he wrote: 'Prince G. this week has been much troubled by silly fretfulness of temper and general spirit of contradiction.' And on 23 September: 'Prince George has been good this week. He shows however too much disposition to find fault with his brother.' October 14: 'Too fretful; and inclined to be lazy and silly this week.' A few weeks later Mr Dalton pleaded for Prince George to 'show application'. Mr Dalton took his job very seriously. Naturally orderly and conscientious, and echoing what he knew the boys' parents wanted, he did his best to instil in them some of his own self-discipline. It seemed from his journal, however, that as time passed he became increasingly unsuccessful.

Prince Eddy gave Mr Dalton very little trouble. By nature the more placid child, he was probably less sensitive than his brother to the minor injustices they both faced. For Mr Dalton time was of the essence. He held punctuality sacred and in Prince George to his surprise he found a willing collaborator. Since Queen Victoria had given her grandson a watch for his eighth birthday and in a letter to him dated 1 June 1873 expressed the hope that it would remind him 'to be very punctual in everything and very exact in all your duties', Prince George had become as obsessed with time as his tutor. As King George V he insisted that all the clocks at Sandringham be kept thirty minutes fast. They remained so until he lay dying, when his son David, who was about to succeed him as King Edward VIII, gave orders for them to be put back. If no one had enough time for Prince George as a child, he intended to ensure that he had plenty of time for himself as an adult.

With his father as his role model, Prince George emulated Prince Edward's behaviour as much as possible. He became known for his energy and boisterousness, his high spirits, his outbursts of temper and his 'naughtiness', characteristics that endeared him more to his friends than to those responsible for his day-to-day management. The servants at Sandringham nicknamed him 'the right Royal pickle' and at about the same time the Right Reverend Samuel Wilberforce, Bishop of Oxford, described Prince George – perhaps with his tongue in his cheek – as 'full of fun and spirits and life' (Smith, 1910).

While the young Prince George was staying with his grandmother at Osborne, he lived up to his spirited reputation by behaving particularly badly at luncheon. Intolerant of 'bad' behaviour in her son, Queen Victoria was unwilling to countenance it in her grandson. She told Prince George that he would have to remain under the table until he agreed to behave. After a while she asked him if he was ready to accept her conditions and, when he said he was, the Queen told him to come out. He did so in what he later described as 'all the majesty of nature'. Nothing could have been designed to shock and humiliate his grandmother more than seeing her grandson demonstrating his contempt for her authority before her luncheon guests by appearing naked. Unable to express anger towards his mother, because of her constant affirmations of love for him and his fear of losing her approval, Prince George took his frustrations out on his grandmother instead. His identification with his sexually exhibitionistic father amused no one and he was suitably punished.

Prince Edward was at once hero and rival to his sons. When Prince George was informed that he could not accompany his father on his state visit to India in the autumn of 1875, the almost ten-year-old Prince was both disappointed and angry. It was some consolation to be told that he was being left behind to look after his mother. Already over-dependent on Princess Alexandra, Prince George remained 'married' to his mother for the rest of his life and after her death remained wedded to her memory.

Princess Alexandra was furious with her husband for leaving her at home. It was a slight that she never forgot and from which she possibly never recovered. Thirty years later, on Prince George's visit to India, she wrote: 'I do still envy you dreadfully having been there and seen it all when I was not allowed to go when I wished it so very, very much.' Bored with her own company while Prince Edward was away, the Princess invited her parents King Christian IX and Queen Louise Wilhelmina to stay with her. Both the Princess and her parents were snubbed by Queen Victoria who, firmly on the side of Prussia in its dispute with Denmark, refused to invite the 'Denmarks' to Windsor for the christening of the Duke of Edinburgh's son. She was angry with Princess Alexandra when she decided to return with her parents to Denmark for the winter, taking her daughters, the Princesses Maude, Louise and Victoria, with her.

Left once more, this time by both his parents, Prince George had yet again to be satisfied with distanced love. While he might have empathized at first with his mother's visit to Denmark, since she too had been abandoned, when she revealed that she would not be back for three months – albeit in time for Christmas – his feelings towards her would have been ambivalent. Anger would have been appropriate, but he would have had difficulty in expressing it. Fearful that his mother might abandon him altogether if he offended her, and aware of his inability to cope on his own, he would have had to suppress his natural emotions and allow them to be replaced with feelings of longing and disappointment such as were to remain with him all his life. In the event, the two boys remained at Sandringham in the care of Mr Dalton.

When Prince George wrote to his mother in Denmark, he explained politely that he would quite understand if she was too busy to respond. Her long-awaited reply came from Marlborough House after her return to England on 6 December 1875. It was probably not what he was hoping for.

My own Darling Little Georgie,

Mother-dear was so delighted to get so many nice dear little letters from her little boy, and I should certainly have answered these long ago but you told me not to do so if I could not find time – which really was the case; and I was much touched by my little Georgie remembering how busy his Mother-dear very often is . . . I have just received your dear last letter and I too nearly cried that I should not see my darling boys tonight to give them a kiss each before going to bed. But now I am looking forward with delight to to-morrow afternoon. Sisters were delighted with their letters and meant to answer them. I have got some lovely presents from dear Papa which I shall bring to-morrow. Thank Mr Dalton very much for all his letters which I was very glad to get.

The Princess ends her letter: 'and with love to all, ever darling Georgie's own loving Mama'.

A similar letter from his father had arrived ten days earlier on 26 November. The Prince on board HMS *Serapis,* anchored off Goa in India, wrote:

My Dearest Eddy and Georgie,

As I have not time to write to you each a letter, I write to you both together and thank you very much for your letters of the 3rd from Sandringham. They were not quite so well written as the last ones and Eddy made several mistakes in spelling, so I hope you will be more careful next time. I had some wild-boar hunting last Tuesday, which is called in India 'pig-sticking'. We all rode with heavy spears, and when a boar is seen, everybody rides up to him to try and spear him. I speared one and then General Probyn gave him another thrust which killed him. On Monday I shot a crane, just like the one that is near the kennels at Sandringham. I am so sorry to hear of poor old Nelly's death. She has been buried near 'old Tom' I hear.

Now good-bye dear boys, and hoping soon to hear from you again, I remain,

Your very affectionate Papa, A.E.

Best love to sisters.

What was Prince George to make of the letters from his absent parents? An overwhelmingly sentimental love letter from his mother on the one hand and a reprimand and description of the wilful destruction of wildlife by his father, in a letter that he had to share with his brother, on the other. At the time Prince George could not have appreciated the irony of any of it, but as an adult he was unable to trust women and had difficulty in controlling his temper, most often with his children. His son and heir, the Duke of Windsor, was known to faint when exposed to his father's temper. Prince George always feared loss of control and as an adult was phobic about flying. Offered a flight in 1918, shortly after the formation of the Royal Air Force, he refused on the grounds that it was too dangerous, although in reality he probably feared handing over control to the pilot. His need to stay in control of his violent rages made it impossible for him to invest control in someone else.

Prince Edward was seldom happier than when killing animals. Black bucks and cheetahs, elephants and bears, jackals and tigers became targets for his gun and were substitutes for the many women, often similarly targeted by him, whom he had left behind in England. He told his sons with pride that in Nepal, with the help of 10,000 beaters provided by his host, he had personally shot six tigers in one day while seated on an elephant. Armed with his gun and penetrating their lairs from the safety of the *howdah* he took the animals quickly and by surprise. Surrounded by other guns, there mainly for his own protection, he was able to experience the illusion of power. By the time he was due to return to England the Prince had enough trophies, endangered plant species and stuffed animals (shot by himself) to furnish the gun room at Sandringham.

Twenty years later big-game hunting and shooting parties allowed Prince George similar outlets for his feelings of victimization. As Prince Edward had done before him, Prince George took out his anger at his neglect by his parents on defenceless animals.

Prince George's childhood was both emotionally and physically disrupted. His mother, who constantly told him that she loved him, seemed content to leave him in the care of his tutor for months at a time; his father, when not emotionally involved elsewhere, was occupied with converting Sandringham into a pleasure palace in which he could hold house parties and entertain his friends. This palace reflected Prince Edward's hostility to his past (no antiques) and to his future (his children's play areas were transformed into adult play areas, notably a billiard room and a bowling alley).

Mr Dalton was always there, always available and always supportive. He seldom took a holiday and, when he did, exchanged friendly letters with his charges on an almost daily basis. He never forgot his concern for them and his duties to them. His letters were appreciated by Prince George whose replies usually ended: 'With much love to all, I remain your affectionate little Georgie.'

Prince George was accustomed from childhood to writing to his deaf mother. Despite the advent of the telephone in 1876, he continued to use the same form of communication to keep in touch with his former tutor. On his death in 1936, a large bundle of letters was discovered written to him by Mr Dalton, most of them in reply to the King's own letters. Conditioned to rely on distanced communication for the exchange of affection, he was to remain quietly non-verbal – other than with his children – for the remainder of his life.

In 1877, when Prince George was twelve, Queen Victoria drafted a memorandum setting out the procedures she expected to be followed for the education of her grandsons. Determined not to follow his mother's instructions, however, Prince Edward planned to remove the boys from what he felt was her unwarranted interference. He decided to cut short their home tutoring and send them away to boarding school, thus removing them from their grandmother's influence over their education. Hoping to enhance the boys' feelings of security, he banished them from home – where love was on offer in abundance but withheld whenever social or state duties demanded – to an environment peopled by strangers where they would be subject to harsh disciplines. In so doing he not only replicated his own arm's-length mothering but ensured that his children's eventual reactions to parental rejection would mirror his own.

Fortunately for the boys, the one immature and backward and the other not yet ready to abandon his clinging attachment to his mother – which suggested that he believed she still had much to give him – the scheme came to nothing. The Reverend Dalton tried to convince Queen Victoria that boarding school was entirely unsuitable, at least for the fragile and oversensitive Eddy, and that if her grandsons were to continue to be educated together then the training ship *Britannia* was an appropriate compromise.

Queen Victoria was opposed to the Royal Princes becoming naval cadets. Referring to Prince Eddy in particular, she said that 'the very rough sort of life to which boys are exposed on board ship is the very thing not calculated to make a refined and amiable Prince, who in after years (if God spares him) is to ascend the throne'. It was in fact the very 'roughness' of naval discipline, with its emphasis on the group rather than on the individual, which in Prince George's case at least was further to suppress the feelings of rage that as an adult he passed on to his children.

Queen Victoria expressed concern that as naval cadets the two boys might also be exposed to 'undesirable' companions. It was well known that what was referred to at the time as 'unnatural practices' were common among men denied female company for months or years at a time. Whether she had this in mind when she finally agreed that they could become naval cadets – but only if Mr Dalton accompanied them – is not known. Neither is it known whether Mr Dalton succeeded in his role as chaperone.

Prince George was pleased when the time came to be enrolled with his brother on the training ship *Britannia*. Not yet twelve years old, he was the youngest cadet aboard. Prince Eddy, who was recovering from typhoid fever, was rather less enthusiastic. Their father, however, was particularly delighted. It was his view that no one could be expected to rule unless first they had learned to obey. Presumably he had his heir in mind. Prince Eddy had other ideas. He learned neither to obey nor showed any real interest in his ultimate role. Prince George, although unaware of his destiny, was the ideal pupil, however. He settled in quickly and soon developed an aptitude for ships and their handling.

Although both boys had passed the two-day entrance examination some months earlier, they were later found not to be up to the standard of their classmates. It was Mr Dalton, promoted from tutor to governor, who took them to Dartmouth where they joined the *Britannia*. Their arrival was a unique event. Never before had an heir to the throne (and his brother) been allowed to mix freely with his future subjects. At first the two boys were in the strange position of experiencing positive discrimination. The other cadets, brought up with only fairy-tales as a source of information on Kings and Queens, were curious to know the facts about life in a royal home and interrogated the two boys about their life-style. Flattered at first by the attention, the boys were soon to become irritated by the curiosity of their shipmates. Their father had insisted that his sons be given no form of preference, and it was not long before more negative discrimination followed. Bullying is inevitable in any closed community and George was certainly the youngest cadet aboard, while his brother Eddy, his only possible ally, was fragile and effeminate. Years later Prince George commented to his librarian at Windsor Castle, Sir Owen Morshead:

> It never did me any good being a Prince and many was the time I wished I hadn't been. It was a pretty tough place and, so far from making allowances for our disadvantages, the other boys made a point of taking it out on us on the grounds that they'd never be able to do it later on. There was a lot of fighting among the cadets and the rule was if challenged you had to accept. So they used to make me go up and challenge the bigger boys – I was awfully small then – and I'd get a hiding time and again. But one day I was landed a blow on the nose that made my nose bleed badly. It was the best blow I ever took because the doctor forbade my fighting any more.

Most helpless victims of older bullies grow up to unload their feelings of humiliation and suppressed rage on to other helpless victims. The Prince's treatment of his two oldest sons, the Duke of Windsor and King George VI, was later to confirm the validity of this truism.

At first it seemed that Prince George had found his *métier* in an environment disciplined but structured, unchanging and constant and which, above all, allowed him to escape from an insecure family hothouse peopled by unpredictable adults. For the first time in his life he knew what to expect from each day in which there were no painful separations and no boring lessons with Mr Dalton. His time phobia faded. It became obscured by the gradual realization that an equal amount of time was available to everyone and that he would not, as previously, be constantly kept waiting by his notoriously unpunctual mother. He found himself among equals. He was more or less with people his own age among whom he learned to fend for himself, and for the first time he developed a sense of self-sufficiency. In contrast with the life-style to which he had been accustomed, in the Navy there were no servants: no nursery maids, no house maids, no parlour maids. Prince George was intoxicated with a freedom that he had never before experienced. It was some time before he realized that he was in fact still in a prison but one in which he was no longer incarcerated with only his older brother for company. As the youngest cadet aboard the *Britannia,* he was surrounded by older 'brothers', his surrogate mother Mr Dalton was by his side and 'Motherdear' herself was with him in spirit. His letters to Princess Alexandra and hers to him were his lifeline. Presumably she also wrote regularly to Prince Eddy, but few of these letters survive. The Princess's letters to Prince George were emotional in content and in style and continued to be so even when her son was a grown man. Prince George was aged twenty-five and already an officer in command of a gunboat when she ended a letter to him 'with a great big kiss for your lovely little face'.

Prince George may not have been the largest, oldest or strongest of the cadets aboard the *Britannia*, but it was not long before the hostility for which he had been notorious from the nursery onwards began to surface. His anger took a form that was perhaps overtly acceptable but covertly vicious. Described by sycophants as 'having a keen sense of fun', Prince George's 'fun' was frequently at the expense of others. His practical jokes had sadistic undertones, especially when the vulnerable victim would climb into his hammock at night to find two marlinspikes placed where they would do the most harm. If his father was hoping for one of his sons to be a leader, George was doing his best. He was not so much a leader, however, as a ringleader. Constantly challenging authority, he always took his punishment like a 'man'. His training aboard *Britannia,* represented as an exercise in democracy, turned out to be an exercise in autocracy. Prince George learned that authority always triumphed over the 'little people', however much they might struggle to overturn it, and that authority also possessed a power he envied and which he showed by his rebelliousness that he wanted for himself. As an adult, King George ruled as an autocrat, if not over his subjects certainly over his family. Autocracy was also the aim of many of his fellow graduates. Fifty-six years later, two of them were Admirals of the Fleet, three were Admirals, six were Vice-Admirals and four were Rear-Admirals (Nicolson, 1952). When Prince George was fourteen he graduated from the *Britannia* and almost immediately joined the 3,912-ton steamship HMS *Bacchante* for a cruise that was to last for three years.

4

None of us could speak, we were all crying so much

W HEN PRINCE GEORGE enrolled on the *Britannia* in 1877 he was the youngest of the six naval cadets on the training ship. He graduated in July 1879 having done well in most subjects, particularly mathematics and sailing. His success says as much for his ability to turn his crippling anger outwards and to sublimate it in physical activity as for his examination skills. A less physically robust boy might well have been damaged at the outset by having to adapt to such an abrupt and draconian change in environment. His brother Eddy, although almost two years his senior, coped less well in a milieu that was far removed from anything either of them had previously known.

At the age of twelve, and with little prior warning, Prince George found that he was no longer a big fish in a tiny pond, in which he had been treated with a deference he had taken for granted, but an insignificant fish in the vast and probably frightening pond of *Britannia*. By now he had come to accept that the attention paid to him by his parents was at best intermittent and at worst inconsistent, although his mother's love for him and his for her was never in question. Princess Alexandra continued to make it clear to 'Georgie' that he would always be her baby, that she hoped he would never grow up and that he would always be special to her. Prince George found it hard to reconcile his mother's erratic behaviour towards him with her constant pledges of affection. Had he not had her letters to which he could refer from time to time to reassure himself of her feelings, he might well have doubted the veracity of her protestations of love. The intensity of his mother's involvement with her son ('quality time'), alternating with periods of neglect when family and constitutional pressures took her away from him, helped to produce an over-anxious and difficult child who in adult life had difficulty in forming close relationships.

There is a tantalizing quality to such love, a hint to a child that were he not to cling to its source it might slip away. Having grown up to experience his mother's feelings for him as either overwhelmingly loving or completely absent, Prince George's reaction was to believe that people were either wholly for or wholly against him. At the outbreak of the Great War he was bewildered when his German family, whom he loved, turned against him. It took him until 1917 to accept that they were his country's enemies. From then on he despised them. From the time he left home at the age of twelve until his death in 1936 he saw everything in black and white. There were few grey areas.

In 1879, when Prince George was fourteen, the all-or-nothing attitude to life with which he had been brought up was about to face a critical test. Having been banished for two years for training on the *Britannia,* he was about to be sent on a three-year world cruise, two years of which were to take him completely away from his home, his parents and everyone else (apart from his brother and his tutors) with whom he was familiar. Such a parting from a beloved mother must have been very hard for a fourteen-year-old boy.

In the 1870s opinion was not divided about the influence of boarding schools on children. Even the most liberal held the view that separating a child from his parents for five years and sending him to boarding school, or into the Navy, would make a man of him. But what sort of man? A man who would grow up to value discipline above love; a man trained to obey orders, to salute the flag, to respect uniforms and uniformity; a man who believed that it was more important to be correct than to be fair; a man accustomed to the company only of his own sex. Such a man would one day become His Majesty King George V.

Within a few weeks of leaving the *Britannia* and the friends they had made aboard her, Prince George and Prince Eddy bade their tearful farewells to their parents and sisters and embarked upon the corvette HMS *Bacchante.* Objections had been voiced by the First Lord of the Admiralty (Mr W.H. Smith) and the Prime Minister (Lord Beaconsfield), both of whom were concerned that it was hazardous for the heir apparent and the heir presumptive to travel in the same ship. Queen Victoria was angry at the government's attempt to interfere with the education of her grandsons, a matter which she insisted was a private family affair. She was more concerned with the 'roughness to which the boys would be exposed', not because it might do them harm but because the experience might be 'incompatible with eventual Kingship'. Not knowing for certain which of them was to succeed to the throne made her dilemma more difficult. In the end it was Prince Eddy, the heir, who gained least from the experience and Prince George – who was not expected to be King – who benefited most.

After much discussion with Mr Dalton and the entire Cabinet but neither of the two Princes, Queen Victoria eventually gave her consent. This, however, was not before she made absolutely certain that the *Bacchante* was seaworthy by demanding that the ship be sent out twice in a storm. Prince George's long association with the Royal Navy had begun. It lasted for fifteen years, ending only with the sudden death of his brother Eddy, when George became the heir apparent.

On 17 September 1879 Prince Eddy and Prince George together with Mr Dalton and two other instructors, one to tutor them in mathematics and the other in French, left Spithead via Gibraltar for the Caribbean for the first leg of their journey. Eight months later the ship returned to Spithead and, after a short break, a three-week cruise was undertaken to Vigo and back. The third and final cruise, which lasted for just under two years, took in South America, Australia, China, Japan, Egypt and Greece (Dalton, 1886).

Although there were many letters to Prince Edward from Queen Victoria, concerning the importance of avoiding the 'contamination' likely to affect her grandsons if they stayed at home and became involved with the Marlborough House set, little concern was expressed for the feelings of either of the boys as they faced two years in exile.

In a letter sent from Cowes, where, on the day after the start of the cruise, the ship had put in because of bad weather, Prince George made his feelings known to his mother. Nostalgic and homesick after only a few hours at sea, he wrote: 'My darling Motherdear, I miss you so very much & felt so sorry when I had to say goodbye to you and sisters & it was dreadfully hard saying goodbye to Dear Papa and Uncle Hans [Prince Hans, Princess Alexandra's uncle]. It was too rough yesterday to go to sea, so we stopped in here for the night . . . I felt so miserable yesterday saying goodbye. I shall think of you all going to Scotland tonight & I only wish we were going to [*sic*]. Lord Colville will take this letter & he has to go, so I must finish it.'

It was not only Prince George who found the separation hard. Although Princess Alexandra may well have had confidence in the Royal Navy, its ships and its officers, she knew that life at sea was not without its dangers. When the boys had left home two years earlier for the *Britannia,* in a letter to Queen Victoria she spoke of their departure as 'a great wrench but must be got through . . . I trust to God that all may go well with them – and that their first step in the world by themselves won't be a too difficult or hard one – poor little boys, they cried so bitterly.' She knew how difficult it had been for the boys when they were on a shore-based training school not far from home and how Prince George suffered dreadfully from homesickness. It must have been all the more worrying for her to see her boys off for a cruise which in its later stages was to take them away from her for two years.

Although Princess Alexandra loved Eddy, it was not with the intensity of emotion that she felt for her second son of whom she was particularly fond. Her endearments, recorded in so much detail in her letters, imply an attachment that would now be considered excessive. At a time, however, when the main form of communication was by letter, Princess Alexandra and her second son would have had to confide all their feelings to paper. The permanency of the written word has a power that the spoken word has not. Read and reread, the often long-awaited letters with their messages of affection assumed an importance that was never forgotten. The central theme within them was clear. Mother and son loved one another and found no impediment in saying so. For a male adolescent any physical expression of love for the opposite sex parent is usually experienced as embarrassing and uncomfortable and is generally avoided. This leaves the way clear for him later to transfer his loving feelings on to a more appropriate partner. The so-called 'incest barrier' never seemed to get in the way at least of 'Georgie dear's' verbal caresses. His pre-pubertal language implied a reluctance to grow up and leave his mother. Even when he had reached adulthood he wrote: 'think sometimes of your poor boy so far away but always your most devoted and loving little Georgie'.

With regard to Prince George's emotional immaturity *vis-à-vis* his mother, it may have been that mother and son colluded to enable him to remain faithful to her. Perhaps the incest barrier had been suppressed by their need for one another in Prince George's childhood, and it may be that it reappeared later to mar his marriage to Princess May of Teck. If this was the case, sexual contact between Prince George and the 'mother' his wife became when their first child was born would have been at best distasteful and at worst almost impossible. Whatever were his reasons for wanting to remain a child in relation to his mother, the effect of this on his subsequent relationships with women was in no doubt.

An interesting aspect of Prince George's closeness to his mother is reflected in Princess Alexandra's daily hair-brushing routine. Although it was his mother's hair that drew them together, neither of them would have thought of her 'crowning glory' as the symbol of her femininity and her sexuality. Nevertheless her long hair, worn as was the custom dressed on the top of her head, needed a great deal of attention and Prince George always read aloud to his mother at this time. They both enjoyed their hair-brushing/reading interaction. It reassured them both of their love for one another.

It was not only Prince George to whom Princess Alexandra remained close. She had difficulty in allowing any of her children to grow up. Typically she celebrated her daughter Princess Louise's nineteenth birthday with a children's party. She was at her most happy when her children were babies. Her husband was in love with her and attentive to her needs. She was a beautiful icon representing the spirit of a Britain anxious to have done with the Victorian era, and above all it was before the episode of rheumatic fever during her third pregnancy, which was not only permanently to affect her health but also to change her husband's attitude towards her. From that time on, the couple's boisterous and playful relationship with one another was to be replaced by Prince Edward's exaggerated respect for, and sometimes resentment of, his wife's invalid status.

The departure (in tears) of the two boys from their sheltered and privileged home for a life for which neither of them was psychologically prepared was marked with the pomp and circumstance peculiar to royal ceremonial. The Very Reverend Canon Dalton commented that: 'When HRH the Prince of Wales determined to send his sons to sea, it was chiefly with a view to the mental and moral training they would receive as midshipmen in Her Majesty's Navy.' There were 450 men aboard the steamship *Bacchante* and, of the six naval cadets, two were the Princes. Their mental training was directed towards teaching them to control their feelings and learning the importance of the monarchical stiff upper lip. Nothing is known of the outcome of their moral training. Had Queen Victoria been aware that, years later, Winston Churchill was to describe life in the Navy as little more than 'rum, buggery and the lash', she would not only have been shocked but there would have been little likelihood of the two boys being educated at sea.

One can only speculate as to the effect a different system of education might have had on King George V and on the future of the monarchy. Had he not been a bullied adolescent, and abandoned – as he thought – by a mother whom he adored, he might have grown up to have been a more tolerant father. His heir, the Duke of Windsor, may not have needed to look for illicit love to compensate him for the absence of love in his childhood and may thus have avoided setting a trend, the ripples from which were to influence the sexual behaviour of some members of the Royal Family two generations later.

The rigorous training the two royal cadets received would certainly have reinforced any obsessional character traits which they already possessed. Prince Eddy, passive and lazy, was indifferent to routine of any sort and, like his mother, unconcerned with the passage of time which in the

Navy was of the essence. Prince George had been brought up to be particularly conscious of the importance of time. His grandmother had
impressed it upon him (and also given him a watch for his birthday), and his
mother's lack of punctuality, which had made him so anxious, led to an
intolerance of being kept waiting. The importance of punctuality in the
Navy was emphasized in the punishing daily routine. 'Rouse out mids' at
6 a.m., breakfast at 6.45, 7.30 cutlass or rifle drill, 9.00 prayers, 9.30
school and regular drills until 11.00 and then lunch at noon exactly. The
drills continued, depending on the watch, on the half-hour, for an hour
until 3.30 p.m. The next watch fell in at 4.00, supper at 4.45, more drill at
5.00 and the hammocks slung at 7.30 ready for lights out at 8.30. It was a
programme well suited to the anxious and insecure who take comfort in
structure imposed upon them by others. Prince George took readily to the
restraints of discipline.

Princess Alexandra infuriated her Sandringham house guests by seldom
appearing for breakfast before 11 a.m. She infuriated her husband even
more. On one occasion, shortly after King Edward VII's accession, when he
had engagements of state to attend to, Queen Alexandra was to help him
receive deputations and addresses at noon precisely. 'The King sat in the
Equerries room drumming on the table and looking out of the window
with the face of a Christian martyr. Finally at 1.50 the Queen came down
looking lovely and quite unconcerned. All she said was: "Am I late?" The
King swallowed and walked gravely out of the room' (Battiscombe, 1969).
As a child, even before he had been taught to tell the time, Prince George
would have known emotionally when the gratification of his needs by his
mother was unnecessarily delayed. His cruise to the furthest outposts of
his grandmother's Empire (in 1876 Queen Victoria had been declared
Empress of India), which separated him from his parents for two years,
might have made him ask himself whether despite her protestations to the
contrary his deaf mother had not only failed to listen to him but whether
she had also had no time for him.

Prince George took after his father, Prince Edward, whose reluctance
to be kept waiting caused him to seek refuge in eating and sex and to make

sure that he never had to wait for the gratification of either appetite. King George V satisfied his needs through an autocratic insistence on deference, obedience and service. In July 1899, in a lecture to cadets on the training ship *Conway,* he said: 'I think I am entitled, from personal experience of twenty years at sea, to impress upon you three simple qualities which I am sure, if conscientiously acted up to, will go a long way towards ensuring you success. The qualities to which I would refer [qualities which he attempted to instil in all those around him, including his children] are truthfulness, obedience and zeal. Truthfulness will give those placed under you confidence in you; obedience will give those placed over you confidence in you; and although I have mentioned zeal last, it is by no means the least important, for without zeal no sailor can ever be worth his salt.' In other words his own need for instant gratification would be satisfied, provided he received from others an immediate response to his orders.

Prince George was never allowed to forget either the trauma of his separation from his parents or their expectations of him. The portraits of Prince Edward and Princess Alexandra, which looked down at him from the walls of the *Bacchante's* gunroom, not only reminded him of his duty towards his parents but also towards their subjects, whose enthusiastic farewells at Spithead saw him off on his journey round the world as well as his journey into adulthood. The demands of duty and obligation, leadership and example were all to feed into Prince George's increasingly punishing conscience. As a monarch, his highly developed sense of duty led him to meet his obligations and to honour his debts to society. He interpreted the role literally. Like his grandmother Queen Victoria, he neither shared his feelings with his children nor the secrets of the dispatch box with his spouse. He did what he was obliged to do, no more and no less. Trained always to do his best, King George V satisfied the demands of his conscience, although it would occasionally make claims on him he would have difficulty in fulfilling. His harsh conscience found fault with everything. He held himself responsible for mistakes and became depressed or blamed others for them which made him anxious and those around him resentful.

On 6 August 1879, after the tears of the two Princes on boarding the

Bacchante had dried, the first stage of the three-year cruise began agreeably enough. Two months earlier Prince George had celebrated his fourteenth birthday aboard the *Britannia*, but he had not been allowed shore leave because he was studying for his passing-out examination. On the day before his birthday his mother wrote to him from Paris:

> My own dear little Georgie, – Fancy my writing from Paris to wish you joy on your dear birthday, your 14th too. [Princess] Victoria says 'so old and so small'!! Oh my! You will have to make haste to grow, or I shall have that sad disgrace of being the mother of a dwarf!!! But let me wish you many happy returns of that dear day, which we ought to spend together always. My thoughts will be so much with you to-morrow, and I pray to God to bless you and make you grow up a real good boy who will be the pride and pleasure of us all who know you. I hope and trust you will do your utmost to pass a good examination, too. Already 14 and I can hardly believe it yet. Now you are both so big and old boys already.

Prince George was already being taught that discipline and regulations must take precedence over love.

The Prince was certainly small for his age (in an entry in his diary four months late, he notes his weight as being six stone four pounds and his height as four feet ten and five-eighths inches, but even so he could hardly have been happy about his mother's comments. He was to wonder not for the first time quite what it was that his mother had meant by her birthday letter to him and whether he should take her remarks seriously. She had written to him using the endearments to which he had by now become accustomed. He thought he understood why she had not been there for him on his birthday (the reason had been explained to him by Mr Dalton), but he could not understand why she was not even in England! She had told him furthermore what a disgrace it would be for her to be a mother of a dwarf! Not only was his birthday disregarded, but the first years of his manhood, like the months following his birth, were spent apart from his mother. Prince George was not the only one who was troubled. It was equally hard for Princess Alexandra to see her favourite son growing up without her. Unable to face the loss of her loved one, she devalued him in her letters by making him smaller and therefore easier to let go. Failing to understand her reasoning, Prince George was determined to impress her with his size and, if that was not possible, with his power. From the moment of his departure from his mother and his motherland, his ambition was to command others, to climb the heights of the career ladder and so to impress Princess Alexandra that she would be proud of him and continue to love him. By the time he was twenty-six Prince George had attained the rank of Commander in the Royal Navy by merit alone, but he left his mother in no doubt that he was doing it for her. The Naval Commander was still signing his letters to his mother from 'your darling little Georgie dear'.

When the two boys began to count their blessings, they realized that their surrogate mother, Mr Dalton, was to remain with them (as was Charles Fuller, the valet they had known from birth) and be responsible for their general education (the Admiralty appointed him acting Chaplain for temporary service) during the entire time they were under his care. Shore leave made a welcome break from shipboard routine. On Prince George's arrival at Bridgetown, their first port of call, an elderly woman threw a spade guinea of George III wrapped in paper inscribed 'A souvenir of Barbados' into his carriage (Smith, 1932). He attached the George III coin to his watch chain, and the link with value and being valued, with time past and with time present, no doubt pleased him. The gold coin remained on his watch chain for the rest of his life. When the *Bacchante* reached Trinidad, the next port of call, Prince George sent his mother some orchids, blissfully unaware that the name for this traditional floral offering by a male to a loved one is derived from the Greek *orchis* (testicle) because of the shape of its tuberous root.

By the time the *Bacchante*'s first cruise ended in May 1880 both Princes had adapted to life away from home, although Prince Eddy's educational progress continued to worry Mr Dalton. The two boys worked hard not only at their naval duties but in the tasks set them in the humanities and history by their tutor, their 'guide, philosopher and friend'. Mr Dalton was insistent that the boys keep fully written-up diaries, which occupied much of their leisure time. At the various ports of call sightseeing was obligatory and, as the boys became older, riding and shooting were also on the itinerary.

At the end of nine months Prince Eddy and Prince George were pleased to return to Spithead, where they were met by their parents and their three sisters who came aboard for a brief visit. Their shore leave, involving a return to Marlborough House, was taken up with several visits to the dentist, after which Prince Edward, wary of Queen Victoria's concern about the 'contaminating' effect of Marlborough House on their morals, took the family to spend a month at Sandringham. Although Prince Edward tried from time to time to reassure Queen Victoria on the subject of her grandsons' morals, his mother – who had had a taste of her son's cavalier attitude to 'morality' – was not so easily reassured.

On 22 May 1880 Prince Edward wrote to Queen Victoria, who was in residence at Balmoral, in an effort to placate her. 'We entirely agree with *all* you say about our two boys. Our greatest wish is to keep them simple, pure and childlike as long as possible . . . All you say, that they should avoid being mixed up with those of the so-called fashionable society, we also entirely agree in and try our utmost not to let them be with them.' Despite his further reassurances the Queen wrote to Prince Edward again on 6 July reinforcing the message in her earlier letter: 'I must also return most seriously and strongly to the *absolute necessity* of the children, all of them, *not* mixing with the society you are constantly having. They must either take their meals together *alone*, or you must breakfast and lunch alone with them and to this a *room* must be given up wherever you are.'

Hovering over the family, like a cloud, was the knowledge that in a few short weeks the boys' leave would be over and the long two-year cruise begun. Despite Princess Alexandra's feelings in the matter she did nothing to prevent their departure, although there must have been moments when she would have longed to do so. When the time arrived, the Princess's two little boys, as she continued to refer to them (despite the fact that they were now fifteen and sixteen years old), prepared themselves for their longest separation yet. Prince George was crying when he wrote his farewell letter to his mother. '*So goodbye once more my darling Motherdear* please give darling Papa and sisters my very best love and kisses and much love to dear Uncle Hans. *So goodbye darling Motherdear, dearest papa and sister.*'

The two boys returned once more to sea, but this time they found themselves sailing into a war zone. The *Bacchante* had received a message to sail at once to the Cape of Good Hope in case she was needed in the dispute with the Boers over the Transvaal, an independent Republic annexed by Great Britain during the premiership of Benjamin Disraeli. The Boers, who saw their expectations for self-government being frustrated, rose in rebellion. The British were defeated and Gladstone, who believed that the Boers should have self-government, fully accepted the independence of the Transvaal three years later. It was agreed that Britain would be free to veto any treaty with foreign powers, that there would be free trade throughout Africa and also freedom for all Europeans to reside there if they so wished. It was this last clause which was to lead to further trouble. In January 1881, as the Boers began their revolt, the *Bacchante* was anchored in the Falkland Islands. Orders were given for the entire Detached Squadron, including the *Bacchante*, to sail at once for the Cape. She arrived at her destination on 16 February 1881, with the two Princes on board, and anchored at Simon's Bay. Prince George had found time to write another goodbye letter to his mother. Thanking her for giving him a hymnbook, he told her: 'As we sung the hymns I could not help thinking of you. I think this last parting was horrid & I think it was true that it made it much worse, us having to wait in the hall until dear Papa came, because none of us could speak we were all crying so much.'

Queen Victoria was concerned for the future of the monarchy, her grandsons' safety and very likely for some acknowledgement that she had been right to oppose their going to sea. Most probably in that order. She telegraphed at once to her son. 'I must earnestly protest against the Princes serving with the Naval Brigade on shore at the Cape. I strongly objected to their both going to sea, but consented on the suggestion that it was necessary for their education. The proposal to send them on active service destroys the cause of my former consent, and there is no reason for and many against their incurring danger in the South African war.' Prince Edward may have felt that the time had come to put an end to what he had come to see was the boys' mollycoddling by their mother which, on this occasion at least, was supported by their grandmother. He therefore declared himself pleased with the idea that they might see some action.

Queen Victoria clearly resented her son's opposition to her views. Two days after the *Bacchante*'s arrival at the Cape she wrote to her daughter-in-law:

> I am very sorry that Bertie [Prince Edward] should have been sore about the Boys . . . The *Bacchante* going to the Cape, which was done in a hurry without due consultation with me − I *disapproved*. And feeling how valuable these 2 young lives are to the *whole Nation*, I felt *bound* to protect them against useless and unnecessary exposure in a cruel *Civil War*, for so it is, the Boers being *my subjects*, and it being a rule that Princes of the Royal Family *ought not* to be mixed up in it. In any other war, should in time there be one (when George be older) and his ship be *obliged necessarily* to take part in it, I would *quite agree* with Bertie.

It seemed that Queen Victoria considered that for a second son to be involved in war was all right but certainly not for the heir.

Prince George, unaware that his activities were arousing so much family interest, had meanwhile become fascinated by King Ketchewayo, the King of the Zulus, who about eighteen months earlier had been taken prisoner at the battle of Ulundi. The two Princes had been taken to visit him by the Governor of Cape Province, on the farm on which he had been interned. Prince George was riveted by Ketchewayo's stature and size. Although he himself was slowly growing, he was still well below average height for his age. He wrote admiringly in his diary on 26 February 1881, possibly still smarting from his mother's comment about his size, that 'he [Ketchewayo] is 18 stone and is nearly six feet tall, large boned, but heavy in the haunches, with enormous thighs and legs'. The Prince also wrote of Ketchewayo's four wives, describing them as each 'weighing between 16 and 17 stone. They were happily squatting on the ground, wrapt in Scotch plaids' (Dalton, 1886).

The Prince's sympathies were clearly with the victims of the African conflict, and he was able to empathize with the defeated. A few days after his visit to Ketchewayo he wrote to his mother from Cape Town. 'This is really a dredful war is it not? All these poor people killed & also poor General Colley.' This was a reference to Sir George Colley, High Commisioner for South East Africa, killed at the battle for Majuba Hill by the Boers a few days earlier.

The life at sea of the two Princes came to an end on 5 August 1882. The diminutive Prince George had grown into a seventeen-year-old with skills that later would be put to good use in his career in the Royal Navy. He was known for his calmness in an emergency, probably the only situation in which he could be relied on not to lose his temper. Three days later he and his brother were confirmed by the Archbishop of Canterbury who told them that the Christian character was best developed by difficulties and warned them that they must not yield to the enervating influences that must gather round them. Prince George, now fully trained and in full control of his feelings, was ready to take the next step on his journey which would finally end when he became monarch of an Empire on which 'the sun never set' but which had reached its territorial peak.

5

Rum, buggery and the lash

O<small>N</small> 12 A<small>UGUST</small> 1882, having learned a great deal about seamanship during his three cruises aboard the *Bacchante*, the seventeen-year-old Prince George returned to his family to begin what he must have hoped would be a period of leisure before moving on to the next stage of his career. In the event both he and his brother were given only about two months to accustom themselves to a family life which for the past two years at sea had been unavailable to them. They attended concerts and the theatre with their parents and played tennis with their sisters in the garden at Marlborough House. It was a month later, when he arrived with his family at Abergeldie Castle in Aberdeenshire, that Prince George first became fascinated by an activity that was later to become a passion: shooting birds and animals for sport.

Today we are increasingly concerned about the preservation of animals, many species of which were in the nineteenth century decimated by hunting, the favourite sport of the aristocracy. Private parks of staghounds and other animals were also becoming popular among the *nouveaux riches*, but hunting remained on the whole an expensive pastime and the preserve of the upper classes. Since big game hunting was physically demanding, time-consuming and extremely expensive, it was less popular even among those who could afford it. The shooting of small game, which in 1831 had ceased to be the legal privilege and monopoly of landed proprietors, was more accessible, less demanding and certainly less dangerous, while big game hunting remained an activity which was not obstructed even by the Royal Society for the Prevention of Cruelty to Animals. The RSPCA, which was founded in 1824, acquired the patronage of Queen Victoria in 1840. The Queen had great personal concern for animal welfare, as long as it did not refer to the shooting of grouse or stags. The RSPCA satisfied itself that its duty applied only to domestic animals, such as the dogs and horses belonging mainly to the lower orders, and it did not attack the blood sports which, it argued, involved only wild animals which did not share the feelings or obligations of domestic animals. Since the society relied for its influence and income on the support of the Royal Family and members of the aristocracy, it was not encouraged to consider such sport as cruel.

The shooting of small game continues to be acceptable, on the often specious grounds that some creatures have to be culled in the interests of other creatures. Killing of big game for sport has now been banned, however, and the gun has been replaced by the camera.

At a time when the ecological consequences of hunting and shooting were unknown, and the activities rarely questioned, Prince Eddy and Prince George became addicted to both pastimes. The 'gun' and the 'horse', both symbols of power, were the *sine qua non* of a male-dominated sport, and the killing of partridge, grouse, hares and foxes were to keep the Princes fully occupied in the weeks following their graduation from the *Bacchante*. Within five days Prince George had shot his first partridge and two days later thirteen grouse. By Christmas his score had risen to forty-eight plus one fox. On 30 December he noted in his diary: 'Eddy got the brush, and I got the head.'

The wildlife in Norfolk enjoyed a brief respite while Prince Edward, Mr Dalton and three other tutors took the boys first to Lausanne and then to Heidelberg to continue their general education and to study French and German. In re-entering society Prince Eddy and Prince George tried – albeit with little success – to make up for the lost years of their adolescence. Their social life was limited to tennis, walking and rowing on the lake, activities hardly destined to improve their interpersonal skills. Neither of them could wait to get back to Sandringham to resume the blood sports that were to excite Prince George, already an enthusiastic and accurate shot, throughout his later life.

Despite the increasing pleasures of life in England and in particular at home, the two brothers, who had been inseparable companions, were saddened to be parted for the first time. Nineteen-year-old Prince Eddy had to be groomed for his future role as King, and tutors were engaged to coach him for further education at Cambridge. He was also to undergo military training and was enrolled in the 10th Hussars, his father's regiment. Less was expected from Prince George who, having come to love the life that had at first terrified him, continued his career at sea. In all the changes to which the two Princes had been exposed they had always been there for each other and had played an important role in one another's lives. They may have been separated in age by eighteen months, but other than in appearance they might have been twins. Both had been born prematurely and had developed slowly. They had been tutored together at home and, as naval cadets, aged nineteen and seventeen respectively, they were young for their years. Prince Eddy was passive, dreamy, ungainly and addicted to sexual adventure. Prince George was emotional, vulnerable, self-aware and heavily dependent on the approval of a mother, who had let him down by making implicit promises she had not kept. At the age of twelve, an immature, cosseted boy from a home where he had been led to believe that he was indispensable, he had been cast upon the waters. He and Prince Eddy, two halves of a whole, had clung to one another and survived.

Although Prince Eddy had done his best, he had never been comfortable as a naval cadet. Life at sea was not his *métier*, and the experience had diminished him. Prince George, psychologically more robust than his brother, had come to look upon his long absence from the home in which he had felt secure and protected as a challenge. Each of them knew that they had either to sink or swim. While Prince Eddy sank, Prince George swam, and now the time had come for them to part. Parting was not easy for either of them. In the absence of their mother they had mothered each other and, for the second time in their lives, a 'mother' had ceased to be available to them. Two weeks after Prince George had returned to the Navy to join his new ship HMS *Canada* his brother wrote him a sad and moving letter which was not dissimilar from the letters they had both received over the years from Princess Alexandra. 'My dear George, so we are at last separated for the first time and I can't tell you *how* strange it seems to be without you and how much I miss you in everything *all day long.'*

At the age of eighteen Prince George's formal education with his tutors had come to an end. The sea and the Royal Naval College at Greenwich were to be his university. Although his instructors spoke well of him, his grandmother continued to concern herself with his morals. He had been in the Navy for two years when Queen Victoria wrote to him as she might once have written to his father. She reminded him of the pitfalls that had befallen Prince Edward and which now lay before her grandson:

Avoid the many evil temptations wh. beset *all* young men especially Princes. Beware of flatterers, too great love of amusement, of *races* & betting & playing high. I hear on all sides what a good steady boy you are & how you can be trusted. Still you must always be on the watch & must not fear ridicule if you do what is right. Alas! Society is very bad in these days; what is wrong is winked at, allowed even, & as for betting or anything of that kind, no end of young and older men have been ruined, parents hearts broken, & great names and Titles dragged in the dirt. It is in *your* power to do immense good by setting an example & keeping your dear Grandpapa's name before you . . . I am afraid that you will think this a long lecture, but Grandmama loves you so much and is so anxious that you should be a blessing to your Parents, herself and your Country, and she cd. *not* do otherwise than write to you *as she feels.*

'Put not your trust in Princes, nor in the children of man, in whom there is no help . . .' Like the psalmist, Queen Victoria was right to be distrustful of Princes. Like many a parent, she had found the task of raising children, and in particular her son and heir, 'in the way that they should go' daunting. Like many grandparents, she is likely to have believed that providence had provided her with grandchildren so that she might be given a second chance to exercise the maternalism with which, as a young mother herself, she had failed to be in touch. In her poetic letter she was able to express feelings that she might well have had difficulty in verbalizing even to her grandson.

On 1 June 1883 Prince George was appointed to the corvette HMS *Canada*. Two months later Midshipman Prince George sailed on her under the command of Captain Francis Durrant, who took the place of Mr Dalton as the Prince's governor. Prince George looked up to Captain Durrant and admired him and they soon became close friends. Anxious to return to the familiarity of life on board ship, Prince George hoped that this would help him with his distress at being parted from his brother. He was well liked by his shipmates but made only a few close friends. Eddy lived on in his memory, and he saw little reason to 'replace' his brother with an unknown shipmate. His solution then, as it would be later, was to find a replacement love for that to which he had been entitled as a child but which had been denied him. He unconsciously attached himself to other 'carers'. It would have been understandable perhaps had he searched for a 'father' (Prince Edward also having been unavailable), as later he searched for a mother (in his wife), to counteract the smothering love of Princess Alexandra.

In addition to Prince George's parents and brother, one other person was both to have an effect on him and later to influence his attitude to women. In late adolescence Prince George was probably a stranger to any sort of intimacy. He made up for this by the warmth of the many letters written during his years at sea, not only (as ever) to his mother but also to male contemporaries of his parents, whose wisdom he needed and respected. One man to whom he had remained close was Charles Fuller, who as a 'nursery footman' had fulfilled the role of father and mother to the two Princes. Engaged about two weeks after the birth of Prince Eddy, Mr Fuller became particularly fond of the boys throughout their childhood. He served them with love and affection and accompanied them as their valet aboard the *Bacchante*. Although Prince George was now eighteen years old, Mr Fuller continued to show concern for his royal master. While the Prince was growing up it was as if he had two surrogate parents both of whom were constantly at his side; while Canon Dalton concerned himself mainly with his intellectual development, it was Charles Fuller who 'mothered' him. Mr Fuller was always available, always loyal, never (unlike Princess Alexandra) made unreasonable demands of him and attended to his physical well-being. In his letters to the Prince he never failed to fuss over him, to remind him to wear clothing appropriate to the weather, to take care of his health and – presciently – to smoke less. Although Charles Fuller was ordered to accompany Prince Eddy when he went to Cambridge, he remained close in spirit to his favourite, Prince George. A few days after the Prince embarked on HMS *Canada,* Mr Fuller wrote to say how much he missed him.

'My Dear Prince George, – It is just a week today since you left us and you cannot think how much I miss your dear face, the place don't look the same. I used to look at the vacant bed in your dear room at M. House. I scarcely knew what I was doing, but am so pleased to hear from Mr Dalton that you are so happy and quite settled down to your new life.' His brother (Eddy), older men (senior officers) and an ever-present mother (Queen Mary) were all to have a significant effect on Prince George's later life.

Princess Alexandra, trying desperately to let go of her younger son, wrote a 'farewell' letter to Prince George which was less concerned with loosening the bond that tied him to her than with consoling her own anguish at being parted from him. On 12 June, less than two weeks after her son's naval appointment but some weeks before he actually embarked on HMS *Canada*, she wrote:

> My own darling little Georgie, I have only just left you going to bed, after having given you my last kiss and having heard you saying your prayers. I need hardly say what I feel – and what we both feel at this sad hour of parting – it will be harder for you this time to go quite by yourself – without Eddy, Mr Dalton or Fuller – but remember darling when all others are far away God is always there – and He will never forsake you – but bring you safe back to all of us who love you so.

Having probably made her son feel guilty at leaving her, Princess Alexandra went on:

> I need hardly say my darling little Georgie *how* much I shall always miss you – now we have been so much together and you were such a dear little boy not at all spoilt and so nice and affectionate to old Motherdear – Remain just as you are – but strive to get on with all that is good – and keep out of temptation as much as you can – don't let anyone lead you astray – Remember to take the Sacrament about every quarter which will give you fresh strength to do what is right – and also never forget either your morning or evening Prayer – We must all try to console ourselves by thinking how quickly the year will pass and what delight it will be to meet once more . . . And now darling Georgie I must say Goodnight and Goodbye as I am so sleepy my eyes will hardly keep awake and it is nearly two – So goodbye and God bless you and keep you safe and sound till we meet again and watch over you wherever you are – Goodbye, goodbye Georgie dear
> Ever your most loving affectionate old Motherdear.

Princess Alexandra's six (royal) commandments, as spelled out in her letter to her son, would have reinforced his punitive conscience to the extent that he would have either found it impossible to live with and rebelled (as did Eddy) or have ingested the imperatives of obedience and duty his mother had instilled into him and used them not only to control those under his command in the Navy but also those 'under his command' (his children) as a result of his marriage. Continuing to climb the career ladder, Prince George was promoted to Sub-Lieutenant. He obtained a first class in seamanship, left HMS *Canada* after a year's service and transferred to the Royal Naval College at Greenwich where he again did well in his examinations and passed well in torpedo, gunnery, navigation and pilotage. While he was at Greenwich Captain Bernard Currey was appointed Deputy-Governor and Captain Durrant wrote to him to inform him of his duties *vis-à-vis* the Prince:

My Dear Currey, – During your stay at the RN College, Greenwich, with HRH Prince George, it is the wish of the Prince of Wales that you should consider yourself as Prince George's companion and friend, to whom he may always come for advice and assistance, and also you will kindly give that advice unasked if you see any occasion for so doing.

It is His Royal Highness's wish that Prince George should not leave the neighbourhood of the College except to join in such sports as are undertaken by the members of the college as a body – or on the occasions that he will go from Saturday to Sunday evening to visit at such places as will be especially approved by the Prince of Wales (of which you will be notified), and His Royal Highness hopes that you will accompany Prince George at these times – unless some well known friend is accompanying him. All expenses of every description that you may incur for Prince George or whilst going anywhere with him will be defrayed, and I shall be obliged if you will let me have the account of them monthly. Any letters addressed to the Governor of HRH Prince George you will be so good as to open and forward to me with your opinion, if they concern any local matters, so that I may reply to them; the same will apply to any letters addressed to Prince George (after he has seen them) which may require answering, as it will not be desirable that His Royal Highness should answer them himself. It will not be advisable that Prince George should accept any invitations to balls, dinners etc., while he is studying at the College without the sanction of HRH the Prince of Wales.

Bearing in mind that the Prince was still only nineteen years old and, furthermore, third in line to the throne, the degree of protection afforded him by such 'fathers' as Captain Durrant and later Captain Currey (later Admiral Currey), would not in the 1880s be considered excessive. What was excessive was the Prince's transfer of affection to these and other older men, which during a critical period in his early development would have been more appropriately directed to his father. Never having been accustomed to an easy and carefree relationship with his own father, Prince George's deference to surrogate fathers would have left him with an unhealthy respect for authority and, by extension, authoritarianism. By the time he became a father himself he often demanded the blind obedience that had been demanded of him from his sons, to a degree they sometimes found it impossible to satisfy.

The Prince's next posting was to the *Thunderer,* in January 1886, under the command of Admiral Sir Henry Stephenson, Gentleman Usher of the Black Rod. Once again entrusting his son to a stand-in, Prince Edward prepared the then Captain Stephenson for his arrival. He wrote to him in May 1885: 'The command you have received is a most interesting one, but be assured that I shall not forget the wish expressed by you that my second son should serve in a ship under your command, and that there is nothing I should like better, as I feel assured that he could not be in better hands.' What better hands are there for a son than those of his father? In their absence Admiral Stephenson would have to do. In January 1886 Prince Edward reinforced his message. 'I feel that in entrusting my son to your care I cannot place him in safer hands, only don't *spoil* him *please*! . . . he *must* be kept up to his work, as *all* young men of the present day are inclined to be lazy.' Was Prince Edward aware that when his son had most need of a father he himself had not been there? And, in his insistence on other 'fathers' caring for him and their being strict with him, might he be attempting to alleviate his own guilt at his failure to be a father to his son?

Despite the enthusiasm with which it seemed that Prince George enjoyed his career, shore leave was invariably welcomed. In February 1886, while he was serving in the Mediterranean, his father took him for a short holiday to Cannes. At the end of his leave the Prince left by train to rejoin his ship in Naples. Parting was still a problem not only for him but also for Prince Edward. Known to be increasingly dependent on stimulation, he never found it easy to give anything up. He also had been left in need of loving input from anyone who could provide it. He had usually no problems in this respect. His great wealth, his power and his ability to reward those who pleased him with social advancement – which cost him nothing but which was of inestimable value to their recipients – ensured that he would never be short of 'friends'. What may have surprised him was how much he depended on the love of his children. Unable to understand the nature of this need, he would have been unlikely to recognize such a need in others, not least in his son. After their brief holiday together Prince George and his father wrote letters to one another which crossed in the post. The theme of the letters was identical: 'I miss you.' In a letter to his son written on 5 March 1886, Prince Edward comments: 'On seeing you going off by the train yesterday, I felt very sad & you could I am sure see that I had a lump in my throat when I wished you goodbye.' His son's letter to him two days later also emphasized the sense of loss experienced at their moment of parting: 'My dearest Papa, I cannot tell you how I miss you every minute of the day, because we have been together so much lately.' The more accurate underlying message that Prince George was giving his father was that highlighting their feelings of separation lit up the fact that they had not been together consistently earlier. Neither of them had been loved appropriately or for long enough when they were children, when it mattered most. Prince George's homesickness, far from being a sign of protracted adolescence, represented his continuing need for a home that had failed to provide him with sufficient hands-on parenting. This was difficult to achieve when he had been sent away from it at the age of twelve.

When he parted from his father in Cannes he was also leaving some of the companions in his father's party with whom he had grown up. One such was Julie Stonor. Miss Stonor's mother, Mrs Francis Stonor, had been one of Princess Alexandra's ladies-in-waiting. When she died her two orphaned children, Julie and Harry, had more or less been brought up with the Princess's children (which Princess Alexandra felt to be her duty). Prince George had become fond of Julie and during her frequent visits to Sandringham with her brother he had seen a good deal of her. Surprisingly Prince Edward and Princess Alexandra did not disapprove of their son's 'romance'. They were pleased in fact that they would be able to supervise (and presumably control) its development. Prince George's parents believed that his friendship with Julie Stonor would distract him from forming disreputable liaisons with other women while he was away from home.

Having spent so much time together when they were young, however, Prince George and Julie were more like brother and sister and it is doubtful whether there would have been a sexual element in their relationship. It had been made perfectly clear to Prince George that nothing must come of their 'romance', since Julie was not only a commoner but a Catholic. None the less, the Prince missed Julie when he left the Côte d'Azur to rejoin HMS *Alexandra*. As he became older he found, like his father, that giving up anything (or anybody) was difficult. It was at about this time that he started to collect postage stamps which, given his passion for letter-writing, was not surprising. He and Julie exchanged warm letters and they remained good friends. Five years later Julie married the Marquis d'Hautpoul.

Prince George, now aged twenty-one, having had a taste of female friendship, began to think in terms of marriage. Unfortunately all the available European Princesses were too young, and he was moderately concerned that no suitable partners seemed to be available. On 21 October 1886 he wrote to his mother but spoke only of his concern for the marriage plans for his brother Eddy, who was being pressed by Queen Victoria to marry a German Princess, an idea to which Prince George and his Danish mother were opposed. All the granddaughters of Queen Victoria who might have been suitable were too young to be thinking of marriage, and Prince George continued to focus his attention on his naval duties.

While serving in the Mediterranean fleet, Prince George became close to his uncle, Alfred Duke of Edinburgh, his father's younger brother. The Duke of Edinburgh was in command of the *Alexandra,* the flagship of the Mediterranean fleet and also commander-in-chief on the Mediterranean Station. When Prince George took shore leave in Malta he stayed with the Duke of Edinburgh and his family. They became close friends and shared a common interest in stamps. Prince George was to see more of his uncle the following year when he joined his flagship as a full lieutenant. The 22-year-old Prince found himself attracted to his uncle's elder daughter, Princess Marie, who at the time was only thirteen. The attraction was not mutual, however, and when Marie was sixteen she became engaged to, and later married, Prince Ferdinand, heir presumptive to King Carol I of Romania. Within the limits of his circle Prince George managed to become attracted to two girls only, the first was unsuitable and less interested in him than he was in her and the second only thirteen years old.

In 1887 Prince George returned to London for the celebration of Queen Victoria's Golden Jubilee. The Jubilee was an excuse for a grand reunion of European Royalty, most of them directly related to Queen Victoria and the remainder indirectly related through the marriage of Princess Alexandra to Prince Edward. Those attending the celebrations included members of the Royal Houses of Denmark, Norway, Russia, Greece, Prussia, Portugal, Austria and of the several Royal Houses of Germany. Although Prince George knew that a suitable princess would sooner or later be chosen for him, he must have hoped that he would at least have an opportunity to preview those who were available. Since he had already established that most of his first cousins were not of marrying age, and most of his second cousins were already well known to him – and in any event his older brother, as the heir, had prior claim – he would have entertained no real hope of meeting his bride at any of the celebrations. Although he was unaware of it, one of the guests at several of the parties, the twenty-year-old Princess May of Teck – daughter of Prince Francis, First Duke of Teck, and HRH Princess Mary Adelaide, Duchess of Teck, Queen Victoria's first cousin – was, within six years, to become his bride.

· 6 ·

The Gay Hussar

ON 4 NOVEMBER 1891 Queen Victoria summoned Princess May of Teck to Balmoral Castle to be considered as a wife for Prince Eddy, known as the Duke of Clarence and Avondale since his return from India the previous year. Princess May's feelings must have been mixed. She could have been in no doubt as to the nature of the summons and would have liked nothing more than to be the Queen of England. But there were two problems she would have to face. The first was her dislike of her cousin Eddy and the second was his lack of interest in her. Brought up in Kensington Palace, Princess May had known Prince Eddy and the other Waleses, since they had all played together as children. She had preferred the company of Prince Eddy's brother Prince George and his three sisters, rather than Eddy whom she had thought of as 'stupid, immature and a bully'.

On her journey to Balmoral Princess May might have been wondering whether Eddy was able to make a commitment to women. She knew that he had had numerous girl-friends and recently, according to hearsay, had fallen in love with Princess Hélène d'Orleans, daughter of Louis Philippe Albert d'Orleans, the Compte de Paris and Pretender to the throne of France. Princess May was impressed that a woman as beautiful as Princess Hélène loved her suitor. But what if Prince Eddy, despite his womanizing, refused to give her up.

Princess May would have been aware that Queen Victoria and Prince Edward were not opposed to the possibility of Eddy's marriage to the Catholic Princess Hélène, provided she could be persuaded to renounce her religion. Because the Princess was so much in love with Prince Eddy, she needed little persuading to do so. The Compte de Paris, however, was furious that his daughter, at twenty-one still under age according to French law, was contemplating becoming a Protestant. He refused to give permission for his daughter to marry the 'dissolute' and promiscuous Prince about whose sexual orientation rumours abounded. The despairing Princess appealed to the Holy Father himself, but Pope Leo XIII refused his dispensation and the engagement did not materialize.

Despite Princess May's erstwhile friendship with Prince Eddy's sisters, they all supported Princess Hélène's claim, because they knew that she had been secretly in love with Prince Eddy for three years before declaring herself. This seemed to them to be the very stuff of romance (with Prince Eddy playing the role of Prince Charming), and they thought that such a fairy-tale marriage would bring a little excitement to their humdrum lives. Princess May might also have wondered whether Queen Victoria's summons was merely a ploy on the part of the Palace to break up Prince Eddy's relationship with the French Princess who had been forbidden to give up Catholicism for the Church of England.

In a letter to his brother, Prince Eddy wrote: 'You probably know through the girls, who told me, that dear Hélène had been fond of me for some time. I did not realise this at first although the girls constantly told me she liked me, for she never showed it in any way.' He went on to explain to his brother that he had seen Hélène on several occasions and had been impressed with the fact that she had shown interest in him. As a result, he had fallen in love with her and took the view that anyone who liked him must be a very special person. He was also perhaps still smarting from the fact that his first cousin, Princess Alix of Hesse, had recently turned him down.

It was soon after this that Prince Eddy realized that no one woman, no matter how beautiful, could satisfy his craving for affection. Despite his protestations of love for Princess Hélène and his conditional offer of marriage to her, he declared himself in love with Lady Sybil St Clair-Erskine, another lovely twenty-year-old and the second daughter of the Fourth Earl of Rosslyn. Like Princess Hélène, however, Lady Sybil was unacceptable. When she discovered that Prince Eddy was wooing her and at the same time expressing undying love for Princess Hélène, she refused to have anything more to do with him. Prince Eddy had convinced himself that it was possible to be in love with two women at once, but while paying attention to one he would inevitably be turning his back on the other. Genuine commitment would be impossible with either, and each would experience him as disloyal. In the event Lady Sybil made her own decision and shortly afterwards married the thirteenth Earl of Westmoreland.

Possibly because of his lack of experience with women, Prince George was seen by his family as resolute, conscientious and pleasing, while Prince Eddy was regarded as immoral, foolish and prone to involvements not only hostile to women but regarded as 'beyond the pale'. It was at about this time that forensic psychiatrists began to develop theories which led to the association of same-sex preferences with criminality. Havelock Ellis referred to homosexuals as 'moral imbeciles' and 'degenerate lunatics', providing authoritative labelling and medical sanction for prejudice. Increasing social pressures, aimed at consolidating family values, were also being brought to bear by the Church. Homosexuals who threatened these values were punished. All homosexual acts, from sodomy to mutual masturbation – whether in public or in private, with or without consent and at any age – had been criminalized under the terms of the Criminal Law Amendment Act of 1885.

It was against this background that two years earlier Prince Eddy had been the subject of a scandal at a homosexual brothel, the Hundred Guineas, at 19 Cleveland Street in central London. During a police raid on the brothel one of Prince Eddy's closest friends, Lord Arthur Somerset, had been discovered *in flagrante delicto* with a young man. Rather than face a possible charge under the new Act, Lord Somerset fled the country. It was rumoured that Prince Eddy (known as Victoria by his friends) was also an *habitué* of the brothel. Three men were arrested and sent to prison for 'offences' but, according to a report in the *North London Press*, others were claimed to have had their reputations protected because of their social standing. One of these was said to be the Duke of Clarence, another Lord Euston, heir to the Duke of Grafton. Lord Euston, however, successfully sued the editor of the *North London Press*, who was sentenced to a year in prison for libel. Taking the view that discretion was the better part of valour Prince Eddy did nothing.

Prince Eddy, like his father, was considered to be sensual and attractive to women. When they came to know him better, however, they found him listless and dreamy. He was only too ready to turn away from them and pass them over either for the next woman who caught his eye or for occasional same-sex experimentation with like-minded friends. Princess May would not have known, and had she known would probably have been unaware of the significance of the fact, that when Prince Eddy was a student at Cambridge he had mixed with a group of young men, many of whom were known to be homosexual. He had also formed a close friendship with his tutor, James Stephen (a cousin of Virginia Woolf). Mr Stephen, described as a scholar 'with cultivated taste and a natural bent towards dainty and exquisite language', formed an attachment to the Prince. This attachment was so intense that when Eddy left Cambridge to join his regiment his tutor, unable to cope without his friend, gave up academic life. He was admitted to a mental hospital and later died while on a hunger strike begun during Prince Eddy's final illness.

Prince Edward and Princess Alexandra laid the blame for most of Prince Eddy's unsuitable attachments on his regiment, the 10th Hussars, which had a reputation for dissipation and drunkenness. Prince Eddy had a name for 'dissolute' behaviour. Years earlier he had been reported by Mr Dalton to have fraternized with 'ruffians' while drunk and on leave during his service on the *Bacchante*. In view of all this he would probably have thought himself fortunate to find any woman willing to take him on, regardless of the fact that he would one day be King of England.

Well aware of the drawbacks, but conscious also of the glittering prizes that lay ahead, Princess May prepared herself for what she hoped would be Queen Victoria's offer to her. The importance of her meeting with the Queen, however, became overshadowed by the sudden illness of Prince George on 9 November 1891 while he was celebrating his father's fiftieth birthday at Sandringham. On 12 November he was diagnosed as having typhoid fever and was immediately removed to Marlborough House in order that he might receive the best possible medical attention. Princess Alexandra was at Livadia in the Crimea with her two unmarried daughters on a visit to her sister Princess Dagmar and her husband Emperor Alexander III of Russia. The fact that she had chosen to be out of the country for her husband's fiftieth birthday was seen by the Court as an act of revenge, the reason for which was assumed to be Prince Edward's continuing flagrant infidelity. In the event this calculated snub took second place to Princess Alexandra's concern for the health of her son. Summoned back to London, George's mother and sisters arrived on 22 November. On 3 December an entry in his diary notes the engagement of Eddy and May, and Prince George had scarcely recovered from his typhoid fever when on 8 January 1892 the family gathered for another celebration, Prince Eddy's twenty-eighth birthday.

Princess May not only received Queen Victoria's approval but also that of Princess Alexandra, who was delighted that her reprobate son made no objection to the arrangements being made on his behalf. She immediately agreed to accept Princess May as her future daughter-in-law. Both Prince Eddy's parents were fond of Princess May. They had known her since she was a baby and recognized in her qualities that fitted her for the role she would one day be called on to play. Their only anxiety was that she might have second thoughts about the marriage.

The deal having been struck, and with Prince George now convalescing from his illness, Princess Alexandra felt that she could visit her parents in Denmark. Plans for the official engagement went ahead in her absence. The Duke of Clarence proposed to Princess May of Teck on 2 December 1891 at a house-party given by the Danish Minister to the Court of St James, Christian de Falbe, and Madame de Falbe at their country home at Luton Hoo. The wedding was arranged for 27 February 1892, two months later, giving Princess May very little time to change her mind. Princess Alexandra was delighted that Prince Eddy had at last found a fiancée who was not only not German but suitable in every way. Writing to Queen Victoria to tell her how pleased she was with Prince Eddy's choice, she was able also to express her feelings for 'the sad tragedy and blighted life of that sweet dear Hélène'. Not everyone was so delighted with the match. Sir Henry Ponsonby, Queen Victoria's Private Secretary, commented in his private papers: 'I am told he don't care for Princess May of Teck and she appears too proud to take the trouble of running after him for which I rather admire her.'

On 4 January 1892 Princess May and her parents arrived at Sandringham to celebrate Prince Eddy's twenty-eighth birthday. Three days later, having caught a cold while attending the funeral of Prince Hohenlohe, he developed a feverish flu-like illness and over the next few days became increasingly ill. By the time Dr Francis Laking, the Physician-in-Ordinary to the Royal Household, was called to attend to him the Prince was terminally ill with pneumonia. His death on 14 January 1892, six days after his birthday, was painful and slow. It took place in the presence of his parents, his sisters, his brother and his grieving bride-to-be. After days of delirium, incessant coughing and profound suffering which affected his family deeply, Prince Eddy's last words were: 'Something too awful has happened – my darling brother George is dead.' These bizarre words may have reflected Prince Eddy's realization that he was about to die. His defence against this fear was to project it on to his *alter ego*, his beloved brother George.

With the death of her eldest son, Princess Alexandra felt a sorrow made all the more poignant because Eddy, of all her children, had failed to live up to her expectations. His promiscuous need for approval (especially from women) made her wonder whether she had done enough for him as a child. Eddy had certainly never failed to love her and had been obedient and easy-going. She never forgot Eddy and kept his bedroom exactly as he had left it. The bed was draped with the Union Jack, his clothes remained in his cupboard and his soap on his wash-stand. He was not forgotten by others either. Princess May kissed his brow as she left his room, and on his tomb at Windsor a wreath inscribed 'Hélène' was left by another woman who, despite his shortcomings, had also loved him. Nine months later, in a conversation with the 72-year-old Queen Victoria, herself no stranger to sorrow, Princess Hélène said simply: 'Je l'aimais tant,' and, more surprisingly,

'Il etait si bon.' In a note to Alfred Lord Tennyson, the Poet Laureate, Queen Victoria wrote: 'Was there ever a more terrible contrast, a wedding with bright hopes turned into a funeral?' Tennyson's response in his official verse was in the event less poetic than that of Princess Hélène who had truly loved Prince Eddy.

No one, however, mourned Prince Eddy as much as did Prince George. In a letter to a shipmate he expressed his feelings for his brother: 'To me his loss is irreparable, as you know how devoted we always were and we had never been separated until I was eighteen . . . the whole of my life has changed.' Despite the many cousins who had visited the Waleses at Sandringham and the shipmates who had served with him at sea, Prince George had been both a lonely child and a lonely adolescent. The only person with whom he had ever felt at ease, apart from his mother, was his brother. Prince Eddy had been his confidant. They had supported one another and wept with one another in their times of homesickness until finally they grew up. While Eddy searched for love from both men and women, George continued his quest for admiration and approval by serving his country, his parents and later his wife.

Inseparable in the nursery, in the school room and as naval cadets, the two brothers had depended on one another. Drawn together by what they regarded as their banishment from home, they shared their anger and puzzlement at having been abandoned by parents who they both knew really loved them. As their years in exile slowly passed, they came to realize that, although Prince Edward and Princess Alexandra had managed to convince themselves that the separation hurt them more than it hurt their children, this was a myth perpetuated by parents to protect themselves from the pain of their failure to respond to their children's needs. Prince Eddy's death, one week after the twenty-eighth anniversary of his birth, was his final rejection of a mother who should by rights have kept him by her side until he was ready to leave her but who instead had loved him and left him. Both the nation, which thought it knew him, and his family and friends, who did know him, mourned the heir apparent.

Prince Edward and Princess Alexandra, together with their family, spent a few quiet weeks at Compton Place in Eastbourne, the home of the Duke of Devonshire, before leaving for Cap Martin in the South of France. They observed a period of mourning for the remainder of the year, broken only briefly on 23 May 1892 by a visit to Denmark for the Golden Wedding of Prince George's maternal grandparents, the King and Queen of Denmark.

Prince George, whose career as a naval officer had been interrupted at first by his own illness and later by the death of his brother, found comfort both in the isolation and the companionship of life at sea. Having relinquished his command of the *Melampus* in January 1892, a year later he returned to naval duties as Captain and continued to climb the career ladder. From 1893, until he retired from the Navy in 1901, he commanded the *Crescent* finally being promoted to Rear-Admiral.

Soon after the death of Prince Eddy Prince George became increasingly interested in the welfare and comfort of his sailors. He knew how it felt to be away at sea, sometimes for months at a time, separated from home and from family. Sensitive also to the financial hardship experienced by some naval pensioners, he suggested that should their circumstances become such that they would have to 'come on the rates' they should be properly cared for at the Haslar Hospital in Gosport. He had no difficulty in identifying with the impoverished. His hand was held out to them as he would have wished his own father's hand to have been held out to him, even though his own poverty was emotional rather than financial. In a speech made at the opening of an institute at Great Yarmouth for the benefit of sailors, he stressed his appreciation of the benefactors who had made such an institution possible. 'Who appreciated me?' he might have asked himself. 'Where was my benefactor when I most needed him?' Prince George seldom let pass an opportunity when he did not emphasize the importance of both the Merchant Marine and the Royal Navy to the people of England. He was proud of all those who served their country at sea. None the less, despite his promotions, his status as a high-ranking naval officer and the growing appreciation by the country of his virtues, Prince George's sense of low self-esteem persisted.

· 7 ·

One feels capable of greater things

No one could have been more devastated than the 24-year-old
Princess May of Teck when she bade farewell to her dying Prince on
14 January 1892. Only a few weeks had passed since she had been summoned by Queen Victoria to Balmoral Castle to be considered as a bride
for her cousin Eddy, Duke of Clarence. Despite the straitened circumstances that faced Princess May's family, and her realization that by marrying the Duke of Clarence she would be securing the family fortunes, she
had been reluctant at first to accept Queen Victoria's offer. In the weeks
that intervened, however, she slowly began to take an interest in Prince
Eddy and found herself attracted to his physical and emotional frailty.
Although, at twenty-eight, her husband-to-be was older than she, she felt
protective and almost motherly towards him. What Prince Eddy needed,
however, was not the smothering love given to him by Princess Alexandra
but a 'mother' who cared sufficiently for him to allow him to develop into
an adult. Realizing that other women found Prince Eddy attractive,
Princess May soon began to revise her childhood perception of him as
aggressive and dull. She was encouraged in this by her parents, who were
quick to see the marriage as the answer to their financial difficulties.

Princess May's mother, Princess Mary Adelaide, Duchess of Teck, was
the granddaughter of King George III and first cousin to Queen Victoria.
She was ash-blonde, blue-eyed, of a cheerful disposition and, at seventeen
stone, grossly but happily overweight (at the time obesity was associated
with prosperity). While Princess Mary Adelaide did not feel prosperous,
she was, none the less, extravagant and charitable, and she was loved by
her children. Princess May's father, Francis, Duke of Teck, a direct descen-
dent of King George II, was an impecunious army officer who had resigned

from the Austrian Army to marry Princess Mary Adelaide. If he thought that his marriage would put an end to his financial troubles he was mistaken. Princess Mary Adelaide's circumstances were as straitened as his.

Fortunately, Queen Victoria, who was fond of her impoverished cousin, made the south wing of Kensington Palace available to the couple while they awaited the birth of their first child. On 26 May 1867 Victoria Mary Augusta Louisa Olga Pauline Claudine Agnes was born and was thereafter always referred to as May, after the month of her birth. It was not until 1910, when her husband, Prince George, ascended the throne of England, that she reverted to her given name and allowed herself to be designated Queen Mary. Because the 33-year-old Princess Mary Adelaide had been considered by medical opinion to be too old and too fat to give birth, it was thought that she might experience some difficulty during her confinement. Fortunately this was not the case, and during the next seven years she was to have three more children, all of them boys.

Princess May was born in the same room, in the same bed and almost on the same day of the year as Queen Victoria had been forty-six years earlier (24 May 1819). Perhaps her destiny had already been decided for her. Although at the time Queen Victoria took very little notice of her cousin Princess Mary Adelaide's baby, years later, after Princess May had married her grandson Prince George, she expressed herself to be particularly fond of her. In May 1896 she wrote: 'I like to feel your birthday is so near mine, that you were born in the same House as I was & that you bear my name. It is very curious that it should be so.'

Princess May's mother was pleased with her first child. She had been born at full term and was strong and healthy. As Princess May grew older she quickly became self-sufficient. This led to her being mildly exploited by her doting but gregarious mother, who was delighted when her daughter accepted some responsibility for mothering her three younger brothers, a chore with which Princess May herself was possibly less delighted. Princess May's birth was somewhat overshadowed by the almost simultaneous birth of two other grandchildren to Queen Victoria in the spring of 1867. Her daughter-in-law, Princess Alexandra, had given birth to Princess Louise, and the Queen's fifth daughter, Princess Helena (who had married Prince Christian of Schleswig-Holstein), had produced a son, Prince Christian Victor. Princess May was almost a year old when Queen Victoria wrote in her journal that 'Mary T's baby' seemed 'a dear merry healthy child' but mitigated her praise of the baby by going on to write, 'but not as handsome as she ought to be'.

Princess May grew up in a household in which money was chronically short. Her father's financial vagueness and her mother's extravagance led to the family becoming increasingly impoverished. Children are generally unaware of financial hardship unless it is constantly referred to. Princess Mary Adelaide complained frequently that she had nothing suitable to wear for the various drawing-rooms she was expected to attend as a member of the Royal Family, and Princess May must have found this puzzling since her mother was renowned for her lavish stylishness. As she grew older she could not help comparing the grandeur of Sandringham and Windsor with her own relatively simple home, Cambridge Cottage at Kew Green. Her impression that there was some material lack in her home life, despite not being entirely true, would have been emphasized during her visits to her maternal grandmother Princess Augusta of Hesse, Duchess of Cambridge.

Like her daughter, Princess Mary Adelaide's mother was a large and stately lady, with a pronounced German accent. Unlike Princess Mary Adelaide, however, she was in no way extravagant either in manner or in clothes. As Princess May was later to recall, her grandmother was rather mean and none of her grandchildren enjoyed taking afternoon tea at the Duchess's rooms at St James's Palace. It was not only the 'stingy teas' of buns and rusks that she recalled. In an exchange of letters to her Aunt Augusta, the Grand Duchess of Mecklenburg-Strelitz, in 1909 she wrote: 'I still meet older people sometimes who knew dear Grandmama & invariably talk so nicely of her. I wish I had been older to appreciate her properly, but in spite of her great kindness to us we were always rather afraid of her' (Pope-Hennessy, 1959). Aunt Augusta replied that she wished: 'You had been able really to know Grandmama; as it was you could not get in real contact with her, besides she looked and could be rather severe, with her firm old notions and principles, though her heart ever was full of love for all her belongings.'

Princess May was happy to be one of her grandmother's 'belongings' and, as an adult, felt deprived of those 'afternoon teas' of her childhood. The 'stingy teas', which at the time she experienced as being of little value, none the less symbolized a love freely given and later in life became confused with other tea parties and other small gifts which were either on offer or hers simply for the asking. Princess May's passion for collecting trinkets caused her to 'forget' that when, as Queen Mary, she admired the baubles of her friends they were unable to refuse to give them to her. Her more fabled jewellery, however, came to her as the result of the deaths of family members to whom she had been particularly close. Princess Mary Adelaide died intestate in 1897, and her jewellery came into the possession of Princess May's least favourite brother, the feckless, gambling Prince Frank, who claimed that before she died his mother had given it to him. Prince Frank gave it all to Ellen Constance Kilmorey, the wife of the Earl of Kilmorey, who was thought to have been his mistress. When the 39-year-old Prince died unexpectedly from pleurisy in October 1910, after a minor operation on his nose, Queen Mary, who had the right to do so but who was the first monarch to exercise that right, had his will 'sealed'. No one would ever be allowed access to it. Her reasons for doing so can only be guessed at. Since that time all royal wills have been sealed. On Prince Frank's death Queen Mary requested the repossession of the family jewels from her brother's mistress and within a few days all were returned, including eight large cabochon emeralds fashioned into a necklace. These gems, together with those presented to her on her twenty-first birthday by her family and later by the Maharajahs and Princes at the Coronation Durbar in 1911, made up the bulk of her collection. The exhibitionistic Queen Mary did not hide away her finery as the secretive and withholding King George was to hide away his stamps but displayed them on all public occasions. When dining at home alone with the King, she often wore not only a great deal of jewellery but also her tiara.

The Tecks were known as the Royal Family's poor relations. From time to time – and usually after Princess Mary Adelaide had been more than usually importunate – Queen Victoria would help them out financially. When Princess May was eighteen the Queen provided the Tecks with a grace and favour home in Richmond Park. Previously they had spent two years in Florence, both to escape their creditors and because it was thought cheaper to live in Italy. Although Princess May made good use of the time spent in Italy by familiarizing herself with the art and literature of the region, she never forgot what she considered to be a humiliating reminder of a poverty she was unable to understand. In moving to Florence she had left behind the palatial life-style led by the rest of her family. In Italy the paintings of the Italian Renaissance hung in museums. In England many of her relatives had paintings equally good on their walls. The seeds of envy, sown in early childhood, would have been strongly reinforced in one who was surrounded by affluence at which she could only look but in which she was not allowed to share. By the age of sixteen Princess May was aware that education and knowledge, unlike material wealth, were assets immune to bankruptcy.

A year later, on her seventeenth birthday, she began to take a somewhat different view. In a letter to her eldest brother Adolphus ('Dolly') listing her birthday presents she writes: 'Mama gave me her carbuncle & diamond star earrings, 2 little bracelets with pearl clasps, & a plain pair of earrings . . .' She ends her list with 'Gdmama £2'. Clearly Princess Mary Adelaide, extravagant in every aspect of her life, was as magnanimous with her gifts to her daughter as her own mother had been parsimonious. Princess May's birthday list was significant for its omissions. None of her Wales cousins, nor their mother Princess Alexandra, nor her godmother Queen Victoria gave her anything at all. Out of sight and out of mind, as far as the rest of her family was concerned, Princess May may have resolved that in future, whenever the opportunity arose, she would demonstrate that she was a valued recipient of gifts by wearing several items of jewellery simultaneously on public occasions. On 27 February 1892, seven years later, and this time on the 'wedding day' that never was, 'Uncle

Wales and Motherdear' presented Princess May with a present which had been intended for her. It was a *rivière* of diamonds, together with a dressing bag that Prince Eddy was to have given his bride.

Princess May's parents had wisely engaged Mademoiselle Hélène Bricka, an Alsatian governess and companion who became close to the Princess and was someone in whom she was able to confide. Writing to her former governess just before her marriage to Prince George, Princess May complained about her parents: 'I read as much as possible. But my hands are full, my father pulls me one way, my mother the other, it is good not to become selfish but sometimes I grumble at my life, at the waste of time, at the *petitesse de la vie* when one feels capable of greater things.' Princess May's hopes of achieving 'greater things' died with Prince Eddy. His death came as a shock not only to his fiancée but also to her mother, Princess Mary Adelaide. They both had every reason to mourn him, just as had Prince George who immediately wrote to his grandmother telling her that 'no two brothers could have loved each other more than we did. Alas! it is only now that I have found out how deeply I did love him; & I remember with pain nearly every hard word & little quarrel I ever had with him & I long to ask his forgiveness, but, alas, it is too late now.'

Guilt and self-reproach came easily to Prince George. Brought up with his conscience at full stretch, terrified of offending his beloved mother, his tutor and, later, his senior officers, he was ready to blame himself for events for which he could not be held responsible. The demands of a harsh conscience can never be fully satisfied. When Prince George at last ceased to punish himself, it was because by then he had children on to whom he was able to shift the blame for his own real or imagined misdeeds.

As the fiancée of the late Prince Eddy, Princess May found herself in the company of the Waleses, in the first instance at Osborne, the Isle of Wight home of Queen Victoria, then at White Lodge, Richmond, and later – at the suggestion of Princess Mary Adelaide – at Compton Place, the home of the Duke of Devonshire. Princess Mary Adelaide was at first aghast that her plan to marry her daughter off to Queen Victoria's grandson, so that she might restore her family's credibility and perhaps its fortune, had come to nought. But she was pleased that the Waleses had taken her daughter under their wing. In a letter to his sister Princess Amelie of Teck (the Countess von Hugel) the Duke of Teck wrote with some satisfaction that 'May has become the child of the Waleses, I foresee that she will be much taken up with them.'

With the death of Prince Eddy, Prince George became the heir apparent. The Teck family, the Wales family and almost the entire country realized that the logical outcome for all concerned would be for Prince George to marry Princess May. Neither of the two young people concerned, however, was ready to consider this possibility. Both were still grieving, and neither had romantic feelings for the other. Queen Victoria was insistent, however, that the time had come for her grandson to marry. There were few Princesses of the Blood Royal available and it was essential that Prince George have children as soon as possible. The Queen was concerned that he had not as yet made a complete recovery from the typhoid fever from which he had suffered just before his brother's death. He had lost weight and was not sleeping. The Queen knew that if George, too, failed to come to the throne, the next in line would be Princess Louise, his eldest sister, a scatterbrained young woman who was married to a commoner (the Duke of Fife) and who, to make matters worse, had only one child, a daughter.

At Eastbourne Princess May was gradually getting to know Prince George. It irritated her that he was unable to discuss anything other than his relationship with his brother and spoke constantly to her of Prince Eddy, referring to him as his 'darling boy'. Because he had not previously had a sexual partner, Prince George may have envied his brother's successes, and there is perhaps some Freudian significance in his inheritance of his brother's pen, which he was to use for all his correspondence for the rest of his life.

Queen Victoria continued to impress upon her grandson the importance of marrying as soon as possible. Prince George had barely recovered from his illness and was still in deep mourning for his brother when, in her Birthday Honours of 23 May 1892, it was announced that 'The Queen has been graciously pleased to confer the dignity of a Peerage of the United Kingdom upon His Royal Highness Prince George of Wales, KG, by the name, style and title of Duke of York, Earl of Inverness and Baron Killarney'. Had it been Queen Victoria's intention gradually to involve Prince George in affairs of state preliminary to marriage (and eventually the throne) she was not immediately successful. Having attended some dinners with politicians and made an appearance in the House of Lords which made him anxious, Prince George resumed his naval career.

Princess May was encouraged by her parents to resume her social life as soon as possible. Still feeling bereaved at the sudden loss of her fiancé, however, she found it difficult, like Prince George, to focus her thoughts on anything other than Prince Eddy's death. Nothing seemed to distract her. The winter appeared to be exceptionally cold and she felt lonely. She was isolated from a life-style which, encouraged by her ambitious mother, she had been looking forward to but which, sadly, had not materialized. Only two months earlier her spirits had been high. The disappointment was too much for her to bear. She was grieving not only for something she had never had but for a man she had scarcely known. In February 1892 Princess Mary Adelaide, well aware of her daughter's grief, and knowing that Prince Edward and Princess Alexandra and their family would be at Cap Martin in the South of France, contrived an invitation to a villa in Cannes belonging to Lady Wolverton, a wealthy friend. The Duke and Duchess of Teck and their family at once accepted.

Although Princess May was pleased to be out of England and distanced from the sad events of the previous January, she continued to reflect on her loss and hoped for a distraction that would allow her to get on with her life. Writing to her former governess Mademoiselle Bricka on 24 March 1892 she asked her to 'write [me] one of yr *clever* letters & tell me of anything interesting *qui se passe* in the scientific, thinking world, here I hear too much gossip & one is inclined to sleep, tho' this must *not* happen to me, so I read as much as possible . . . I moralise a good deal to myself but this doesn't help much – When I see people chaffing each other, talking in a flighty way, I think of the tragedy of 2 months ago &

wonder how can they go on like this when there is so much sadness in the world, quite forgetting that they have not suffered as I have & do suffer.' Princess May's sad outpouring of feeling continued: 'Sometimes I feel rather miserable & it does me good to talk out my feelings to so sympathetic an ear as yours . . . When I am alone I feel the loneliness, some vague dream of something pleasant having passed out of one's life for ever.' The sadness of loss was soon to be replaced by the happiness of gain. Unbeknownst to Princess May, within a few days of the Tecks' arrival in Cannes, fate and destiny combined to rewrite history. At Cap Martin, a few miles east of Cannes, Prince Edward and Princess Alexandra arrived with Prince George and their family.

After a decorous interval of three weeks Prince George wrote to Princess May suggesting that they dine together since he and his father were proposing, during the next few days, to visit Cannes on the Royal Yacht *Nerine*. He ended his note by confiding in the Princess the news that 'we are going to stay at a quiet hotel, only don't say anything about it. The others will remain here . . . Goodbye dear "Miss May" . . . ever yr very loving old cousin Georgie.'

When Princess May received Prince George's letter she might well have been struck by its probably unintentional conspiratorial tone. Believing themselves invisible – perhaps because they were beginning to have eyes only for each other – the two cousins strolled along the promenades and through the street markets of Cannes, mildly surprised when they were not only recognized but sometimes presented with flowers, purchased in the local flower market by passers-by. With a freedom scarcely imaginable today, the young royal couple were able to spend a few days out and about, either in Cannes or on a return visit in Cap Martin. In the hothouse atmosphere of two expectant families, each pressing for a satisfactory conclusion to the friendship of their children, the relationship began to flourish.

Prince George and Princess May had much in common. Both had mothers who showered them with tokens of their affection: Princess Alexandra with her many and eloquent letters expressing her undying love for her son, Princess Mary Adelaide with the finery she occasionally lavished on Princess May. These priceless symbols of love (which were to furnish the libraries and illuminate the showcases of posterity) had similar effects on both Prince George and Princess May. Like the favourite toys of childhood, the letters and the jewellery became treasured transitional objects. They were never relinquished by either of the recipients who were condemned to search in vain for the 'hands-on' relationship not only denied them by their mothers but by their fathers who had admired their children from the sidelines and cheered them on but who had seldom joined in the game.

Children who at a crucial time in their development are cheated of their birthright by parents who, through no fault of their own, are sometimes otherwise engaged become angry children. Prince George and Princess May were so deceived by the 'pseudo-love' they had both received from their parents that they were unable to give vent to their angry feelings towards them. Repressed anger may lead either to depression or to a self-righteous assault upon others who are more easily able to express their anger, sometimes violently, and who, perhaps in order to redress the wrongs of childhood, may even take the law into their own hands.

In 1898 an anarchist, whose hatred of crowned heads of state was possibly equalled only by his hatred of the uncrowned head of his own family, stabbed the Empress of Austria to death in Geneva with a file. Following this outrage an extraordinary account of the feelings of the Grand Duchess of Mecklenburg-Strelitz, her niece, Princess May, and her niece's husband, Prince George, were committed to paper. Aunt Augusta wrote to Princess May in 1900 outlining her strategy to rid the world of the anarchists: 'My plan would be, to forbid and close all meetings, Associations, and to muzzle the Press entirely, then, take up every man or woman, expressing anarchist views, have them flogged daily, and if decided murderers, have them tortured then blown off from a Gun.' Princess May expressed herself in favour of lynch law for active anarchists and Prince George was in favour of 'exterminating all anarchists like wasps', 'since hanging or shooting was much too good for them'. Later, as King George V, he told the future Lord

Justice Goddard while conferring a knighthood on him at Buckingham Palace in 1932 that he should not hesitate to sentence violent prisoners to be flogged. The Royal Prince and Princess, both denied love as children, may have unconsciously empathized with – but consciously disapproved of – the rage of those whose inner world was so disadvantaged that they rose up against authority. Although they believed themselves to have been nurtured in a loving environment, they confused the written expression of love and the material wealth they had been given with parental care and attention. They not only therefore identified with authority but passed their faulty nurturing on to their own children, thus unwittingly perpetuating paternalistic tyranny.

As the summer of 1892 came and went Princess May and Prince George became increasingly companionable. No hint of romance passed between them. As yet they felt themselves bound together only by kinship and by the death of Prince Eddy. Princess May and her parents arrived back at White Lodge after their holiday in the South of France which was then followed by a dutiful visit to their German relatives. At the end of the year the Prince and Princess found themselves together again at Sandringham to celebrate the birthday of Princess Alexandra on 1 December. Two days later the anniversary of Princess May's engagement to Prince Eddy brought the enforced gaiety to an end. The inspection of the memorial window dedicated to Prince Eddy at Sandringham Church brought Prince George and Princess May together again briefly before Princess May's return to White Lodge for Christmas.

Prince George and Princess May could hardly be unaware that they were expected by their families to consider each other as prospective marital partners. Prince George, as always, did what was expected of him and sent Princess May a brooch for Christmas, a gift 'close to her heart'. Princess May sent Prince George a pin. They each wrote and received polite and rather guarded thank-you letters. On 14 January 1893 the year of mourning for Prince Eddy came to an end and his shadow began to recede.

Princess May now felt free to allow herself to think of Prince George not as a cousin, nor as a stand-in for his late brother, but as an individual in his own right. What she saw was a man of her own height, with fair hair and blue eyes, lively in disposition but short on conversation. He would become animated only when the subject of shooting was broached or when he was demonstrating a brand of humour more cutting than amusing, which concealed the rage buried within him. Princess May knew that she was better educated than her cousin and, his years touring the Empire in the Navy notwithstanding, more worldly. She sensed Prince George's lack of ease and his total lack of experience in the ways of the opposite sex. While she knew herself to be equally naïve, her cultural interests had imbued her with at least some knowledge of romantic love derived from her reading. While she could not envisage Prince George as a Prince Charming who would sweep her off her feet, she knew that marriage to him might provide her with a framework from within which a more realistic relationship could develop.

Prince George's mother was ambivalent about relinquishing her 'Georgie dear' to another woman. While Princess Alexandra wanted him to marry, she was less concerned about gaining a daughter (she already had three of her own) than about losing her beloved son. Events overtook the reluctant trio, however, and on a visit to Sheen Lodge, the home of his sister Princess Louise, Prince George allowed himself to be pushed into the garden to propose marriage to his cousin Princess May. Princess Alexandra had already made her views known to her son in a letter a few weeks earlier. She reminded him that 'there is a bond of love between us, that of mother and child, which nothing can ever diminish or render less binding – and nobody can, or shall ever, come between me and my darling Georgie boy'. While she had to accept that she must give up her son to another woman, she made sure that he knew he was expected to remain faithful to his mother for ever.

Princess May accepted her cousin Prince George's proposal and Queen Victoria immediately gave her consent. She wrote to her grandson telling him 'how thankful I am that this great and so long & ardently wished for event is settled & I gladly give my consent to what I pray may be for your happiness and for the Country's good. Say everything affectionate to dear May, for whom this must be a *trying moment* full of such mixed feelings. But she cannot find a *better* husband than you and I am sure she will be a good, devoted and useful wife to you.' If Prince George felt, as he did when he was banished from home as a child, that he was on his own and now expected to fend for himself, he might have been comforted by the fact that his future wife was at least expected to be 'useful' to him. He had done what was expected of him. He would fulfil his duty to Crown and Country. He would remain faithful to his mother and at the same time would acquire a companion who would look after his interests. He now felt free to devote himself to his other passions, shooting and stamp-collecting.

· 8 ·

Killing animals and sticking in stamps

PRINCE GEORGE'S INTEREST in stamps began during the 1880s while he was serving in the Navy. His uncle Alfred, Duke of Edinburgh, Commander-in-Chief of the Mediterranean fleet, himself a collector, encouraged his nephew in what at first was simply a pastime while the Prince was under his command on HMS *Thunderer*. Uncle Alfred took the view that since as a sailor Prince George would be travelling the world, he would have every opportunity to collect the stamps of the countries he visited.

Prince George enjoyed spending his shore leave with the Duke and his family at San Antonio Palace on the Island of Malta, not only because their shared interest brought him close to his uncle but also because he was attracted to his uncle's thirteen-year-old daughter Princess Marie, who took little or no interest in him.

The Prince may also have been drawn to what was later to become his hobby for less obvious reasons. Uncommunicative, and obliged by Prince Edward and Princess Alexandra to regard the Navy as his career, he accepted the distanced communication of letter-writing as the only means of keeping in touch with his parents. The stamps on the envelopes he received would at first have been of lesser interest than the enclosures, mainly from his mother, contained within. As time passed, the stamps themselves became of interest.

After the introduction of the penny post in Britain in 1840, the leisured Victorians became a nation of letter writers. In the first year alone 132 million letters were delivered in England and Wales; in 1870 the number was 704 million, and by 1913 it had risen to 2,827 million. In the City of London, by 1890, a letter was often delivered within four hours of posting, and there were as many as twelve deliveries a day (Browne, 1993).

Stamp-collecting was a hobby available to everyone, but few, other than some ladies of leisure, took advantage of it. *Punch* noted in 1842: 'A new hobby has bitten the industriously idle ladies of [Victorian] England . . . They betray more anxiety to treasure up Queen's heads than Harry the Eighth did to be rid of them.' Prince George was not in fact the first British monarch to collect stamps. Queen Victoria had always displayed a fascination and respect for the Post Office and the postal system and, unlike any other British monarch since, always paid for her stamps. She was also a stamp collector and it was her enthusiasm that fired her grandson, in 1896, to become President of the London Philatelic Society.

Although Prince George began as a general collector, by 1906 he had focused his attention on the stamps of Great Britain and the British Empire which bore the portraits of either his grandmother or his father and were reminders of his own future status. By 1910 every stamp in his collection bore his image, a gratification unique to the King. When the Duke of Edinburgh died in 1900, King Edward VII, who had always encouraged Prince George's interest in philately, bought his brother's stamp collection and presented it to his son. Collecting postage stamps (together with the letters they embellished) appealed to Prince George's methodical and conscientious nature. His obsessional personality which had served him well in the Navy, where precision and concern for detail can make a difference between life and death, came to the fore in his major leisure interest. Reluctance to throw anything away, or to give anything up, is a trait, needless to say, common to collectors.

A large quantity of letters to Prince George from his mother, from his tutor and from all those concerned for him, whether as servant or friend, were discovered on his death in 1936. All were neatly packaged in bundles and clearly labelled. Prince George also kept a diary, almost without a break, from 1878 until three days before his death. As with every child, communication was of great importance to him. What was less usual was the fact that his mother had difficulty in hearing him, that his tutors had impressed on him the importance of being seen and not heard and that he was forced to rely on letter-writing to communicate his deepest feelings to his mother as an adolescent. It was hardly surprising that as an adult he found it easier to write to his diary and to commune with his image on his stamps than to articulate his love for his wife.

Prince George was a creature of habit, and at the age of six, as soon as his tutoring began, the pattern of his life became apparent. He preferred to know what he was doing at every moment of the day and confided to his diary where he had been and how he felt. Knowing what he had done and what he was about to do made him feel more secure. As he grew older, perhaps as a reaction to his experience in the Navy when time was used to control him, he used time to control others. As King, perhaps as a faint echo of the rigid feeding patterns of his childhood, he would enter the breakfast room each morning between the nine strokes of Big Ben. Luncheon was served at 1.30 p.m. and tea at five o'clock. After dinner King George either read or examined his stamps and he retired to bed at 11.10 p.m. precisely. Uncertain of the shifting sands upon which he stood, he felt safer upon the firm ground of familiarity.

In addition to collecting stamps and preserving his letters, Prince George collected pictures of young children. This may have been to remind him of the time in his life when he had received the most attention from his parents, but was possibly also because as an adult the child still present within him felt more at ease with other children. For a similar reason – or perhaps simply as a reminder of the carefree time when he had been unaware of the responsibilities that lay ahead – he also acquired a number of mechanical toys, although he claimed they were for his children (Smith, 1910).

Later, when he had children of his own, he dealt with his overwhelming love for them by keeping them safely at arm's length. Easily moved to tears, both of sadness and of joy, it was only in old age, when he was able to embrace his grandchildren, that he ceased to guard his feelings. His interest in carrier pigeons, second only to his stamp collection, also reflected, as did the letters that bore the stamps, the silent communication to which he had to resort with his mother.

In 1881, when the *Bacchante* visited Australia, Prince George was particularly fascinated by the carrier pigeons used by a newspaper reporter from the *Adelaide Observer*. The Prince himself sent off four of the birds. The first carried a message to his mother, the second a message to Government House and the third some private instructions. In the case of the fourth bird, Prince George said: 'We will let this poor little thing go without any message, it will arrive at home all the sooner.' It was probably the Prince who was the 'poor little thing' whose dearest wish was to fly home to his mother.

Prince George read and reread every word of his mother's letters. Unlike the ephemeral spoken words used by most mothers to their sons, Princess Alexandra's intimate written messages to Prince George were to remain with him for ever, keeping her constantly by his side. The stamp, later to bear King George V's head, was a reminder to Princess Alexandra of the son she had once banished, while King George V's almost mute relationship as a child with Princess Alexandra ensured his continuing interest in alternative forms of communication. As an adult, King George V had very little to say to those around him. On Christmas Day 1934 this man of few words was to become the first monarch to communicate with his people over the air, albeit by reading a message written for him by his friend Rudyard Kipling. The words of others compensated him for the paucity of his own and he discontinued reading aloud to Princess May only after his accession, by which time his words had acquired the panoply of status and like him were at last accorded recognition.

By the time of his death in 1936, by dint of zealous collecting, King George V had acquired the finest stamp collection in the world. Three hundred and twenty-five volumes bound in Moroccan leather were needed to house it. The King was never happier than when he was in the stamp room at Buckingham Palace, oblivious to his surroundings, in the company of his friend, adviser and collaborator Edward Bacon. Edward Bacon – later Sir Edward – took the same train from South Croydon, three times a week, to mount the King's stamps, to discuss his most recent acquisitions and to take lunch with him. In 1913, within a few months of his appointment, Edward Bacon (by sad coincidence) became, like Queen Alexandra, profoundly deaf. Unfortunate though this obviously was for Mr Bacon, his affliction enhanced his companionship with a man brought up with little to say because (as he believed) no one had listened to him. Closeted together in the stamp room, insulated from all sounds and distractions, the two friends retreated from the outside world. They were so absorbed in their mutual interest that time went unnoticed. When the King entered his stamp room, the page and footman in attendance knew that their services would not be needed. In all the years in which they had worked for him, when the King was occupied with his stamps they had been sent for only twice.

Probably as early as 1890 King George V began to collect stamps seriously. It was not until his marriage to Princess May three years later, however, after he had focused his attention on the stamps of Great Britain and the Empire, that he joined the Philatelic Society and was immediately elected to Honorary Vice-President. Three years after this he was elected President. His fellow members of the society added significantly to his collection by giving him a present of postage stamps as a wedding gift. Since wedding presents are usually intended for both bride and groom, it is not known whether Queen Mary felt snubbed by the partisan nature of the gift. Although she showed little or no interest in her husband's hobby, she was probably grateful that when the King was occupied with his stamps he was able to find some relief from the pressures of his constitutional duties.

The stamps became a ritual, compulsive in nature and addictive in quality. Both before and after his marriage the King spent three afternoons a week in the stamp room. Since his only companion was Edward Bacon, who was unable to hear him, it represented a comforting return to the peaceful, quiet period in his life when little or nothing was expected of him. He was fascinated by his stamps and by the facsimiles of the crowned heads of Europe which put him in touch once again with some of the relatives with whom he had grown up. In the privacy of the stamp room, where no one was allowed to disturb him, the King arranged and rearranged his collection. His stamps satisfied his obsessional need for order, reflected his concern with how others saw him, nourished his narcissistic self-sufficiency and, ultimately, fulfilled his expectation of loneliness.

A study of the books King George V read, first as a child and later as an adult, provides a picture of his hopes and aspirations for the future and his curiosity about the past. In the same orderly manner that he was later to classify his stamps, he made a list of all the books he had read since 1890 (Gore, 1941). He was interested not so much in the historical past as in his own (royal) past, and among the many biographies were that of his grandmother *Queen Victoria* by her Private Secretary Sir Arthur Ponsonby, Grace Williams's *The Patriot King* (William IV), E.F. Benson's *Edward VII, King Edward and His Times* by André Maurois, *Victoria the Widow and Her Son* by Hector Bolitho and Sir George Arthur's *Queen Alexandra*. It is not given to everyone to read biographies of their parents and not everyone would wish to do so. It is probably fair to say that the happier one's past the less need there is to re-examine it. King George was fascinated by his past, however, and could not learn enough about it.

Another interest that was reflected in the King's reading was his passion for hunting and shooting. His involvement in blood sports rivalled that of his father King Edward VII, and when, in the last few years of his life, his days of shooting were coming to an end he exchanged violent sport for violent and macabre novels. On his bookshelf were kept *The Massacre of Glencoe* (John Buchan), *The Murder of the Romanovs* (Paul Bulygin) and David Lloyd George's *War Memoirs*. He might also have sought a better understanding of women from reading *Lady Chatterley's Lover* (D.H. Lawrence) or from *The Story of My Life* by his cousin Marie, Queen of Rumania, the first girl to whom he had been attracted but who had not reciprocated his feelings.

King George V overcame the disability of his crippling shyness by his determination to excel in his leisure pursuits. In the last shooting season before the Great War King George, who was one of the finest game shots in the country, fired 1,760 cartridges in a single day. On another day he brought down thirty-nine birds with thirty-nine consecutive cartridges. His attachment to shooting was such that sometimes his family complained that he loved his shooting companions more than his children. This passion for shooting, this sublimated anger, this attempt to right the wrongs of childhood by 'fighting back' leads us to ask whom he was targeting. Surely not his parents? His mother's protestations of love, however, obscured the fact that she and Prince Edward may have been the real targets for his aggression. He did, in all fairness, give the birds a chance to escape; sportingly allowing them to fly almost out of range before he shot them down, he gave them an opportunity which, as a fledgeling, had not been offered to him.

On his shore leaves during his naval training Prince George had frequently taken part in the sporting facilities provided by his hosts. He shot kangaroos and peacocks in Australia, wild buffalo and elk in Ceylon and turkey buzzards and other wildfowl in Argentina. He was never happier, however, than when he was shooting on the Sandringham estate, close to his childhood home.

While aboard the *Bacchante* Prince George had engaged Henry Feltham to teach him how to box. It was not long before the tutor realized that it was not so much boxing in which the Prince was interested as in 'having a go'. Mr Feltham, it is recorded, had to use a certain amount of force to terminate the Prince's aggression towards him. Although Prince George had been brought up to have an exaggerated respect for his superiors during his naval training, this did not prevent him from 'playfully' taking every opportunity to act out his hostility towards authority. He made apple-pie beds for his senior officers and enjoyed playing practical 'jokes' on them.

Prince George, a true Victorian, did not neglect the philanthropy which was a characteristic feature of the landed gentry in Britain. The social ills of Britain in the nineteenth century, in the absence of a welfare state, could hardly be remedied by individual effort. Charitable endeavour, while doing little to mitigate the plight of the poor, at least relieved the consciences of the rich. Prince George was concerned especially with child welfare and, in particular, supported disadvantaged children with whom he could readily identify. Although as a child he had not himself been materially deprived, his concern for those emotionally in need suggests that he had much in common with them. One of his favourite charities was the Gordon Boys' Home, opened in memory of one of his heroes, Charles Gordon, who fell defending Khartoum against the Mahdi in 1885.

Presiding at the festival dinner of the home in 1897, Prince George was struck by the number of sick and impoverished boys who were resident there. He was moved to congratulate all concerned with the excellent 'discipline' of the home, perhaps seeing it as the remedy for childhood ills and a sad reflection of his own experiences. Discipline and duty, instilled in him from birth and reinforced by his tutor Mr Dalton, were the guiding principles of his life

Queen Mary, like her husband, was also a collector of images, although she was less interested in postage stamps than in other forms of royal iconography. Her understanding and knowledge of art, which had begun in Italy, had been further encouraged by her friendship with Gian Tufnell, the niece of Lady Wolverton, in whose Cannes villa she and her mother had taken refuge in the months following Prince Eddy's death. Gian Tufnell had been Princess Mary Adelaide's second lady-in-waiting from 1895 until her marriage to Lord Mount Stephen, an elderly Canadian railroad millionaire, two years later. Queen Mary and Lady Mount Stephen shared common memories and, with Lady Mount Stephen's expert help, Queen Mary began to accumulate mementoes and became as well known in Bond Street as she was in the small antiques shops of King's Lynn and Cambridge.

In touch perhaps with her own fragility, she was attracted to Chinese snuff boxes, Battersea enamels, porcelains and miniatures. Each piece had to have a provenance, preferably one which connected it with her family. She was disappointed when after the death of the second Duke of Cambridge, Queen Victoria's cousin, in 1904 his sons sold their father's uncatalogued effects in various sale rooms. In a letter to her Aunt Augusta in 1909 Princess May wrote: 'If only I could find the history of all these things, how interesting it wld be, but alas there is no inventory, nothing.' She told her aunt how busy she was making sure that her own possessions were carefully listed, together with their histories. She made the point that she had acquired a wonderful collection of family things since her marriage 'without spending much money over it'. An *objet* is often more valued by a collector when it is a 'bargain' or a gift. While children are entitled to something for nothing and no child should be expected to reward his parents for the love that is his by right, adults are usually expected to pay for the acquisitions they amass in an attempt to compensate for missed parental love. The 'child' in Queen Mary clearly took precedence over the adult.

Queen Mary and King George were no more or less influenced by the past than those with similar upbringings. What made them unique was their ability to surround themselves with artefacts denied to those with less leisure and fewer financial resources. It was through these unique collections that they were able to categorize, classify, replicate, react to and unconsciously memorialize their past experiences.

Queen Mary's re-creation of her emotionally minimalist past was the Doll's House designed for her in 1920 by Sir Edwin Lutyens, the architect of New Delhi. Lutyens had just completed the Cenotaph in Whitehall when he was commissioned by some friends of Queen Mary to build a doll's house in the style of a Palladian country house in which all the objects, including the royal occupants, were to be one-twelfth of life size. Menkes (1991) points out that as much space was given to the strong-room which housed the Queen's jewels as to the nursery for the children. The diminutive garden was designed by Gertrude Jekyll, and the two hundred miniature books for the King's library – many of which were written specially – were contributed by, among others, Arnold Bennett, A.E. Houseman, Aldous Huxley, Robert Graves and Rudyard Kipling, who wrote 'If' specially for the project. Sir Alfred Munnings, Heath Robinson, Mark Gertler and 'Fougasse' were among the artists who painted or drew the seven hundred tiny prints and watercolours. The vintage wines in the cellars included an 1874 Château d'Y Quem. The Doll's House, which was completed in 1924 in time for the Wembley Exhibition, was eventually relocated in Windsor Castle.

While King George and Queen Mary were happy to lead parallel lives, neither of them lived emotionally in the present. It could not be said of King George V, as was said of his father, that his life was spent in the pursuit of pleasure or the avoidance of boredom. His dislike of society turned him in on himself, but with his stamp collection for company he was never lonely, and when he found it necessary to give vent to his ever-present and explosive rage there was always his gun.

·9·

The Queen has gladly given her consent

O N 3 MAY 1893, at the home of the Duke and Duchess of Fife at Sheen Lodge in Richmond Park, the 27-year-old Prince George proposed marriage to the 26-year-old Princess May and was accepted by her. On the following day the official announcement appeared in the newspapers: 'Her Majesty received this evening the news of the betrothal of her beloved grandson, the Duke of York, to Princess Victoria Mary of Teck, to which union the Queen has gladly given her consent.'

A shadow was cast over the day by a surprising announcement in the *Star,* a London newspaper, which reported that Prince George was already married to the daughter of a British naval officer in Malta. The Prince was at first amused to think that there were some who thought of him as being a sexual adventurer, but as time passed the joke, such as it was, turned sour. It was not until 1910, however, after years of being haunted by allegations of bigamy, that legal steps were taken to quash the rumour. After an article in a French republican newspaper stated that the King 'foully abandoned his true wife and entered into a sham and shameful marriage with a daughter of the Duke of Teck', the editor, E.F. Mylius, was immediately arrested. He was successfully prosecuted for criminal libel and sentenced to twelve months' imprisonment. There was no evidence to support the slur on the King's character, but it was not until the trial ended that his honour was finally vindicated (Rose, 1987).

On 3 May 1893 the nation's only concern was with the news of the royal engagement, and preparations were immediately put in hand for the pageant that was to make Princess May's and Prince George's wedding day the century's most colourful event. In honour of the occasion the

Princess's portrait was painted, and because she was slim-waisted and tall she looked particularly becoming in her court dress. An editorial in *The Times*, however, struck a pragmatic note. Referring to the recent death of Prince Eddy (Duke of Clarence), it conceded that the 'betrothal accords with the fitness of things, and, so far from offending any legitimate sentiment, is the most appropriate and delicate medicament for a wound in its nature never wholly effaceable'. Queen Victoria was entirely delighted, not least because the heir of the heir apparent had chosen for his bride the first consort of English birth since James, Duke of York, married Anne Hyde, daughter of the first Earl of Clarendon in 1659.

Princess Alexandra wrote to her son from Malta two days after the announcement of the engagement. The message the letter bore was ambivalent. 'With what mixed feelings I read your telegram! Well all I can say is that I pray God to give you both a long and happy life together, and that you will make up to dear May all that she lost in darling Eddy and that you will be a mutual happiness to each other, a comfort to us, and a blessing to the nation.'

The leader in *The Times* and the letter from his mother brought home to Prince George that he was Princess May's second choice. It was a difficult role for any man, but it was too soon to expect the shadow of Prince Eddy to disappear and unreasonable to expect it to do so.

Prince George and Princess May had been close companions since childhood, and since the death of Prince Eddy they had been drawn closer to each other and understood each other's feelings. Although the marriage might in a sense have been arranged, this was only because there was no other suitable candidate for either of them. From the time of Prince Eddy's death both of them knew that they were being considered for one another and were happy with how events turned out. Although either one of them could have refused the match, neither of them did so.

Prince George in reality had little or no experience of women other than his sisters and his mother, all of whom, in their different ways, had mixed feelings about the marriage. His mother never denied that she found it difficult to let him go, and his sisters had previously championed the cause of Princess Hélène. Only Queen Victoria knew where her duty lay. She had to secure the accession and had a thousand years of royal ancestry and a compliant grandson to back her up. Prince George had been trained to obey all orders that came from above, and when the Queen informed him of his duty he had no problem with accepting her command. He might even have felt relieved that a decision had been taken for him in a matter of which he had no previous experience.

Princess May also knew her duty. She was pressed to accept Prince George's proposal not only by her ambitious and financially impoverished mother but also by her sense of destiny. Her disappointing childhood, the nagging realization that she was cut out for better things than always to be a poor relation of the Royal Family and her conviction that fate had demanded that she would marry the younger brother were sufficient to make up her mind. It was unlikely that either Prince George or Princess May was 'in love', but they certainly liked one another and were happy that it should be so.

It soon became apparent that the Prince and Princess were opposites in almost every way. Princess May, brought up with nothing, had been taught to expect everything; Prince George, brought up with everything, had learned to expect nothing. The Princess had an importunate, greedy and grossly overweight mother who adored material possessions and who envied the wealth of others. She had led her daughter to believe that a person's worth was represented by their degree of personal adornment. Prince George, on the other hand, had been brought up to believe in simplicity and hardship, in duty and obedience, in the unavailability of women other than his mother and in the written rather than the spoken word.

By the time his father, King Edward VII, died in May 1910 Prince George had been married to Princess May for almost seventeen years. Five months later, shortly after his accession to the throne, the young couple, now King George V and Queen Mary, exchanged letters with each other. The King, who was at Sandringham, had, perhaps belatedly, become aware that his wife was beginning to wonder whether he really liked her. He wrote: 'Fancy this is the first letter I have written to you since our lives have been entirely changed by darling Papa having been taken away from us. You have never left me for a single day since that sad event.'

Aware that his relatively carefree days had ended, King George seems to have realized his need for a strong replacement for his father. He explained to his wife that, although he had never been able to show his feelings for her, he loved her dearly. He told her also that her strength and support following the death of his father had been an enormous comfort to him: 'My love grows stronger for you every day mixed with admiration & I thank God every day that he has given me such a darling devoted wife as you are. God bless you my sweet Angel May, who I know will always stick to me as I need your love & help more than ever now.'

Perhaps only partly reassured by her husband's declaration, Queen Mary replied: 'What a pity it is you cannot tell me what you write for I should appreciate it so enormously – It is such a blessing to know that I am a help to you.' King George's response the next day was only one of many letters written over the years protesting feelings for his wife that he was able to express (not surprisingly) only in writing. 'I am glad my letter pleased. I really am full of feeling and sentiment & am very sympathetic but somehow I always find it difficult to express what I feel except in a letter, especially to the person I love & am always with like you darling.'

King George and Queen Mary had both been brought up to devote themselves to public ceremonial at the expense of devotion to family. If either of them had realized that they had themselves been cheated, and were now in turn cheating on their own families, their strong sense of occasion – at least in the run-up to their marriage – would have obscured this realization. King George had his early spontaneity dampened by too rigid a work schedule from the time that Mr Dalton had entered his life, and Queen Mary learned belatedly to suppress her own feelings in the face of positive feedback from her husband.

The wedding took place at the Chapel Royal, St James's Palace, on 6 July 1893. Prince George and Princess May were married by the Archbishop of Canterbury and the Bishops of London and Rochester in the presence of the Royal Family and most of the crowned heads of Europe. After the ceremony the royals returned to Buckingham Palace for the signing of the marriage register. At five o'clock, with the wedding breakfast concluded, the Prince and Princess drove in their carriage through the streets packed with cheering Londoners to Liverpool Street Station where they took the train to Sandringham where they were to spend their honeymoon.

Prince George and Princess May were given two homes by Prince Edward and Princess Alexandra: York House in St James's Palace and York Cottage at Sandringham. It was at York Cottage that the couple, now the Duke and Duchess of York, were to live for more than thirty years, and it was here that Princess May came to realize that she and her husband were unequal partners in the marriage. York Cottage had previously been known as Bachelors' Cottage. A few hundred yards from Sandringham House, it had been built by the side of a pond to accommodate male guests for whom there was no room in the main house. The cottage had very little to commend it. Its neo-Gothic appearance was unattractive and it reflected a variety of architectural styles. Colonel Ellis, who claimed to be an architect but who turned out in fact not to be one, was hired by Prince Edward to refurbish it and make it habitable for the young married couple. He failed miserably.

The exterior consisted of black-and-white Elizabethan gables mixed haphazardly with Gothic turrets, pebbledash stucco and local stone, with several small more or less useless, non-functioning balconies. The interior of the cottage, although reasonably large, was little better. Most of the rooms were small and dark and furnished rather gloomily in the unattractive suburban style of the day. The Prince's sitting-room was particularly dark, because its windows were obscured by a laurel.

Queen Victoria's granddaughter, Princess Alice, Countess of Athlone, recalls in her memoirs (Athlone, 1966) that she would stay regularly with her Uncle George and her sister-in-law Princess May at York Cottage.

> It was a poky and inconvenient place, architecturally repulsive and always full of the smell of cooking. George adored it, but then he had the only comfortable room in the house, which was called the 'library', though it contained very few books. The décor of this room was hideous. The walls were lined with a red material worn by Zouaves! Uncle George's much treasured guns were on display in a glass-doored cabinet. He was one of the best shots in England and I think his love of York Cottage was in great measure the outcome of his passion for shooting. The drawing room was small enough when only two adults occupied it – but after tea, when five children were crammed into it as well, it became a veritable bedlam.

The cottage was also too small for live-in staff, but its disadvantages were partly compensated for by its surroundings. It was a novel situation for the happy couple to have a home of their own and they enjoyed the experience. It was not long, however, before Princess May realized that Prince George was entirely indifferent to his surroundings. Having spent so long in the Navy, a house to him seemed to be nothing more than a place to stay in between voyages. He liked the size of the rooms, many of them not much larger than ships' cabins.

Princess May saw her home in a different light. Her interest in it was that of a bride looking to build the nest in which she could bring up a family. In marrying a Prince of the realm, she had not considered that she would be condemned to life in an overcrowded ship's cabin. Neither had she considered that Prince George would furnish the house himself and in a style which she found totally unacceptable. The Prince, with his father and his eldest sister Princess Louise, had bought all the fabrics, carpets and wallpapers from Maples which was noted for its 'modern' furniture. Princess May was given no say in how her new home would look and she found herself living in a house in which many of the paintings were replicas and nearly all the furniture reproduction.

Prince George, who had been brought up in the shadow of an older brother destined to be King, was not himself an 'original'. He was the second son, it was the unexpected death of his brother that had made him heir presumptive to the throne and he had even taken his brother's place at the altar. Throughout his life he had been a replacement and destined always to be number two. Prince George was not his wife's first choice, and neither was Princess May his.

From this false start the Prince and the Princess were to jockey with each other over the next few years for first place. Princess May had an additional rival to contend with. She found herself living next door to a woman still in love with her husband.

10

I am very glad I am married and I don't feel at all strange

A T FIRST PRINCE George and Princess May, a country boy and a sophisticated girl, seemed to have little in common. The Prince's main interests, other than stamp-collecting, took place outside the home, whereas the Princess preferred life indoors amongst the artefacts and *objets* which were often reflections of her family background. She loved her new home, arranging it and rearranging it in an effort to make it more attractive. While the Prince's home life had been interrupted by his two years aboard *Britannia,* followed by a further three years on the *Bacchante,* Princess May's life had been similarly disrupted when her parents left London, which they could not afford, for Florence, but at least Princess May's move to Italy provided her with a new interest centred around the paintings and the architecture of the city.

Prince George, a Victorian English gentleman, while well acquainted with the world geographically knew little about its culture. Princess May, a typical English rose, had yet to bloom. The personality of the Prince allowed him to play his ceremonial roles without difficulty. The personality of the Princess demanded that she involve herself in all matters relating to the arts and, unusually for her time, the needs of women. On his marriage the Prince was a dutiful and highly disciplined naval officer. When the Princess married she had little experience of life other than that which she had learned from nineteenth-century literature. The press eulogized her intellectual attributes and informed their readers that 'no young lady of the present day . . . is more thoroughly grounded in the English classics, or more happily at home in modern literature than is our future Queen'. She was described also as a brilliant linguist and familiar with the works of Goethe and Schiller. When Prince George set up home with his new bride he expected life to continue as before. When Princess May pledged her troth to a potentially wealthy Prince of the realm she anticipated a radical change in her life-style and hoped perhaps that she might be able to remedy some of the more obvious defects in her husband's education.

For one accustomed to life at sea, running a home might seem little different from running a ship. At the age of twelve Prince George had been expected to look after himself, to carry out running repairs to his clothing, to prepare simple meals and to batten down the hatches when navigating difficult waters. At the same time, however, he had also been provided with a valet and other attendants. He was like the other cadets but different from them. He was special. He had special privileges. A special cabin to be shared only with his brother. He had been a special child and had a special mother, albeit one who had let her son leave home with scarcely a word of protest. He had been trained to live by the rules and not to question them, and he expected others to do the same. But in his rule book nothing was as it seemed. His mother wrote love letters to him, and his father loved other women. He had been sent away to become independent but had been provided with servants. He had adapted to life without parents but remained dependent upon their approval, as he was later to depend on the approval of his wife and his subjects. He was expected to become a parent, but he had role models whose attitudes to him were at best confusing.

Princess May had lived by more flexible rules and continued to do so. But her role models were as confusing as her husband's. Like Prince George she had a dominant mother and a weak father, but unlike Prince George she was entirely in control of her feelings. She found no difficulty in identifying with her dominant mother and looked forward, with a crusading zeal, to shaping the Prince's behaviour to correspond more closely with her own. Princess May was acutely aware of her husband's educational deficiencies. The comment that 'his planned education ended just where and when it should seriously have begun. [He was] below the educational and perhaps intellectual standard of the ordinary public school educated country squire' (Gore, 1941) encapsulates the problem that Princess May decided she would attempt to remedy. She took it upon herself to continue her husband's education by reading to him and conversing with him in French and German.

Prince George, a resourceful and essentially a practical man, looked after the interests of those who were dependent upon him and, in return, he expected that his own dependent needs be satisfied. His employees, like him, had been brought up to know their place and like him they expected to do as they were told. The Prince could give as well as he had got. A physical, rather than a cerebral man, he had probably survived his fragmented childhood for being so. Had he been more thoughtful and introspective he might have coped less well with the stresses of his reign.

Women had as yet played only a small part in Prince George's life. He noted in his diary that a year or so before his marriage he had 'shared' a girlfriend with his brother in St John's Wood. It has been suggested that the two brothers were kept so short of money that they could afford only one girl between them. It seems more likely that where the sexually adventurous Eddy would lead the more timid George would follow. His two brief emotional forays, the first with his cousin Marie and the second with his childhood friend Julie Stonor, had also been abortive and he soon turned his back on them. Women seemed not to need him and he would have no need of them. He would emulate instead his father's passion for shooting and, with a firm grip on his gun, make a life for himself. He was, above all, unaware of a woman's nesting instinct and her need to furnish her own home. He believed that in preparing the cottage with the help of his mother for his wife's arrival he had saved Princess May the trouble of decorating it herself.

Princess May was distressed that she had not been given the opportunity to choose her own decorations but deemed it inappropriate to complain. Like her husband, she had also brought some emotional baggage to the marriage. She needed to be admired not only for her appearance but for her intellectual qualities. As a child she had relied on the education she had had with Mademoiselle Bricka to compensate for her material deficits, and from her she had learned that for a woman who had little to fall back on financially education was an asset.

Before her marriage, while she was considering whether she wanted to spend her life on the Sandringham estate, Princess May could not have anticipated Prince George's controlling personality. Life at York Cottage had to proceed at his pace. Used to being the captain of a tight ship, and not knowing any other way, he expected to continue in the same manner in his home. Princess May, wise beyond her years, struggled to play the role imposed upon her by her husband and knew that if their relationship was not to be emotionally sterile she must proceed slowly. Unwilling to reproach her husband for fear of rocking the boat of a marriage as yet barely afloat, she looked around her for a scapegoat. It was not long before she found one.

In the early days of her marriage it was the close proximity of her mother-in-law that troubled Princess May the most. She wrote in her journal: 'I sometimes think that just after we were married we were not left alone enough and this led to many little rubs which might have been avoided.' She soon began to realize that Princess Alexandra believed that there was room for one Princess only at Sandringham. Any change in York Cottage had to be approved by 'Georgie dear's' mother who often arrived uninvited, daughters and dogs in attendance, and felt herself free to criticize not only her daughter-in-law's home but the marriage. Princess Alexandra made it clear from the beginning that she resented Princess May for taking 'Georgie dear' away from her. It was understandable resentment from a woman whose philandering husband had left her with only the comfort of her children. It was no consolation to Princess May to discover that Princess Alexandra was just as demanding of her two unmarried daughters as she was of her son and his new wife. She had already made it plain that she would not allow Princess Victoria, who was anyway considered insufficiently attractive to find a husband, to marry. The Princess was told that she was needed at home to look after her mother. Princess Maude had had a few suitors, but her mother always found reasons to send them away. Both girls had at first been fond of Princess May, but they soon began to resent her and envy her the marital status to which they themselves aspired but which they were prevented by their mother from achieving.

The royal biographer John Gore, very conscious of the rights of women and particularly sensitive to what Princess May was going through, looked back at the early years of the royal marriage. In his personal memoir of King George and Queen Mary he writes: 'Sometimes the Duchess's intellectual life there [at York Cottage] may have been starved and her energies atrophied in those early years. For she came from a younger more liberal generation, with far more serious notions of woman's spheres of usefulness, and very strong ideas of the responsibilities demanded of the first ladies of the realm. For many women, then and now, the daily call to follow the shooters, to watch the killing, however faultless, to take always a cheerful appreciative part in man-made, man-valued amusements, must have been answered at the sacrifice of many cherished, constructive and liberal ambitions' (Gore, 1941).

Prince George was almost certainly unaware of the growing disharmony within his family. Since the season had begun soon after the wedding, much of his time was spent shooting. The Prince, who was becoming increasingly obsessional, had taken to wearing a pedometer and recording the distance he walked during a day's shooting. His average was somewhere between eleven and twelve miles. Despite some of the more irritating incidents that marred the honeymoon period for his wife, he at least was happy. He wrote to an old naval friend, Flag-Lieutenant Bryan Godfrey-Faussett, on 16 July 1893: 'I can hardly yet realise that I am a married man, although I have been so for the last 10 days. All I can say is that I am intensely happy, far happier than I ever thought I could be with anybody.' He went on to tell his friend how contented he was to be spending his honeymoon in the 'charming little cottage' that his father had given him, describing it as a haven of peace 'after all we went through in London'.

After living for so long at sea, Prince George found himself in an alien environment. He was certainly happy at York Cottage because the rooms reminded him of the small cabins that he was used to, but he was at first embarrassed to find himself alone with a cultured adult woman. Such was the strength of Princess May's personality, however, and her obvious desire to make the relationship work, that within a very short time he fell in love with her, and he remained in love with her for the rest of his life. His feelings for his wife were reciprocated. On 9 July 1893, during the first week of the honeymoon, Princess May wrote to Mademoiselle Bricka to tell her how she was feeling. 'Georgie is a dear . . . he adores me which is touching. He likes reading to people so I jumped at this & he is going to read me some of his favourite books . . . I am very glad I am married and I don't feel at all strange.' The Princess told Mademoiselle Bricka that she felt as if she had been married 'for years' but thought the cottage too small, although she was certain that she would be able to do something with it.

Her comment that she felt she had been married to (had known) Prince George for years is an illusion common to all those who fall in love. The feeling of partners that they have known one another 'for ever' is thought to be a reminder of their first, not altogether satisfactory, infantile 'love affair' they had with the mother. Since it was the custom for infants to be removed from their mothers immediately after birth, neither Princess May nor Prince George had been given the opportunity to bond with theirs. If the primary love affair is as unsatisfactory as this, the need to bond with 'a mother' remains and may be acted out in adult life. It says much for the genuine love that Prince George and Princess May had for one another, as well as for the Princess's instinctive realization that she would always have to play a maternal role with her mother-fixated husband, that throughout the forty-three years of their marriage they remained loyal to each other. It is an interesting footnote that when Queen Victoria first saw her eldest son, Prince Edward, she told the nurse to take him away because he was so ugly. Prince Edward did not bond with his mother but he did spend his life searching for the love she had denied him. Princess Alexandra in her wisdom, however, unlike Princess May, preferred to mother her children rather than her husband.

Prince George had always enjoyed reading aloud. He had read to his mother every evening during the hair-combing ritual and he quickly experienced a similar closeness with his bride. It says much for the success of their marriage that the possibility of another damaging mother–child relationship, such as he had with his mother, was at first not an issue. It did, however, become a problem after their first child was born. Prince George then placed his wife on a pedestal (where she remained until his death in 1936) and worshipped at her feet, as he had once worshipped his mother. Queen Mary was happy to play the role of mother. It suited her as much as it did Prince George. She would become a mother figure as often as he wished. She would be a mother to her husband and a mother to her people, but she did not believe that her duties as a royal mother included being a mother to her children. Her 'jewels' were in her crown, rather than in her nursery.

Events now moved quickly for the newly-weds. At the end of July 1893 they were invited by Queen Victoria to spend Cowes Week at Osborne House on the Isle of Wight. Princess May's spirits, already high, lifted further as she realized that, as Duchess of York, doors were beginning to open for her. Kaiser Wilhelm (son of Princess Victoria – the Princess Royal – Queen Victoria's grandson and Prince George's first cousin) was placed next to her at dinner on her first night at Osborne. Princess May liked Wilhelm, an arrogant and quarrelsome man who seemed never to have recovered mentally from a birth injury that had left one arm twelve inches shorter than the other. Prince George's parents, firmly on the side of the Danes, disliked the man – and his Napoleonic reaction to his disability – intensely, and their daughter-in-law's pleasure at being in the place of honour next to him did not endear Princess May to them. Princess May, however, was beginning to enjoy her new role. One month later she passed another milestone. She discovered that she was pregnant.

11

What a hard task it is for us women to go through this very often

PRINCESS MAY DID not enjoy her first pregnancy. She disliked the changes in her body, believed she looked unattractive and began to withdraw from social life. She was comforted to find that she had an ally in Queen Victoria who had also never liked being pregnant. 'Having children is the only thing I *dread*' was the Queen's comment during her first pregnancy. In a letter to her Uncle Leopold, the King of the Belgians, she wrote: 'Men never think, at least seldom think, what a hard task it is for us women to go through this very often.' Queen Victoria's views had not changed when, fifty-four years later, seven months into Princess May's first pregnancy, she wrote in similar vein to her eldest daughter Princess Victoria: 'It is really *too dreadful* to have the first year of one's married life & happiness spoilt by *discomfort & misery*; I have a most lively recollection of what it was before you were born – All sort of fuss & precautions of all kinds and sorts – displaying every thing & being talked abt & worried to death of wh. I think *with* perfect horror – in addition to wh. *I* was furious at being in that position.'

Queen Victoria's non-maternal views did little to comfort Princess May. She continued to resent the gradual disappearance of her waistline and saw herself in appearance becoming more and more like her obese mother. The changes in her body were entirely outside her control and she did not like it. Her chaotic upbringing with a mother whose 'can't afford it' responses to her daughter's needs but 'can afford it' responses to her own had taught Princess May to play controlling role-play games in order to get what she wanted. Now no amount of control would change the course of events.

Princess May's mother had brought her daughter up to believe that it was how you looked that was important, rather than who you were. Since

Princess Mary Adelaide was not happy with her 'poor relation' perception of herself, she used her appearance to compensate for her lack of financial status. Princess May soon began to realize that what might have been true for her mother (who probably had little going for her until her daughter married Prince George) was also true for her. She was able to reassure herself that, as Duke of York and particularly as Duke of Cornwall, Prince George enjoyed an income from the vast ducal estates such that whatever future worries she might have they would never be financial ones. None the less, she was not comforted. With her swollen body she felt that no matter what her financial status she would be judged on her appearance. Resenting the child within her, she thought of how her mother had tried to compensate for her semi-illusory poverty by overeating. Princess Mary Adelaide had made obesity a feature of her life, had taken pleasure in the affectionate name 'Fat Mary' given to her and had presumably been untroubled by physical changes during her pregnancies. Princess May knew that her mother had not been happy, either as Queen Victoria's impoverished cousin or as an overweight woman. Her mother was greedy and had not been satisfied with the love of her husband and children, her only genuine assets. She was, in addition, shameless and believed that the world owed her whatever she could lay her hands on. Although she loved her mother, Princess May also resented her and had no wish to become 'Fat May', greedy not for food, like her mother, but for love and approval.

Essentially a shy and private person, and feeling that she had been thrust into a central role on the royal stage before she was ready for it, Princess May disliked the attention her pregnancy attracted and she was unaccustomed to being fussed over. While for many women pregnancy fulfils compelling biological imperatives, Princess May's material imperatives far outweighed her biological ones. To make matters worse, her mother-in-law used the pregnancy as an excuse to interfere in Princess May's personal life. For this reason, Prince George and Princess May decided to escape temporarily from York Cottage to their London home, a wing at St James's Palace which they had named York House. There they would wait until the baby was due, at which time they would install themselves, as planned, at Buckingham Palace for the delivery.

Princess May disliked York House. Despite the sunny spring of 1894, the house seemed as dark and depressing as York Cottage and, like the cottage, it was full of tiny rooms which had also been furnished by Prince George and his mother before the wedding. The Princess felt enclosed and trapped by the gloom, the minuscule rooms and the reminders of Princess Alexandra's intrusion into her marriage with which she was surrounded. No happier there than she had been at Sandringham, she decided to make a second move to White Lodge, Richmond Park, her old home. Her doctors forestalled any further upheavals by 'suggesting' that she remain there to deliver her baby. Princess May seemed to be panicking. She had gone home to her mother and her familiar bedroom to escape from the swollen body which she found so unattractive. Possibly trying to make up for her own deficiencies as a mother, Princess Mary Adelaide was over-attentive to a daughter who wanted to be ignored, and she and Prince George fell out over it. Although the Prince might have been pleased that he had at last found a 'mother' on whom he could justifiably vent his anger, Princess May was distressed because she did not want any family divisions. On 23 June 1894 her first child, a boy (later to become King Edward VIII), was born at White Lodge.

During her pregnancy the Princess's female cousins complained that May never wanted to discuss pregnancy or babies, and they labelled her unmaternal. Since she also found breast-feeding, body odours, incontinence and even handling the baby repugnant she was unlikely to have bonded with her son. She seldom took him into her arms and could not wait to place him into the care of the nanny, Mary Peters, a young woman of twenty-seven with impeccable references. Peters had been taken on shortly before the baby's birth on the recommendation of Lady Eva Dugdale, the Princess's Lady-in-Waiting, for whose family she had worked. It seems clear now but was probably less so then that, agitated and distressed as she had been during her pregnancy, Princess May had become depressed after her confinement.

As the time for the christening approached, Queen Victoria voiced her disapproval of her son's and daughter-in-law's choice of names. As was expected, she wanted to name the baby after her beloved Albert, a name she continued to insist upon for all her male grandchildren. The baby's parents, however (probably more so his father), wanted him to be named in memory of his uncle Eddy. Queen Victoria pointed out that Eddy's real name was Victor Albert, and a compromise was reached. The child was christened Edward Albert Christian George Andrew Patrick David. Because 'Eddy' had such sad connotations for his grandparents, however, it was decided that the boy would henceforth be known as David.

Queen Victoria was particularly delighted with the arrival of her great-grandson. His birth ensured that the direct succession to her crown was established for three generations. Fifteen hundred callers to White Lodge signed their names in the visitors' book and the country rejoiced that both mother and baby were apparently well and making good progress.

Six weeks after her son's birth Princess May went to St Moritz for a month with her mother and brother, in the hope that the bracing alpine air would improve her mood. Prince George went to Cowes for the sailing, and the baby remained at White Lodge with Mary Peters. Any opportunity for the infant David to bond with his mother had long since passed.

Princess Alexandra wrote to Prince George to let him know that she did not approve of Princess May leaving on his own not the baby but her son. It did not occur to her that the baby had been abandoned by both his parents. 'I was sure you wld miss yr sweet *May* & tutsoms baby very much & it was a pity she had to leave you for St Moritz, but never mind once in a way does not matter so much.' Princess Alexandra's scarcely concealed message – that she would never have left Prince George so soon after he had been born – was a reminder to the Prince that she would miss no opportunity to denigrate the woman who had taken her son from her. Mary Peters now came into her own. She had become inordinately attached to the baby and, in the absence of any evidence of maternal interest on the part of his mother, saw herself not just as a surrogate but as David's actual mother. Unlike Princess May, who had belatedly recognized that she was not cut out for motherhood and was happy to leave the day-to-day management of her child to a nanny, Mary Peters never left her charge for a moment.

On his return from Cowes Prince George immediately resumed his royal duties. He laid a number of foundation stones: the Cripplegate Institute in London; the New General Hospital in St Mary's Square, Birmingham, and the new Post Office building in Liverpool. Although

Princess May was probably not fit enough to accompany her husband on these occasions, she did attend the weddings and funerals that occurred during the following months.

In August 1894, while Prince George and Princess May were apart, he wrote to his wife to complain how irritating he had found Princess Mary Adelaide while her daughter was pregnant: 'I am very fond of Dear Maria, but I assure you I wouldn't go through the six weeks I spent at White Lodge again for anything she used to come in & disturb us & then her unpunctuality used to annoy me too dreadfully. She was always most kind to me & therefore it made it impossible for me to say anything.' Prince George also pointed out to Princess May that her mother had, in addition, come between them in London because of her too frequent visits to St James's, 'so that I saw you very little & it used to make me angry'. Prince George was beginning to realize that when someone's bad behaviour is masked by tender expressions of concern it makes it difficult to express anger towards them. Was he also wondering whether 'darling Motherdear' had so anaesthetized his true feelings, with her sentimental expressions of love for him, that in his eyes she could do no wrong? Was he prevented, for the same reason, from voicing his disapproval of his mother-in-law's unacceptable behaviour?

Prince George's and Princess May's courtship had been virtually non-existent, and there had not been sufficient time for them to get to know one another before Princess May became pregnant. Other events were also to come between them. Princess May's pregnancy was not a comfortable one. She was distressed by the birth and depressed after it, and when she felt physically well enough her mother had taken her away to Switzerland. Her note from St Moritz was sad and to the point. 'I well know how true it is & it used to fidget me dreadfully when I was laid up to feel that we could hardly ever be alone without being interrupted.' Prince George's reply was equally frank. 'It is one of the small things in life which can just prevent one being absolutely happy & if it could be altered my happiness would be perfect; you know what I mean.' Both Prince George's and Princess May's mothers professed to have loved their children when they were babies, but, like other mothers from their social background, when their children needed them most they had left them in the care of surrogates. Now, when the two mothers were no longer needed, they interfered with unsolicited help and advice and came between the newly-weds.

Years later in *A King's Story*, the memoirs of HRH the Duke of Windsor, David recalls his earliest memories of life at Sandringham. 'My parents first materialise on the threshold of memory as Olympian figures who would enter the nursery briefly to note, with gravely hopeful interest, the progress of their first born. For better or for worse, Royalty is excluded from the more settled forms of domesticity.' The Prince goes on to reassure his readers (or more probably himself) that 'affection was not lacking in my upbringing' and excuses his parents for their detached behaviour by adding: 'the mere circumstances of my father's position interposed an impalpable barrier that inhibited the closer continuing intimacy of conventional family life'. It was probably less the circumstances of 'my father's position' that had interposed that impalpable barrier than the belated realization by his parents that it had perhaps not been children they wanted but each other. Affection, of a sort, was certainly not lacking in the Duke of Windsor's childhood. He had been loved by a nanny and as an adult he was to find that love again with Mrs Wallis Simpson. His need for this love was so compulsive that he found it easier to give up his throne rather than his 'nanny'.

Prince George and Princess May were barely beginning to know one another again when, in November 1894, the Prince was summoned to the funeral of his uncle, Tsar Alexander III, in St Petersburg. The sad and early death at the age of forty-nine of Princess Alexandra's brother-in-law shocked the royals of Europe, sixty-one of whom travelled to Russia for the funeral. The Tsar's body lay in state for seventeen days in the spectacular red-and-white fortress church of St Peter and St Paul on the banks of the Neva. On 19 November 1894 Prince George was one of the pall-bearers as the coffin was lowered into the Romanov vault. The marriage of the Tsar's son Nicholas to Prince George's cousin Princess Alix had been planned to take place one week later in St Petersburg. It was decided that, despite the death of the Tsar, the wedding should not be postponed. Once again it was Prince George's duty to be present. When the Russian Provisional Government asked King George to grant the Imperial Family

The infant Prince George photographed in 1867

The Times Picture Library

Prince Edward and Princess Alexandra with their baby son Prince
George and his older brother Prince Eddy, the Duke of Clarence, 1867

Prince George aged fourteen with his mother Princess Alexandra

The Times Picture Library

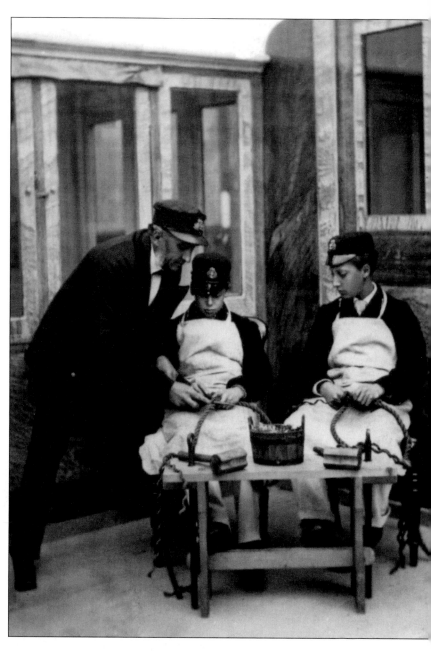

Prince George (centre) with his brother Prince Eddy, Duke of Clarence,
learning to tie knots on the training ship HMS *Britannia*

Prince George aged
nineteen in naval
uniform, 1884

The Times Picture Library

The Princes Eddy (left) and
George while in the Navy

The Times Picture Library

Prince George and Princess May of Teck, taken on their wedding day,
6 July 1893

King George V's children, clockwise from top left: Prince Bertie (the future George VI), Edward, Prince of Wales, Prince Henry, Prince George, Princess May and Prince John, 1916

Framed portrait of King George V's wife, Queen Mary, 1911

Prince George in naval uniform, signed 'Papa, 1896'

King George with Major-General H. Hudson cheered by men of the
25th Infantry Brigade, Fouquereuil, France, 11 August 1916

King George visiting war graves
in Belgium with Rudyard
Kipling, c. 1925

The Times Picture Library

King George and Queen Mary during a shooting party at Sandringham, c. 1934

King George making the first ever Christmas broadcast in 1934

King George's last journey; his subjects pay their respects at Littleport,
near Ely, as the royal train bearing the late King's body passes by on its
way from Sandringham to London, January 1936

political asylum in Britain in 1917 he again saw it as his duty to agree immediately to do so. But under pressure from the British public, whose anti-German feelings extended to Tsar Nicholas's wife, the German Princess Alix of Hesse, he withdrew the invitation. When it became known that his entire Russian family had been murdered by the Bolsheviks, on the night of 16–17 July 1918, the King never forgave himself.

While St Moritz, after the birth of David, was Prince George's and Princess May's first separation, the Tsar's funeral in St Petersburg was their second. Both of them found parting increasingly difficult. The Princess wrote to Prince George from Sandringham and told him 'what agony it was to take leave [from him]' and Prince George wrote from St Petersburg and told her that 'I should get ill if I had to be away from you for a long time'. It was clear that they had eyes only for each other and apparently for no one else, including their new baby.

It was another three years before it was discovered that Mary Peters – the nanny who had been so highly regarded by her previous employer – had been physically abusing David. Peters, an unmarried and obsessional woman with a cruel streak, had become so possessive of her charge that she resented sharing him with his mother. Princess May expected her son to be brought down from the nursery every day at teatime so that she might play with him for a few minutes. These few minutes were too long for Mary Peters. As she handed David over to his mother she would twist or pinch his arm so that he would cry and be handed straight back to her. The bruising on his arm was only discovered when a new under-nanny, Charlotte (Lala) Bill, was taken on to help Mary Peters in preparation for the birth of Princess May's third child. Lala Bill was horrified at the damage done to David's arm and, plucking up her courage, reported it to Lady Dugdale. The nursery staff were terrified of Mary Peters whose behaviour was always unpredictable and frequently violent. They had all kept quiet for fear of reprisals against the baby or themselves. Throughout this time neither Princess May nor Prince George had noticed there was anything wrong. While the abuse was going on Princess May had given birth to a second boy, Albert Frederick Arthur George (known as Bertie), later to become King George VI, and she was now pregnant for the third time. Apart from the constant bruising of Prince Edward's (David's) arm, Mary

Peters had also resented the arrival of Bertie, whose needs separated her from David. In retaliation she often neglected to feed him. Neither Princess May nor Prince George showed any interest in their babies until they were old enough to understand their parents' instructions. By the time, belatedly, they did take notice of them, permanent psychological damage had been done.

Princess May's third child was a girl and once again Queen Victoria was influential in the choice of name. The baby was christened Victoria followed by Alexandra Alice Mary. Princess Mary, as she was known, was born on 26 April 1897, two months before Queen Victoria's Diamond Jubilee. She grew up, shy and timid, to become the Countess of Harewood and the Princess Royal. Prince George and Princess May now had three children under the age of three. Mary Peters had been dismissed, although not without some difficulty as she had to be forcibly removed, and spent the remainder of her days suffering from 'a nervous breakdown'. Subsequently this was attributed to the fact that while she had been in the royal employ she had not had a holiday for three years. After her departure the full extent of her abusive behaviour was revealed. Both David and Bertie had been abused in one way or another by a so-called care-giver and both grew up to be terrified of everything.

Having become accustomed to the abusive vehicle in which 'love' was delivered to them, they suffered from the sudden loss of their nanny. It was a loss that neither of them ever got over. As an adult David was not only prone to bouts of depression but required repeated assurances from women that he was lovable. Since his many affairs were reported only in the American press, the people of Britain knew little or nothing about them. It seemed that David was doing his best to get even with a monarchical system that had not only deprived him of his first nanny but, years later, when he was prevented from making Wallis Simpson his Queen, his second one. Affected by the cruelty of Mary Peters and the bigotry of his father and overwhelmed by the oppressive regime which had dominated his early years, as an adult, David was mentally to join forces with yet another repressive regime. The autocracy of his royal childhood easily became replaced in his mind with the autocracy of Nazi Germany, a political system with which he found he had considerable empathy. His family, all of whom were either directly or indirectly to blame for his future behaviour, closed ranks and were to use the excuse of his relationship with Mrs Simpson to rid themselves of him. The final blow came when his brother Bertie refused David's request that his new wife (now the Duchess of Windsor) be referred to as Her Royal Highness, and only Adolf Hitler was to promise David that, in the course of time, he would be restored to the British throne. David's brother Bertie fared rather better as an adult. Although he had not aspired to the throne he accepted his new role with dignity. Mary Peters's cruelty, however, and his parents' neglect when he was a baby may have contributed to his persistent digestive problems, his tendency to outbursts of uncontrollable rage and his stammer.

Neither Prince George nor Princess May seemed to have considered that it was their indifference to the welfare of their two older children that was responsible for abuse which would today have attracted the attention of the social services. In the event little changed, and as York Cottage became steadily more cramped Prince George was often heard shouting to Lala Bill: 'Can't you stop that child from crying?' Far from uniting them, Prince George's and Princess May's children irritated both their parents.

Like other royals, Prince George and Princess May produced their off-spring not so much for one another but for England and the Crown. If they thought about it at all, they believed that they were fulfilling their obligations simply by giving birth to them. While pregnancy for Princess May was a disagreeable duty which could not be delegated, servants were hired to do the rest. It would not have occurred to either Prince George or Princess May, nor indeed to any other upper-class parents whose means allowed them to employ nannies, that there were further responsibilities. They thought they knew their duties as parents, but these duties definitely did not include hands-on involvement with their children. Providing the 'best' carers ensured that the physical welfare of the babies was taken care of in the nursery, and thus any future monarch would have a good start. Once the nursery was left behind, the children would be trained in social behaviour appropriate to their status by yet another team of carers, and by the age of six their formal education would be taken over by tutors.

Prince George and Princess May passed the time as well as they could. Prince George found his life somewhat boring. He was aware that it might be some time before he would accede to the throne and would have liked to have been more involved in political issues, but, in much the same way that Queen Victoria had failed to prepare Prince Edward for the throne, his father had given him little or no preparation for that office. He spent his time like any other country gentleman. At Sandringham he would either shoot, visit the farms on the estate or attend to his stamps. When in London the Prince and Princess gave occasional dinner parties to which family members would be invited. Both Prince George and Princess May felt themselves to be in a backwater. From time to time, as the children became older, they played cricket with them in the garden and, amusing themselves with their own interests, waited for the days to pass.

On 17 August 1897 life suddenly changed. To mark the Queen's Diamond Jubilee they travelled to Ireland as representatives of Queen Victoria and Prince Edward. Despite the misgivings of some members of the Royal Family – notably Princess Mary Adelaide – the visit, as reported by Prince George, went off well. The Irish question, then as now, was an important political issue. With a touching *naïveté* that endeared him to those who knew him, Prince George hoped that his visit might remind the people of Ireland (whom he loved dearly) of their good fortune in being part of the British Isles. Others had different ideas. In 1859, almost forty years earlier and only thirteen years after the great famine of 1846, an anti-English society, the Fenians, had been created with the sole purpose of working towards the establishment of an independent Irish republic. Religious differences and jealousies had come to a head in 1869 when Gladstone passed an Act for the Disestablishment of the Irish Protestant Church to accord with the largely Roman Catholic population of Ireland. Resentment had been caused when it was realized that the Protestant Church would still keep the greater part of state endowments, secular as well as religious. Prince George intended to demonstrate his religious tolerance – and presumably hoped others would follow his example – by planning a visit both to the Catholic Cathedral in Londonderry and the Presbyterian Church on the same day.

It was against this political division that the royal visit took place. From the moment the Prince and Princess left Euston for Holyhead the tour was a social success. For the journey Princess May wore a gown of blue Irish poplin and an Empress bonnet in which a sprig of green foliage had been placed. On their arrival at Kingstown Harbour they were welcomed by cheering crowds which lined the road to the Viceregal Lodge. The highlight of the tour was the Prince's investiture, at the request of Queen Victoria, with the order of St Patrick, at St Patrick's Hall in Dublin. A local newspaper report said it was 'like an historic picture in a gorgeous frame, so much did the mere onlookers seem to be entirely separate from the figures within the enclosure, moving in a world of their own and speaking a language of their own; clad in the garb of chivalry with mantles, stars, collars, maces, batons, and tabards; reading strange formulae from rolls of parchment'.

The Prince was so impressed, both with the welcome that the royal party received throughout the country and the ceremonial that accompanied the visit, that on his return to England he asked Queen Victoria to establish a royal residence near Dublin. Lord Cadogan, the Lord Lieutenant of Ireland, and Lord Salisbury's Cabinet approved his request but the Queen – possibly with more foresight than her government – refused it.

The Prince and Princess had both been brought up to value appearances. The Prince's naval training insisted on the importance not only of performing every duty thoroughly but of being seen to do so. The ships on which he had served were built to fight wars both aggressive and defensive, and their armaments and their structure were of magnificent design. In the absence of war, the only indications of a battleship's intended purpose were ceremonial and flags, uniforms and decorations. A Royal Prince's peacetime 'invasion' of Ireland, dressed in the uniform of a British naval captain, and his 'triumphal' progress through the country satisfied a young man's dream of power and glory. The tour successfully over, the Prince and Princess returned to England to great acclaim. The unusually prescient press, however, insisted that 'this unanimity, this superabundant hospitality, [must be] attributed to the removal from the popular mind of any suspicion that the visit of Queen Victoria's grandson was to be regarded in any other than its personal aspect'. The three royal children, who had not seen their parents for four weeks, also welcomed their return.

12

George says that he isn't ready yet to reign

APART FROM HIS marriage to Princess May in 1893, the Irish tour was so far the high spot of Prince George's adult life. He had naïvely hoped that showing the Union flag would be sufficient to compensate the Irish people for what they perceived as the mother country's neglect. This endeared the Prince momentarily if not to politicians, who suspected that the Irish problem was not so easily resolved, then to the man in the street whose life was touched, if only superficially, by the pomp and pageantry of the royal visit. On 9 September 1897, the Prime Minister, Lord Salisbury, wrote to Prince George congratulating him on the 'remarkable success' of his visit, but he went on to strike a more realistic note. 'The devotion to your person you have inspired is not only a result gratifying to yourself . . . but it will have a most valuable effect upon public feeling in Ireland, and may do much to restore the loyalty which during the last half century has been so much shaken in many districts.'

If the Prince believed that the friendly meetings which he had with the Lord Lieutenant of Ireland, Lord Cadogan, during his visit would serve as the model for an *entente cordiale* and divert the Irish from the idea of becoming independent from England, such a belief was doomed to failure. It was not the only time that the somewhat grandiose Prince was to be proved blind to a disaster in the making. More than a decade later, on the eve of the Great War, he thought that family ties and friendly discussion with his cousin Kaiser Wilhelm would be sufficient to enable him to change the course of history. The Kaiser had other ideas. The two cousins had grown up in similar backgrounds, had similarly neglectful parents and shared the same gene pool. Both tended to repress their anger. While George had found an acceptable outlet for his anger, Wilhelm had not. Shooting animals for sport was preferable to shooting people, but the Kaiser's withered arm denied him Prince George's 'legitimate' outlet for the anger generated by his insensitive upbringing.

The excitement induced in Prince George and Princess May by their state visit to Ireland was to be short-lived. Soon after the couple's return, it was dispelled by the news that Princess May's mother, Princess Mary Adelaide, was seriously ill. Six months earlier she had been operated on for kidney stones since which time her health had gradually deteriorated. Her doctors finally diagnosed cancer, and on 27 October 1897, two days after an exploratory operation, she died without regaining consciousness. Princess May was with her mother to the end, and Prince George, who had been at Elvedon shooting with Lord Iveagh, returned at once to White Lodge to be with his wife. At the funeral, although distressed by her mother's death, Princess May remained in control of her feelings. With no socially sanctioned outlet for her anger, Princess May had made do with the admiration she received to suppress her rage, and in the absence of admiration she resorted to control. The interment took place in the royal vault at St George's Chapel, Windsor, where the Duchess – as manipulative in death as she had been in life – had demanded to be buried. Two years later Princess May's father, the Duke of Teck, already frail at the time of his wife's death and living in seclusion at White Lodge, also died.

After her parents' death, a change occurred in Princess May's demeanour. Although she had loved her mother and grieved for her, the loss of her parents empowered her. For years she had lived in the shadow of the larger-than-life Duchess and, with her death, her daughter not only blossomed but adopted her mother's persona. The mantle of a gregarious, demanding and dominant woman who had been denied the wealth to which she believed her royal birth had entitled her now fell on to Princess May's shoulders. Unlike her mother, however, Princess May was reserved rather than gregarious and, if she was demanding, it was not apparent. Although since her marriage Princess May was no longer materially impoverished, she often felt the need to be reassured of her wealth. In reassuring others of it by her extravagant appearance she became reassured herself. Her clothes were not only regal but sensational, her erect stature, her upswept hair made her tower over other women. She dressed in the most avant-garde clothes and her attention-seeking colours and her mother's jewellery proclaimed her increasingly regal manner.

As the months passed Princess May's new strength of purpose and resolve became more evident. It was as if she had looked into the future and liked what she saw there. In the past she and Prince George had experienced major losses. First with the death of Prince Eddy and now with the passing of Princess Mary Adelaide, both had been pushed one rung up a ladder on which they had not expected to find themselves. With the road ahead clear, a lifetime of service to Britain, the land of their birth, beckoned. Falling into step, the Prince and Princess began to march to a jingoistic drum, the beat of which obscured the territorial acquisitions, the new populations, the new spheres of interest on which British power had encroached. Cape Town and Cairo, Rhodesia and Nigeria, Kenya and Uganda, the Americas and the Indian Ocean, China and the Antipodes were now either partially or entirely controlled from Westminster. Prince George and his Princess had within their grasp an Empire on which the authority of *Pax Britannica* was imposed by Queen Victoria, Empress of India, from the throne room at Windsor Castle.

On 22 June 1898, anticipating the military demands that life was soon to make of him, Prince George took command of the first-class cruiser HMS *Crescent*. The main objective of the cruise, possibly disappointingly for the Prince, was target practice, a skill he did not lack. On 25 August 1898, however, his final spell of service on the high seas on which he had been educated, and on which he had grown to manhood, finally ended. He relinquished his command for the last time and returned to dry land. If he thought that he could now relax and devote himself to shooting birds he was mistaken. There would soon be other targets to aim at.

On 10 October 1899 the two Afrikaner republics, the Orange Free State and the Transvaal, declared war on the English. Almost at once a series of major defeats were inflicted on the garrisons at Mafeking, Kimberley and Ladysmith, and British interests became seriously under threat. The

Boers were well prepared for battle and knew the terrain well. They were an amateur army of not more than 45,000, but they were trained in commando methods by Germany, which had also armed them. It took three years and 450,000 men from all corners of the British Empire for Britain to achieve its main objective, which was to control the vast wealth of the region.

Believing that they had right on their side, the British were both baffled and angry when almost all continental Europe, particularly Germany and including France (which had resented the criticism in the British press of its handling of the Dreyfus affair) and Belgium (which was offended by Britain's attitude to its behaviour in the Congo), took the side of the Boers. The war eventually took a turn for the better after popular opinion, both at home and in the British Colonies, rallied the armies of the Empire behind the British soldiers. Winston Churchill, war correspondent of *The Times,* having recently returned from the battlefronts, used a characteristic rhetoric that was to remain with him throughout his life as he thundered: 'Imperial troops must curb the insolence of the Boers . . . For the sake of the Empire, for the sake of our honour, for the sake of our race, we must fight the Boers.'

The war in South Africa touched directly on the Royal Family. Much to Princess May's distress, all three of her brothers were sent to the front. Had Prince George been allowed to do so he would have joined them. He had not forgotten that in March 1881, while on his world cruise aboard the *Bacchante*, he had visited Cape Town and met the Zulu King Ketchewayo, then a prisoner of war. The Prince had expressed sympathy both for the captive King and for his cause. In 1899, however, he believed with his fellow countrymen that Britain had a duty to 'civilize' Africa. It was a need to exercise control over Africa's economy, however, rather than a wish to bring Western customs to the natives, that drove many to seek their fortunes in Africa. Others believed that it was the duty of the British to civilize Africa, even at the point of a bayonet. The aims of those who convinced themselves of the morality of colonialization were reflected in the poetry of Rudyard Kipling. The Prince's lifelong admiration for Kipling's fervent nationalism reflected his ability to express political opinions which confirmed the Prince's own prejudices.

> We broke a King, and we built a road,
> A court-house stands where the regiment go'ed
> And the river's clean where the red blood flowed.

Patriotic to a degree, Prince George had a keen sense of justice. Not only had he been taught the importance of obedience to orders while in the Navy but he had learned also to be fair. Had his children blindly obeyed their father's orders he would no doubt also have been fair to them; had they been old enough to understand his commands doubtless they would have obeyed them.

Prince George and Princess May had six children in all. After the traumas inflicted upon them by their nanny, Mary Peters, the two older boys were compensated by a period of quiet neglect in the hope that they would overcome the abuse they had suffered. Lala Bill was as kind and permissive as Mary Peters had been sadistic and controlling, but despite her efforts the consequences of Mary Peters's treatment were to affect the boys' lives. From 1897, after the birth of Princess Mary, all three children were brought up simply and without ostentation at Marlborough House and Sandringham. Their attendants were instructed to instil in their charges the ideals that had been given to their parents by their own parents. The children were quietly encouraged to fulfil the duties imposed upon them by their position and status in the monarchical hierarchy.

On 23 April 1900 Prince George was invited by his cousin, Kaiser Wilhelm, to attend the eighteen-year-old Crown Prince's coming-of-age party. Despite the anti-British hysteria that prevailed in Germany as a result of the South African war, the Prince accepted the invitation. He was fond of his cousin Wilhelm and, being largely uninstructed in the intricacies and protocols of European politics, believed – as he had believed in Ireland three years earlier – that his charm and status were sufficient to overcome these hostile attitudes. Queen Victoria's two grandsons got on well enough socially, but Prince George's hopes that family ties and a gala opera performance would unite the two nations were never to be realized. Just as Queen Victoria had kept her son Prince Edward in the dark over affairs of state, Prince Edward in his turn had denied Prince George any information on political matters, only changing his attitutude later when he acceded the throne. Had Prince George possessed the necessary data he might conceivably have used it to advantage. By maintaining a family network, a royal mafia might have evolved concerned not only with maintaining family harmony but harmony in the countries over which they ruled. But Queen Victoria had not been forthcoming. Had she seen fit to enlighten her family, some of the power struggles of the late nineteenth and the early twentieth century might conceivably have been − if not avoided − at least the subject of informed debate. Time instead was frittered away with days at the races, visits to Lords for the test match with Australia (where to his joy the Prince met Dr W.G. Grace) and everlasting shooting parties.

It was shortly after the birth of their fourth child, Prince Henry (known as Harry), in 1900 that Prince George and Princess May learned that they were to be entrusted with a visit to the Colonies and Australia and New Zealand the following spring. Queen Victoria gave her blessing to the tour that had been under consideration for the past two years. The visit was to express the gratitude of the mother country to the Overseas Dominions for rallying behind England during the Boer War. It also entailed the opening, on behalf of Queen Victoria, of the First Federal Parliament of the newly created Commonwealth of Australia by Her Majesty's favourite grandson, HRH Prince George the Duke of York. Other parts of the Empire also scheduled to be visited included Natal, Cape Colony, Canada and Newfoundland.

The arrangements had scarcely been finalized when Queen Victoria's long life began slowly to come to an end. The Queen died in her bed at Osborne House on 22 January 1901 in the arms of the Kaiser and surrounded by almost her entire family. On his mother's death Prince

Edward succeeded to the throne as King Edward VII, Prince George became the direct heir and he and Princess May became known as the Duke and Duchess not only of York but also of Cornwall. Eventually, on King Edward's sixtieth birthday in November 1901, they were given the title of Prince and Princess of Wales.

In the interests of safeguarding the monarchy, King Edward VII, having lost one son in Prince Eddy, was at first reluctant to permit Prince George to tour the Colonies and asked Lord Salisbury if the journey might be delayed. The Prime Minister refused to sanction any postponement on the grounds that the people of Australia were expecting the Prince and Princess and would be very disappointed if they did not arrive in Canberra in time to open the Parliament. Prince George's feelings about the tour were mixed. Never at ease with those of higher intellectual status than his own, he complained, with good reason, that he found it difficult to discuss issues of government policy with Dominion statesmen because he had not been properly briefed.

On 16 March 1901 the dazzling, white-painted, twin-screw, 6,910-ton, 10,000-horse-power Orient Line SS *Ophir* sailed from Portsmouth with a complement of 550 passengers and crew. The ship's company included a hundred Marines, thirty-seven bandsmen of the Royal Marines, Chatham, twenty boys, various cooks, barbers, butchers and bakers, three ladies-in-waiting and Canon Dalton, aged sixty (still in the service of his former pupil), as Chaplain. The crew consisted entirely of men on the active list of the Royal Navy. The Royal Yacht was accompanied throughout the voyage by HMS *Juno* and HMS *St George*, which formed the royal escort squadron. Splendour once again was on the march.

On the day of departure on a journey that was to encompass the globe and last for eight months Prince George wrote in his diary: 'Papa proposed our healths & wished us God speed and I answered in a few words & proposed the King and Queen. I was very much affected & could hardly speak. The leave taking was terrible. I went back with them to the yacht when I said goodbye & broke down quite.'

This was not the first time that the highly strung Prince George had said goodbye to his parents and gone to sea. He was as affected on this occasion as he was when he enrolled on the *Britannia* at the age of twelve, and he wanted his parents to know what it had been like. He wept then and he wept now. He wrote to them from Gibraltar, the *Ophir*'s first port of call, to explain how sad he had felt when they had parted from one another a few days earlier: 'May and I came down to our cabins and had a good cry and tried to comfort each other.' What he did not say in his letter was that at least on this occasion he had someone who felt as he did and who was able to comfort him. Having been brought up to experience all partings as painful, he was reluctant as an adult to stray far from Sandringham unless obliged by affairs of state to do so. He was particularly averse to travelling abroad, about which he is said to have commented: 'I've been there and I don't like it.'

Twenty-four years later he was to inflict on his children the pain that his parents had inflicted on him by sending his two older boys to a naval academy. He would have rationalized this behaviour by reassuring himself that life in the Navy had made 'a man of him', when in reality it had kept him as a child. Still self-conscious, timid and anxious in social situations, years later King George V was to describe the State Opening of Parliament in February 1911 as 'the most terrible ordeal I have ever gone through'.

In the absence of Prince George and Princess May, Queen Alexandra and King Edward VII seemed pleased to have been given a second chance to take care of children. Queen Alexandra did her best to compensate for her intermittent neglect of her own two sons by allowing her grand-children to miss lessons and insisting that they should have 'fun'. Both grandparents seemed determined to expiate whatever guilt they may have felt at sending Eddy and George to sea at too early an age. The Queen neglected to write to Princess May to tell her of David's and Bertie's change in routine, but their governess, Mademoiselle Bricka, wrote to the Princess to say how upset she was that David's education was being neglected. When the indignant Princess May complained to her mother-in-law, the Queen replied defensively that she thought it 'the only thing that could be done as *we all* noticed how precocious and *old fashioned* he

[David] was getting – and quite the ways of a *single child*! – which would make him ultimately "a tiresome child".'

The Queen, who had still not forgiven Princess May for taking her 'darling Georgie dear' away from her, now seemed to be getting her revenge by taking 'David darling' away from his mother. The free and easy relationship between grandparents and grandchildren sometimes fulfils a need in both. It gives an opportunity to grandparents to right the wrongs they may have perpetrated on their own children and to prove what good parents they could have been, and it provides the children of repressive parents with a chance to experience a form of (grand)parenting that would otherwise be denied them.

By the time Prince George and Princess May returned from their world tour on 1 November 1901 David, Bertie, Mary and Harry had become so detached that the youngest of them, who was only a few months old when his parents left, failed to recognize them. The other children also demonstrated their disapproval. Mary clung to her grandmother's skirts and within six months Bertie developed a stammer. It was only the seven-year-old David who allowed his parents to embrace him. Prince George was relieved to be home. There is an account in his diary of the enthusiastic reception he was given the following day on the state drive through the streets of London. 'Most touching, got back to York House at 3.30. We do indeed feel grateful that it has pleased God to bring us back home again safe and sound.'

Neither Queen Alexandra and King Edward nor Prince George and Princess May, and certainly not the four children, thought that there was anything unusual about leaving small and dependent children for eight months. One of the earliest memories of David, Duke of Windsor, is his recollection of being cared for as a seven-year-old by his grandmother while his parents were on the *Ophir*. He writes:

> If the superimposition of four noisy children upon the Royal Household
> during my parents' absence was ever a nuisance, my grandparents never
> let us know it . . . If my grandparents were not entertaining distinguished

company at lunch, they liked to have us romping around in the dining-
room. In this congenial atmosphere it was easy to forget that our governess was waiting for us upstairs with her French and German primers.
If we were too long in going, she would enter the dining room timidly to
warn us that we were already late for our afternoon lesson. Usually my
grandmother would wave her away, and my grandfather, puffing at his
cigar, might add reassuringly to the governess, 'It's alright. Let the children stay with us a little longer. We shall send them upstairs presently.' So
unconcerned were my grandparents over the lapses from the school-
room routine that on taking us to Sandringham for a two weeks' stay, they
left poor Mlle Bricka behind in London lest she should spoil our fun.

(Windsor, 1951)

David's somewhat idealized recollections only thinly obscure his contempt for the governess who was *in loco parentis* and his pleasure at her dis-
comfiture. His memories of his benevolent, unconditionally loving
grandparents are distorted by wishful thinking which enables him to compare his parents' behaviour towards him unfavourably with theirs.
Carrying on the tradition in which he had been brought up, Prince George
thought it high time for the two older boys to be educated in the same way
as he had been. Ignoring the misery he had endured at being parted from
his parents with only his brother as a confidant, he engaged Henry Peter
Hansell as tutor for his two sons until the time came for them to enrol as
naval cadets.

Prince George and Princess May had returned from their travels to a
monarchy with different values from those of Queen Victoria. She had
taught King Edward VII little of his duties as a constitutional monarch, had
been more preoccupied with her son's shortcomings than with his assets
and had never forgiven him for his role in his father's last illness. The
Prince had hoped, more or less from the time of Prince Albert's death, to
play a greater role in the stewardship of the country, but as long as Queen
Victoria lived this was not to be. It was only with great reluctance that in
1892, by which time her son was fifty-one, the Queen allowed him limited
access to state papers.

Because of his mother's unwillingness to trust him, the King insisted belatedly that he would not treat his son in the same way. His decision not to withhold official secrets from his heir might well have been prompted by his near-fatal illness on 14 June 1901, twelve days before his Coronation. A diagnosis of appendicitis was made by the Royal Surgeon Sir Frederick Treves ten days after the King had complained of abdominal pain. Sir Frederick reluctantly removed the appendix but not before a life-threatening abscess had developed. The Coronation eventually took place on 9 August 1901 after a prolonged convalescence. For almost two months Prince George remained in a state of acute anxiety. Not only was he concerned that his father might die but, should that unhappy event occur, he knew that he was in no way ready to take on the role of monarch. King Edward, realizing that at the age of sixty he had outlived his father by almost twenty years, more conscious than ever of his mortality, now spared no effort to prepare Prince George for the task that lay ahead.

Despite his travels and the warmth of his reception throughout the Empire, however, Prince George remained diffident and self-conscious. His father did what he could to coach him in his royal duties, but his years at sea, his lonely pastimes and his clinging attachment to his mother had not prepared him psychologically for the role that he would have one day to play. It was hardly surprising that King Edward's life-threatening illness provoked anxiety in him, and it was with great relief that he welcomed his father's recovery. Princess May's concern for her father-in-law equalled that of her husband. 'Oh, do pray that Uncle Wales may get well,' she commented to Mademoiselle Bricka and in an understatement went on to say: 'George says he isn't ready yet to reign.'

The death of Queen Victoria, the turn of the century and the Coronation of King Edward VII heralded a change in the country's perception of the monarchy. The King's expansive, outgoing personality contrasted sharply with the mystique, the privacy and the essential propriety of the Victorian era, a period which almost within weeks of Queen Victoria's death was confined to a past that few regretted. The Queen's depression had cast a gloom over the country which had lifted completed only with her demise. Although her mourning for Prince Albert was unnaturally prolonged, there had been occasions on which she had been distracted from it. Her friendship for her favourite Prime Minister, Benjamin Disraeli, in the 1870s did much to bring her out of her seclusion, as did the Golden Jubilee celebrations of 1887. King Edward, however, was expected to raise up his subjects' spirits and he did not fail to live up to their expectations. The country was ready for a physical and social spring-cleaning. Only Prince George and Princess May, the last of the eminent Victorians, were opposed to the proposed changes. Prince George was more in tune with his introspective grandmother than with his socially extrovert father. Shy and often inarticulate, he was to have only another eight years in which to prepare himself for the ordeal ahead that he dreaded.

Princess May had no such anxieties. She had already had eight years since their marriage to prepare herself for Coronation. She was ready. Drawing herself up to her exaggerated height, bedecked with the jewels of her status, she stood in the wings and impatiently awaited her cue.

· 13 ·

Wake up, England

THE BLACK VEIL of mourning that had obscured the monarchy during much of Queen Victoria's reign was about to be lifted. The Edwardians emerged from their palaces, hobnobbed with their subjects, swept aside sexual taboos, endowed the accumulation of wealth with respectability and cast a festive spirit over the land. This did not please everyone. Lord Salisbury and the ascetic Arthur Balfour, his successor as Prime Minister, were cast in a very different mould from the fun-loving, sexually promiscuous King Edward VII. They disapproved of the King and the King disapproved of them. Having caught a whiff of his own mortality during his recent illness, at the age of sixty-one the King threw himself wholeheartedly (social engagements permitting) into grooming his anxiously awaiting son for the succession.

Prince George, at the age of thirty-six a Victorian among Edwardians, was still haunted by the anxiety he had felt when he thought that his father might not recover from the removal of his appendix. He feared that he would too soon be flung into kingship for which he was unprepared. Realizing that there was much work to be done before he could confidently step into his father's shoes, he made every effort to understand the protocols and procedures appropriate to his future status. During his trip to Australia he had already had a taste of international diplomacy. On his return he wrote a statesman-like (although, as ever, grandiose) letter to the Colonial Secretary, Joseph Chamberlain – whose concern for the colonies equalled his own – telling him of his conviction that in Australia there existed a strong feeling of loyalty to the Crown and a deep attachment to the mother country. The Prince went on to point out that this was due to 'our having paid them a visit' and that the time was fast approaching when the mother country could profit by it. With the ordeal of Australia behind him the Prince felt himself ready to benefit from his recent foray into diplomatic flag-waving by taking a further step along an unfamiliar road. He was deeply conscious that he was not a 'man born to be King' but a stand-in for his late lamented older brother. If he hoped to be able to join in the euphoria which followed the end of Queen Victoria's reign, and celebrate the beginning of an era of prosperity, his hopes were dashed. There were changes but they were not changes of which either he or the Conservative government of the day had any experience. The beginning of the twentieth century concerned itself not with the interests of the landed gentry but with the growing political representation of the working classes. The problems of poverty, unemployment and ill health – barely acknowledged by nineteenth-century governments – were concerns that in the general election of 1906 caused the Conservatives to be swept out of power and a Liberal government to be voted in.

The prosperity to which everyone had looked forward at the end of the Boer War had not materialized. The cost of the war to the Empire had been immense. Twenty thousand lives had been lost and £200 million had been spent. Trade was in recession, industry was depressed and in the first budget of King Edward VII's reign taxation had been increased to one shilling and two pence in the pound. In addition King Edward VII (and indirectly Prince George) was becoming increasingly disturbed by rumours that his ill health made him unfit to hold office. The King, however, managed to convince himself that it was rather the conflict with his parents, which had resulted in his mother's refusal to allow him access to state papers until 1892, than his ill health which had left him unprepared for his monarchical role. Queen Victoria's responsibility in the matter, however, had to do with his exclusion from the family circle, more or less from the moment of his birth, rather than with his exclusion from governmental information. A worried man since his illness, King Edward was determined that his heir be better prepared for kingship than he.

Against a setting of social unrest, an upsurge in republicanism and a general lack of understanding by the public of the role of the monarchy in the affairs of state, Prince George and Princess May struggled to prepare themselves for the part they believed the nation expected them to play. As King Edward's health went slowly downhill, Prince George's sense of purpose visibly strengthened. Until his illness the King, although only five feet seven inches tall, weighed sixteen stone and had a waist measurement of forty-eight inches. His appetite was voracious – he ate five meals a day – and he smoked twelve large cigars and at least twenty cigarettes a day (Souhami, 1997). Prince George, the 'sardine' rather than the 'whale', had always been both impressed and overwhelmed by size. His childhood had been spent in the shadow of a dominant, boisterous, powerful and intolerant father and as his father shrank physically the Prince expanded intellectually.

King Edward was determined that Prince George be given every opportunity to fulfil his future role. To this end, immediately before the Australia tour began he appointed Sir Arthur Bigge (formerly Private Secretary to Queen Victoria since the death of Sir Henry Ponsonby in 1895) as the Prince's Secretary. In many respects he was similar to Prince George. Like the Prince he was conscientious, meticulous and regimental, honest and loyal, qualities that were to keep him by the side of his pupil for the next thirty years.

Sir Arthur Bigge was a teacher such as the Prince had became accustomed to in Canon Dalton. Like Canon Dalton he was the son of a vicar, but unlike Dalton he did not follow his father into Holy Orders but joined the army, where he was commissioned in the Royal Artillery. As with his former tutor, Prince George was to display the same bouts of rage and impatience that had been a feature of his boyhood. Bigge was undeterred both by this and by his pupil's royal status. He dealt with whatever problems arose in a straightforward, man-to-man manner. He told the Prince that he felt it no longer appropriate for him and Princess May to continue living in York Cottage because of its unsuitability for entertaining. On another occasion he expressed disapproval to King Edward for deferring the investiture of his son as Prince of Wales until after the *Ophir* cruise.

Sir Arthur Bigge was the prompter should Prince George forget his lines, and it was probably also his talents in promoting the interests of the

Prince that were responsible for putting him on the front pages of the newspapers on 6 December 1901, a few weeks after his return from his world tour. In an emotional speech at the Guildhall, Prince George, summing up his experiences, caught the imagination of the people, probably for the first time. He spoke with emotion of the welcome he had received in the colonies. 'I appeal to my fellow countrymen at home to prove the strength of the attachment of the Motherland to her children by sending to them of her best.' He concluded his speech by addressing the businessmen in the audience, reminding them of the 'commercial needs of the Empire' and pointing out that the 'mother country must wake up if she intends to maintain her old position of pre-eminence in the Colonial trade against foreign competitors'. The Prince's 'wake up, England' speech came across as a rallying call to a nation in danger of sliding into a despondency felt all the more after the heady expectations that followed the successful conclusion to the Boer War. The King furthermore made the point that in the future trade and commerce would be the only real connection between the mother country and the colonies.

A few months later Prince George successfully passed another test. In January 1902 he was invited to visit Germany to congratulate the Kaiser on his forty-third birthday. This visit came at a time when Anglo-German relations, hitherto reasonably amicable, were at an all-time low. The British Colonial Secretary, Joseph Chamberlain, always an advocate of an alliance with Germany, made a plain-spoken reference in a speech at Edinburgh to the behaviour of the German Army during the Franco-Prussian war of 1870, to which the German Chancellor, Prince von Bülow, had taken offence. A few days later, during the Budget debate in the *Reichstag*, several deputies retaliated by criticizing the behaviour of the British Army during the South African war. Earlier statements made by the German Chancellor were recalled, notably his ominous and prescient comment in 1899 that 'in the coming century, the German people will be either the hammer or the anvil'. Against a background of political and diplomatic tensions and increasing Anglo-German hostility King Edward decided that it would be unwise for Prince George to visit Germany. The Prince was disappointed that his father intended cancelling his visit. Recalling similar anti-British hostility on the part of the Germans two years earlier, when he attended the Crown Prince's coming of age, he was not put off. He liked his cousin the Kaiser and did not share his father's resentment of all things German. In the event the visit did take place and the German Chancellor and Prince George found themselves in harmony. The Kaiser was pleased to see his cousin and sent a telegram to King Edward to tell him so. 'Georgie left this morning for Strelitz all safe and sound and we were very sorry to part so soon from such a merry and genial guest. I think he has amused himself well here.'

In the years that lead up to the Great War Prince George did his best to interest himself in international affairs. Despite every effort, however, he found himself unable to compete with his far more socially extrovert, worldly-wise and cosmopolitan father. He was particularly impressed with his father's visit to France in 1903, which laid the foundations for a Franco-British *entente* to counter German aggression in Europe. Prince George envied the King's role in helping to stage a dramatic display of friendship between the two countries and in encouraging the exchange of visits between the two fleets, notwithstanding the fact that following the ratification of the *entente* in 1904 Germany had scared France by threatening war. The arrival of the British Atlantic Fleet at Brest in July 1904, and the return visit of the French Fleet to Portsmouth a month later, was welcomed with such enthusiasm by the people of France and England that the alliance, far from breaking down as the Germans had hoped, was further cemented. Germany's intention of demonstrating that the Fatherland and not Britain was the master of Europe had failed.

Prince George appreciated the help given him by Sir Arthur Bigge to prepare for the time when he would take over the affairs of state from his father, but his heart was in the country rather than in the field of international affairs. He wrote many letters to Bigge on whom he was becoming not only dependent but almost child-like in his devotion to him. He looked on Bigge as a father, firm and benevolent – as indeed his own father had been and continued to be – but, unlike his father, Bigge, who dedicated virtually twenty-four hours a day to Prince George's well-being, was always available for help and advice. With Bigge the Prince avoided the flat and somewhat colourless style that he used in communicating with his father, with whom he was always conscious of a need both to please him and to reassure himself of his love. His letters to Bigge were franker, much warmer and in some respects not unlike the carefree style he adopted in his letters to his mother. In a letter to his mentor from York Cottage, dated 1 January 1902, Prince George writes:

> My Dear Bigge, – First let me thank you for your most kind letter receivd. this morning & for all yr good wishes to us for the New Year. The one that is now over has indeed been an eventful one for me and mine; it has been a sad one and a happy one & there is much to be thankful for, as you say. I must again repeat how grateful I am to you for all you have done for me during this past year. I thank you for yr kind help & advice & for yr great loyalty. I feel that I can always rely on you to tell me the truth how-ever disagreeable & that you are entirely in my confidence. To a person in my position it is of enormous help to me. I thank you again for it from the bottom of my heart.

Prince George's easy relationship with Bigge is also illustrated in a letter written a few days later, again from York Cottage. No formal phraseology and careful editing here.

> A Colonial Office Box has just arrived but I had no key to open it with, I sent it up to Sidney Greville to unlock it; it only contained a telegram from Hely-Hutchinson expressing thanks from officers & men of Cape Peninsular regiment to me for becoming their Col. in Chief. You had bet-ter get a key for me if they are going to send me boxes, otherwise I cant open them. I am returning you all the letters and papers you sent me & have written on them all. I am sending this pouche by the messenger. I hope you will have some decent weather & get some good hunting. Believe me, Your sincere friend, George.

Throughout 1905 the Prince's diary was full. In January he visited Ireland to shoot with Lord Ardilaun, in February he attended debates in the House and visited the Motor Show for the first time. While waiting for Princess May to give birth to Prince John, their sixth and last child, at York Cottage the Prince played golf. He also played cricket on the lawn at Sandringham with the two older boys. None of this was particularly stressful, yet he had made a note in his diary in April that he had not seen his younger children for three months. The birth of the Waleses' youngest son, on 12 July 1905, had as ever brought Prince George and Princess May closer to one another. Although they lived side by side it was in harmonious isolation. Their interests seldom overlapped and, other than on state occasions, when circumstances brought them together, each was content just to know that the other was there. When either of them was 'unavailable' through illness, or in Princess May's case following childbirth, their need for one another drew them close. Illness in the other worried them both. Each felt safe only when the other was well. Prince George was content to sit by his wife's bedside and read to her for much of the day. His touching vigil was understandable. In the event the Princess made her usual rapid recovery from childbirth. The attending doctor, Sir John Williams, left after eight days, and as ever the baby was handed over to a nurse. Preparations for the royal tour of India began. On 19 October 1905 Prince George and Princess May left London for Bombay via Genoa, where they embarked on HMS *Renown*. Barely four years after their eight-month voyage to Australia they were once again separated from their children, this time for six months.

The visit to India had a profound effect on Prince George and Princess May. Both were moved by the awesome responsibility undertaken by the mother country for the welfare of the sub-continent. They were struck not only by lives far removed from their own but by a religious faith that allowed for hope and salvation for a people who had little other than spiritual assets on which to fall back. If either of them were to consider the importance of feelings rather than possessions in their own lives, India would have been the catalyst. In keeping with the received wisdom of the time and to maintain colonial rule, the needs of the governed were emphasized by Whitehall at the expense of those of the governors. The Prince and Princess were in accord with this attitude but possibly for different reasons.

As HMS *Renown* docked in Bombay the Prince in particular would have been struck by the ubiquitous poverty, which was emphasized not so much by the contrasting splendours of the royal visit but by the extravagant pageantry of the welcome provided by the Indian Princes. Politely, if somewhat patronizingly, Prince George asked his wealthy hosts how he might help them with whatever problems they might be facing. The Maharajah's main problems of course were how to maintain their lavish life-styles in the presence of increasing calls for social reform. To his credit the Prince also took an interest in the social and health problems of the impoverished population. In 1905, apart from the usual endemic tropical diseases and famine, India was experiencing an outbreak of bubonic plague. Conscious of the great suffering of the hungry the Prince provided for a great feast to be attended by thousands. Finally, after further lavish entertainments, the tour came to an end in Calcutta, the capital of British India.

In almost his last act as Viceroy Lord Curzon had not only distressed the people of Bengal by partitioning their province but had also succeeded in antagonizing the members of the hitherto low-key Indian Congress Movement. Naïve as ever in political matters, on his departure for England Prince George addressed Gopal Gokhale, the President of the Congress Party. 'I have been reading your speech at Benares, in which you said it would be better for India if the Indians had a much larger part in the administration. I have now been travelling for some months in India . . . and I have never seen a happier-looking people, and I understand the look in the eyes of the Indians.' Prince George asked: 'Would the peoples of India be happier if you ran the country?' Gokhale replied: 'No, Sir, I do not say they would be happier, but they would have more self-respect' (Gore, 1941).

It was clear that the protagonists had offended each other. Prince

George left India full of admiration for its peoples but distrustful of its leaders. On his return to London, sensitive perhaps to the fact that the day of the Raj might be drawing to a close, he called for 'a better understanding and a closer union of hearts between the Mother Country and her Indian Empire'. Unusually for the time, the Prince was concerned about the way the Indians were treated by the British. It was not the first occasion on which he was to identify with the downtrodden and the disadvantaged. Possibly with memories of the bullying he had experienced as a naval cadet, he was later to comment: 'Evidently we are too much inclined to look upon them as a conquered & down-trodden race and the Native, who is becoming more and more educated, realises this.'

Prince George was not averse to exercising his own form of bigotry. A few weeks after the end of the Indian tour the Prince and Princess were invited to Madrid for the marriage of Queen Victoria's granddaughter, Princess Ena of Battenburg, to King Alfonso XIII of Spain. Prince George was furious with his cousin Princess Ena for converting to Catholicism. When a bomb was thrown at the royal carriage, killing twenty and injuring more than fifty (but sparing Princess Ena and the bridegroom), he attributed it to the wrath of God.

He could be equally angry with any change from established custom. In January 1906 he and the Princess were on a visit to Burma when news of the Liberal landslide victory in the General Election reached them. On his return he told his father that 'I see that a great number of Labour members have [also] been returned which is rather a dangerous sign, but I hope that they are not all socialists.' The Prince struggled to remain in touch with, and to understand, the political changes of the Edwardian years. He hoped that when his time came to rule, with the help of Sir Arthur Bigge, he would be prepared for every eventuality.

· 14 ·

I know what's best for my children

WITH THE BIRTH of their sixth child Prince John on 12 July 1905 the family of Prince George and Princess May was completed. Princess May's experience of motherhood had been gained not so much from Princess Mary Adelaide as from Mademoiselle Bricka, an unmarried Frenchwoman whose personal experience of mothering was non-existent. Unaware, as were most upper-class families of the time, of the benefits of hands-on mothering, Princess May left the care of her children to nannies and nurserymaids while Prince George – when he was not shooting or attending to his stamps – was seen by them as a bad-tempered bully. Their opinion of their father, who made only rare appearances in the nursery, confirmed his possibly apocryphal comment that 'he had been afraid of his father, and by God his children would be afraid of him'. Not one of Prince George's children was to receive an education likely to bring out whatever talents they possessed, and all grew up to experience them-selves victims of injustice. The two older sons had been ill-treated by a sadistic nurse, the result of which was that one was compelled to seek compensation from other women for his mother's neglect and the other suffered chronic digestive problems. Had Princess May even been aware of her children's needs she would have been incapable of showing them affection in her formal and remote role of Queen Mary. In common with others of their class the royal parents saw nothing amiss in leaving their young family for months on end.

Prince George's view of himself as a father differed from that of his children. He considered himself to be fair and just, a disciplinarian who 'knew what was best for his children'. He claimed to love them (although he never told them so), but the love he gave them was conditional upon their obedience. Despite evidence that today would suggest the contrary, Prince George thought of his father as a good father and his fear of him did not seem incompatible with the belief that he was kind and loving and had a genuine concern for his children. He had no problem either with accepting that Princess Alexandra had been a good mother and that he was her favourite child. Yet he grew up to be shy, self-conscious, insecure, prone to outbursts of uncontrollable rage and dependent for approval not only on his peers and all authority figures but also on his children.

Prince George's insistence that his children love him was exploitive. He was unaware of his character defects, and there was no evidence that he ever queried them. Had he done so he would certainly not have laid the blame for such defects at the door of his parents, whom he saw as above criticism and beyond reproach. This led him to subject his children to the same conditions as those in which he had grown up: absentee parenting, inadequate and sometimes cruel surrogates, poor tutoring and an insistence on the same life-style which had caused him and his brother to be so unhappy. The paradox of Prince George's childhood was that, although he had been led to believe by his mother that he was her 'darling Georgie dear', he seemed not to have been sufficiently 'dear' for her to be there when he needed her most.

Prince George's older son, Prince Edward (known as David), bore the brunt of his father's frequent displeasure. Prince George had grown up in the shadow of an older son, the Duke of Clarence, whose needs had always taken priority over his own. His tutor Mr Dalton had had to proceed at the pace of Prince Eddy, and not only had his own education been held back but his career had been indirectly determined for him, since a naval academy, rather than a boarding school, had been selected as more suited to Prince Eddy. While he could not blame Eddy for deserting him by dying, he could (and eventually did) 'blame' his oldest son David, whom he saw as another Eddy.

Traumatic events, such as Prince George's separation from his parents and his brother's untimely death, are not always readily recalled, but the emotion associated with those events persists throughout life. In the Duke of Windsor's autobiography, *A King's Story,* the eight-year-old Prince Edward (David) recalls how his father, in the winter of 1902, on his parents' return from the world cruise that took them away from their children for eight months, added insult to injury by suddenly terminating 'the feminine suzerainty' of the nursery.

David and his brother Bertie were told abruptly one evening that they would be woken up the following morning by a man named Frederick Finch. David, who claimed to have no memory of an event which he seems conveniently to have blanked out, repeats a story that years later Finch had disclosed to a friend: Finch had described his master 'as a handful or, if I might use the word, a "stubborn" character'. The Prince went on to recount an occasion

> when [Finch] played the role of 'rod in pickle' to me. Evidently one afternoon when my sister was supposed to be taking a nap, I had invaded the nursery and on one pretext or another had kicked up a fuss. My father was out shooting, and no one dared disturb my mother. My sister's harassed nurse 'Lala' Bill, stormed into Finch's room crying, 'That boy is impossible. If you don't give him a thrashing, I will.' Finch marched me off to the bedroom, laid me face down on the bed, and while I kicked and yelled, applied a large hand to the that part of the anatomy nature has conveniently provided for the chastisement of small boys. I yelled more out of hurt pride than pain; and, as Finch was leaving the room with the air of a man who had performed a distasteful but inescapable duty, I shouted after his receding back that I would get even with him. 'You just wait!' I cried. 'I will tell Papa what you have done.' Later that evening my mother heard the whole story from the nurse. I was summoned to her room; but instead of my being embraced and mollified I was admonished first for my bad behaviour in the nursery and next for my mistaken judgement that a servant had no right to punish me. I was sent back to Finch's room to apologise for having been such a nuisance.
>
> (Windsor, 1951)

Prince George's oldest son had been so humiliated by his experience that understandably he chose to 'forget' it. He presumably also 'forgot' that his mother had not stood by him. David had already been the victim of physical abuse by his nurse Mary Peters, mainly because for three years his mother had failed to recognize what had been taking place under her nose.

While Prince George is frequently quoted as saying that the kind of education which he received was good enough for him and it must therefore be good enough for his sons, nothing was further from the truth. His own education was pitifully inadequate and the arrangements that he made for them ensured that that of his sons would be equally inadequate. As soon as the two older boys were out of the nursery, Prince George engaged Henry Hansell, a Norfolk man recommended by one of his shooting friends, as tutor to David and Bertie. Hansell had been educated at Magdalen College, Oxford, and had worked as a schoolmaster for several years. He was, however, a poor teacher, who 'without sharing Dalton's intellectual appetite shared his humourless solemnity' (Rose, 1986).

Both Hansell's pupils thought that their father had made a poor choice. Their tutor turned out to be an indifferent teacher and without the charisma required to retain the attention of small boys. Neither of them liked him and as a result he was unable to inspire in them a desire to learn. Perhaps realizing his limitations, Hansell eventually told Prince George that the boys would be better off at a preparatory school. Having set his mind on David and Bertie being educated at home in the same way as he had been, Prince George disagreed. As an adult, David, by then the Duke of Windsor, wrote: 'If he [Hansell] harboured strong views about anything, he was careful to conceal them. I am today unable to recall anything brilliant or original that he ever said. Looking back over those peculiarly ineffectual years under him, I am appalled to discover how little I really learned' (Windsor, 1951).

Prince George's own early experiences aboard the *Britannia* were painful ones. He had frequently been bullied and in his letters to his mother he had described the feelings of sadness and homesickness he was obliged to endure during his long absences from home. None the less, as soon as David and Bertie were old enough to graduate from Mr Hansell's efforts their father insisted they be enrolled as cadets in the Royal Navy.

David, like Prince George at a similar age, was growing up to be rebellious, and he was constantly being reprimanded for refractions of the rules laid down by his father. Neither of the boys was interested in the sports, games and other aspects of the curriculum introduced by Henry Hansell. But when they complained to their mother, who was more concerned with the tapestries on which she was working than the education of her children, Princess May told them to do as their father had instructed. David learned to sew, an interest that remained with him into adult life, probably because it was the only way he could guarantee being close to his mother. Such closeness, however, was illusory. As Duke of Windsor, he later wrote poignantly that he could only remember one parental embrace as a child. This had been in public when his grandparents had taken all the children to meet their parents on their return from their tour of Australia and the colonies. He also confessed that he never saw his mother alone without a servant or lady-in-waiting in attendance.

While Princess May more or less ignored her children, Prince George constantly, and often abrasively, involved himself in their development. His expectation that they blindly obey him frightened them and must have resulted in the suppression of their natural feelings. Harsh with both his sons – even when they were six and eight respectively they were expected to address him as 'sir' – Prince George seldom gave them so much as a peck on the cheek, preferring to shake hands instead. The Prince loved his children but seemed to be afraid of being too close to them (possibly for his benefit rather than for theirs) and used anger and formality to keep them at a distance.

The injunction to be 'seen and not heard' permeated the boys' childhood. Bertie, who had developed a stammer soon after Prince George and Princess May returned from Australia and who had great difficulty in expressing himself, was probably quite pleased not to be heard. He believed himself to have been doubly rejected, first by his parents when they left on their world tour and on his parents' return by his grandfather to whom meanwhile he had become attached. While there may well have been some psychological factors in the development of his stammer, these were not addressed. There were, however, psychological reactions to his impediment on Bertie's part. Mr Hansell added to his embarrassment at his inability to speak clearly by reporting him to his father when, not unnaturally, he was having problems with French and German conversation. '[He] had difficulty enough in expressing himself in his own tongue let alone in a foreign language – to his father. There followed one of those summonses to the Library where Bertie, his knees knocking together as he stood tongue-tied before his father, suffered bitter humiliation, anguish of spirit, self-pity, exhaustion and pure frustration' (Wheeler-Bennett, 1958).

A summons to the library, a room furnished not with books but with guns, terrified David and Bertie. It invariably meant that they had done something of which either Mr Hansell or their father disapproved. They were expected to file in and stand to attention in front of Prince George's desk until ordered to stand 'at ease'. Hands in pockets were forbidden. Whenever they forgot this instruction Lala Bill had to stitch up the pockets on their suits. Their father's command to attend the library was so frightening, particularly for David, that on occasion he was known to have fainted in anticipation.

Prince George may have thought that he was being jovial and friendly when he 'chaffed' his children. His sadistic sense of humour, however, had always been an outlet for his hostility and the children soon came to realize that 'chaffing', or sarcasm, was a form of wit that invariably discomfited them. The Duke of Windsor in his memoirs explains how much his father's strict and bellowed instructions inhibited his development. The laws of behaviour, he says, as revealed to a small boy tended to be ruled by a vast preponderance of 'don'ts'.

David was entered at the recently established Royal Naval College at

Osborne. A year later he was joined by his younger brother. On the day that he was escorted by his father to Osborne, at the age of twelve, tears were streaming down his face. Prince George's message to his son as he began his four-year training course was: 'Now you are leaving home, David, and going out into the world, always remember that I am your best friend.' David could not be blamed if he doubted the veracity of his father's message. When his brother Bertie arrived at Osborne, shortly after his thirteenth birthday, he was placed almost at the bottom of the intake. David said later that 'quite apart from my Royal parentage and homes, the fact that I had never been to school before caused me to be regarded as a freak'.

Prince George insisted that his sons be treated in the same way as the other cadets. Their day started at 6.30 a.m. with a plunge into cold water. 'It indicated no lack of respect that a royal or aristocratic bottom could be flogged by a petty officer wielding a bamboo cane, with a naval doctor in attendance to see fair play' (Howarth, 1987). The beatings were neither fair nor playful but a further humiliation for two children whose parents had always demonstrated a lack of understanding of their needs. Other humiliations followed. The older cadets, looking for younger boys to bully, soon picked on David. Victims attract bullies and David had had plenty of experience at being a victim. On one occasion red ink was poured over his head just before the evening parade. On another he recalls a boy being strapped to a gymnasium horse and being severely beaten on the instructions of his father Captain Edwyn S. Alexander-Sinclair. David knew all about such fathers. His sense of injustice and his feelings of inferiority, compounded by his lack of height, were reinforced on a regular basis. He grew up only when his father died, by which time, having found someone to help him escape, he was able to summon up sufficient courage to turn his back on his family, his throne and his country.

As time passed David and his younger brother fared no better at Osborne. They both remained at the bottom of the class as they did later at the Royal Naval College, Dartmouth. The bullying continued at

Dartmouth with the senior cadets devising ever more sadistic ways of tormenting the younger boys and probably the two Princes in particular. The senior officers turned a blind eye to practices which they deluded themselves would 'make men' of their victims. Having undergone similar experiences in his own youth and knowing what his sons would be going through, Prince George also turned a blind eye. The Duke of Windsor, who on the whole preferred Dartmouth to Osborne, describes an especially disagreeable form of bullying by the cadet captains.

> One evening while we were undressing in our dormitory, the cadet captain rang the gong for silence. He told us that we were a lazy bunch of 'warts' and that we needed a good shake-up. He went on to announce that henceforth the time allowed for undressing and putting on our pyjamas before running down to the wash-house would be reduced from one minute to thirty seconds. Although we were used to doing everything at the double and obeying orders unquestioningly, this order was the last straw. The inevitable result was a series of summonses to the washhouse after 'lights out' and a harsh application of the gong rope to any boy who had failed to meet the deadline.

The Duke goes on to describe the chaos as the terrified boys 'tripped in the passage and fell up the stairs in [our] frantic struggles to reach the dormitory and get undressed and pass the cadet captain, standing by, watch in hand, under the gun. Every evening produced a few minor casualties; and we fell into bed panting and scared, waiting for the delinquents to be called for punishment' (Windsor, 1951).

Humiliating and degrading rituals are commonplace in enclosed environments such as prisons, boarding schools and the armed services. These rituals are exaggerated examples of earlier parental bullying which the perpetrator has to offload on to others before he can feel free to move on into adult life. The rituals may serve a useful purpose for the aggressors but do nothing for their victims. At the end of the twentieth century bullying seems to have changed little from David's graphic description of it three generations earlier. British newspaper headlines in September 1987 – 'Army bullies jailed for torment of new recruits' and 'Ex-soldiers gaoled for degrading rites' – drew readers' attention to a story concerning sexual initiation rites in the King's Own Scottish Borderers. Two former soldiers had admitted to ordering recruits 'to get on top of one another and have sex' and forcing them to sit in a cold bath containing urine and human excrement. The recruits were also put into a cupboard in which CS gas was released. The defence lawyers at the court-martial said that the two accused had themselves been through initiation ceremonies and believed that 'there was no harm in it'.

Prince George must have experienced similar ceremonies and also concluded that 'there was no harm in it'. Unable and presumably unwilling to abuse his children as he was once abused, he allowed his feelings of victimization to be passed on to his children 'by proxy'. Like other children who have been humiliated and degraded, David would have felt too embarrassed to tell his parents of his ordeal. He did, however, hint in one of his letters to his mother that 'there is an awful rush here, and everything has to be done so quickly'. If he had hoped that his mother would read the heartache between the lines he was disappointed. In her reply Queen Mary merely reminded him to leave time to clean his teeth at night.

Knowing what makes a bad parent is as important as knowing what makes a good one. Without an understanding of their own childhood to guide them, parents may bring up their children in the same way as they themselves were brought up. Neither Prince George nor Princess May could have had any insight into their own upbringing. Indeed they both probably idealized their respective childhoods and glossed over the defects if ever they became aware of them.

Awareness of the effects of bad parenting often seems to skip a generation. King Edward VII and Queen Alexandra were bad parents but good grandparents. The same could be said of King George V and Queen Mary. Nothing pleased King George V more than to play with Bertie's daughter

Princess Elizabeth. She was devoted to her grandfather whom she referred to as 'Grandpapa England' because he told her that the national anthem ('God save the King') was his song. While recovering from his penultimate illness King George asked for Princess Elizabeth who he said was a 'tonic' for him. Pretending to be a pony so that she could ride on his back, he would encourage her to pull his beard. No adult had played so with him when he was a child, and neither had he played with his male children in such an uninhibited manner. The essential warmth within him, which had until now been denied expression, had at last found an outlet.

· 15 ·

An overgrown schoolboy

As THE REIGN of King Edward VII slowly wound down and Prince George prepared himself for the ordeal ahead, the political views of the heir to the throne were becoming increasingly rigid and conservative. Not only did he abhor change but he was more interested in the past than in the future. Too much unfinished business, left over from his own past, prevented him from relinquishing the anger that kept him attached to his childhood and from concentrating on what lay ahead. Whether the Prince had any insight into the cause of the intense rages that often overwhelmed him is not known. The balance of probability suggests that he did not.

In the early part of the twentieth century, despite – or more likely because of – the increasing influence of Sigmund Freud, such introspection was unfashionable. Freud's professed atheism, and his insistence that a general shift towards secularism was afoot, would have little appeal to the scion of a family whose life-style was heavily slanted towards dogma, ritual and the spiritual values of Christian belief. Prince George's anger was acted out rather than thought out. He shut his eyes to the 'all or nothing' love of his mother and the totally inadequate education which had been thought fit for him. His search for a father figure, on to whom he could (inappropriately) unload some of his pent-up rage, brought him into conflict with his long-time confidant, Admiral of the Fleet, Lord Fisher of Kilverstone.

He had been a seventeen-year-old midshipman on the *Bacchante* when in 1882 he first came into contact with Captain J.A. Fisher. Three years later he met him again while undergoing a training course aboard HMS *Excellent*. Captain Fisher, Commandant of the *Excellent,* was the same age as

Prince Edward and it was not long before Prince George bonded with the older man.

In a letter to Queen Victoria, when her grandson had completed his training course, Captain Fisher wrote:

Madam, Having received your Majesty's commands through Sir Henry Ponsonby to write to your Majesty about Prince George I have the honour to report that during his six months' stay on board the *Excellent* under my command his attention to his work and the manner in which he has performed all his duties has been all that your Majesty could desire. He has with great tact and good judgement and quite of his own accord declined many invitations kindly meant to give him pleasure, but which would have taken him too much from his work besides bringing him more prominently into public notice than Your Majesty might have thought desirable under the circumstances. His Instructors have reported to me that his aptitude for the practical work of his profession is very good, and Your Majesty may perhaps consider this is the chief point, as it will not probably fall to his lot to write learned reports or make mathematical investigations. Quite incidentally, this morning I heard the remark made by one of his late mess-mates that it was a subject of general regret that Prince George had left the *Excellent* and his pleasant and unassuming manner has been a matter of general notice. Trusting your Majesty will pardon me if I have written at too great length, I have the honour to be Your Majesty's most humble and grateful servant and subject, J.A. Fisher, Captain. HMS *Excellent*.

On the following day Prince George was promoted to Lieutenant. Also on the following day Captain Fisher, whose sycophantic letter to the Queen was, to say the least, patronizing about her grandson's lack of literary skills and his inability to make mathematical investigations, wrote to Sir Arthur Bigge, the Assistant Private Secretary to Queen Victoria, passing on more of the same. 'Prince George only lost his first class at Pilotage by 20 marks. The yarn is that one of his examiners, an old salt-horse sailor, didn't think it would do to let him fancy that he knew all about it.' It was clear that Captain Fisher was unimpressed with the Prince's intellect, but none the less Prince George and Fisher continued to correspond with one another for the following twenty years.

As Prince George became increasingly constrained by the demands that his inheritance was imposing upon him, his almost phobic urge to break out caused him to lash out at those who in one way or another he felt were responsible for his anxieties. One of these was his old mentor, Sir John Fisher. By 1904 the Prince's rationalization for his anger took the form of disapproval of Sir John's naval policies and of the ruthless manner in which the Prince believed he implemented them. One issue on which he disagreed with the now Second Sea Lord was the latter's plan to increase the strength of the Home Fleet by reducing the strength of the Mediterranean Fleet in the event of an attack by Germany. Generally acknowledged to be well ahead of his time, Fisher had made an effort to keep on the right side of the Prince by informing him of the changes he proposed making in such matters as the training of officers and the development of the submarine. He did his best not to antagonize Prince George, although he had never been particularly impressed with his old pupil's judgement. The Prince alternated between his desire to please the Second Sea Lord and his irritation with the responsibilities thrust upon him in the lead-up to his accession. He told Fisher that he saw an enormous future in submarine warfare, although others in the Admiralty and elsewhere saw its 'sneaky invisibility' as 'unethical'.

In a letter addressed to Sir John Fisher in August 1904 and headed 'Private', the Prince wrote:

Many thanks for your letter and the preamble on the new designs of fighting ships which I have read with great interest and shall, of course, keep secret. I am sure that they will be splendid fighting machines and I so agree with you about the increase of speed. I don't think you will get the Foreign Office to accept the Merchant Ship with the White Ensign & the

Maxim gun. Why not build a very large destroyer with good speed for this kind of work, which also would be useful with your fleet. Of course the 'Snail' and Tortoise' classes ought to be abolished; they are utterly useless for anything . . . I much appreciate that you say you will show me everything & tell me everything later on. I will certainly try and give you my best advice & be quite frank always & tell you exactly what I think the King will say. Believe me, Always most sincerely yours, George.

The tone of the Prince's letters to Fisher, child-like in their effusiveness and in their desire to please, and bearing more than a hint of wanting to play one authority figure off against another, are very much those of a son to a mildly exasperated father. In a letter to his own son Cecil, written on 10 April 1903, Fisher had said he had promised the Prince that he would burn all his letters 'directly I have read them, as then he says, he feels he can write freely, which he certainly does!' Fisher's attitude to the Prince – many of whose letters he neglected to burn – and his views, with which he was only too familiar from his time on the *Excellent,* finally provoked the Prince into an open hostility that never completely disappeared. The more fragile his father became, the more his anger seemed to increase. As he anticipated the demise of King Edward it was as if he was at last in touch with the suppressed anger of his childhood. He had been left then and feared, as his father grew older, that he would be left again before he was ready to stand on his own feet.

Apart from antagonizing John Fisher Prince George also succeeded in antagonizing Lord Curzon (with whom he had fallen out on the India tour), Herbert Henry Asquith and Lloyd George. Growing up in the political conservatism of the Victorian era, and accustomed to the deference paid to him by successive conservative Prime Ministers, he found the views of the Liberals, elected in 1906, not entirely to his taste. His outspoken and often needlessly offensive attacks on ministers such as Asquith, whom he referred to as 'not quite a gentleman', and Lloyd George, whom he disparaged as 'that damned fellow', did not endear him to a government wrestling with topical issues, not the least of which was the Irish question.

Prince George's hostility to the Liberals, the party that represented change, with which the insecure Prince was unable to cope, was infamous. Following an anti-Liberal outburst at the home of Lord Londonderry, the poet and literary critic Edmund Gosse was heard to say that the Prince was 'an overgrown schoolboy, loud and stupid, losing no opportunity of abusing the government'. Gosse might also have had a view on why the Prince's sons were also the victims of their father's abuse and were to remain so until his last illness robbed him of some of his aggression. In 1907 Gosse, who could be said to be an expert on schoolboys, had anonymously published the prize-winning *Father and Son*, an intimate account of his own early life.

The Prince acquired a reputation more for outspokenness than for diplomacy. He could be very dictatorial and, despite the lip-service he paid to democratic values, in his dealings with his family he was anything but a democrat. As far as he was concerned only one person in the Royal Household had rights – himself. All others were expected to be dutiful and unquestioning. No issues were ever debated with his children, and his absolute authority had to be obeyed, with questions neither asked nor answered.

As Prince George's anxiety, which amounted almost to a sense of impending doom, increased, Princess May, who hitherto had remained in the background as far as the children's upbringing and their welfare was concerned, did her best to protect them against their father's increasingly frequent outbursts of temper. Her first duty, however, was always to her husband and to the monarchy. 'I always have to remember,' she once said of her sons, 'that their father is also their King.' Prince George, who was dependent on Princess May, was comforted by the knowledge that his wife would always support him. None the less he began to suffer from what was described as 'frayed nerves', which was manifested both in physical as well as psychological symptoms. His physicians were no more able to 'cure' his chronic indigestion – perhaps a symptom of the malignant anxiety that was 'eating him up' – than they were his sense of inferiority manifested by his fear of speaking in public. This was particularly severe when he felt that the members of the audience were of superior intellectual status. He accepted an invitation to be guest of honour at the annual dinner of the Royal Academy in 1908 but absolutely refused to address them, although clearly expected by his hosts to do so.

Two years later the news that Prince George was dreading finally came. On 6 May 1910 his father, King Edward VII, died from the effects of chronic lung disease. His death took place in the presence of Mrs Alice Keppel, his long-term mistress. Queen Alexandra looked tactfully out of the window while they made their farewells.

· 16 ·

I have lost my best friend and the best of fathers

PRINCE GEORGE WAS grief-stricken at the death of his father. 'I have lost my best friend & the best of fathers,' he wrote. 'I never had a word with him in my life. I am heart-broken and overwhelmed with grief but God will help me in my great responsibilities & darling May will be my comfort as she had always been.' His addendum that 'We've seen enough of the intrigue and meddling of certain ladies' was a clear enough reference to his late father's paramours, but when he went on to say that 'I'm not interested in any wife, except my own' the meaning was unclear, and it was difficult to know for whom the words were intended. If they were meant to reassure Princess May they were superfluous. Whatever the Prince's faults infidelity was not one of them. That he needed his wife now more than ever was confirmed by the above diary entry. If he was reassuring himself that as a red-blooded male he would have to resist the impulse to stray, such reassurance was more the result of wishful thinking than of reality. It is possible that he was addressing Queen Alexandra to whom he was still inappropriately attached, telling her that unlike her late husband her son would never be unfaithful to her. It was not long, however, before Queen Alexandra was to put his faithfulness to her to the test.

On Monday 9 May 1910, three days after the death of King Edward VII, the accession of King George V was proclaimed by Garter King-of-Arms from the balcony of Friary Court, St James's Palace. 'That the high and mighty Prince George Frederick Ernest Albert is now, by the death of our late Sovereign of happy memory, become our only lawful right Liege Lord; George V by the Grace of God, King of the United Kingdom of Great Britain and Ireland and of the British Dominions beyond the seas, Defender of the Faith, Emperor of India, to whom we acknowledge all faith and obedience, with all hearty and humble affection, beseeching God, by whom Kings and Queens do reign, to bless the Royal Prince George the Fifth with long and happy years to reign over us.'

Princess May became not only the Queen Consort of Great Britain and Ireland and of the British Dominions beyond the seas but Empress of India. Her own ambitions, and those of her late mother Princess Adelaide Duchess of Teck, were fulfilled at last.

On 20 May 1910, after three days lying in state in Westminster Hall, King Edward VII's remains were taken to Windsor Castle and the coffin placed in the vault below the Prince Albert Memorial Chapel. At the funeral Queen Alexandra, accompanied by her sister Marie Feodorovna, the Dowager Empress of Russia, insisted on standing at the foot of her husband's coffin. Although this may well have been the custom in St Petersburg it was certainly not the custom at the Court of St James. Queen Mary, relegated to an inferior position, deemed it unseemly to invoke protocol and challenge her mother-in-law's presumptuous action.

The as yet uncrowned King George V had no difficulty in accepting that there were two women in his life. Ever since Queen Alexandra had presented him and Princess May with York Cottage as a wedding present, his mother and his bride had vied with each other for his attention. It was inevitable that his attachment to his mother would persist into his adult life and he probably thought it entirely appropriate that it should be so. It was equally inevitable that his devotion to her would transfer itself on to all those who, from the nursery onwards, had selflessly served his needs. Among these were his nursery attendant and valet Charles Fuller, his tutor Mr Dalton, Edward Bacon (who helped him with his stamps), his Private Secretary Sir Arthur Bigge and various others, the chief of whom was Princess May, on whom he depended.

Queen Mary would have been happier with her maternal role towards her not-yet-grown-up husband had she been given a free hand to manage both it and their home without interference. She realized that Queen Alexandra's primary motive in giving them the cottage at Sandringham was to keep her son close by. When the time came for the Queen Dowager (as Queen Alexandra was now known) to move out of Buckingham Palace, in order to make room for the new incumbents, problems arose. She was as reluctant to move back to Marlborough House as in 1901, on the death of Queen Victoria, she had been to move from her home at Marlborough House to Buckingham Palace. There was no question of her not moving, but she refused to give her daughter-in-law the satisfaction of knowing when the move was to take place. She felt that only at Sandringham could she take comfort in familiar surroundings. The house had been built for her by her late husband King Edward VII, and she remained there until her death in 1925.

The Dowager Queen also seemed to be reluctant to hand over some of the Crown jewels to which she had become attached and which were now due to the Queen Consort. The fact that she eventually both handed them back and moved out of the Palace did little to reduce Queen Mary's frustration. She was anxious to get on with redecorating Buckingham Palace in a style more suited to her own tastes than those of her mother-in-law. In a letter to her Aunt Augusta, the Grand Duchess of Mecklenburg-Strelitz, Queen Mary wrote of her irritations at the delay: 'the odd part is that the person causing the delay & trouble remains supremely unconscious as to the inconvenience it is causing, such a funny state of things & everyone seems afraid to speak'. The 'everyone' who was afraid to speak was presumably King George, who, torn between his loyalty to his wife and his loyalty to his mother, shut his eyes to the problem in the hope that it would go away. There is certainly no evidence that he discussed his wife's feelings with his mother, deciding, probably wisely, to stay out of a conflict in which there could be no winners. Queen Mary had an ally in Mademoiselle Bricka. In a letter to her old governess some months before the Coronation, she wrote: 'Life is *too* fatiguing for me, I have *too* much to do, to think of, I am getting worn out and people bother one so, I am sick of the everlasting begging for favours of all kinds!'

When the time came for Queen Mary to redecorate Buckingham Palace there were more problems. She did not care for Queen Alexandra's furniture and began to replace it with heirlooms – which had been stored away and not seen since the days of King George IV and King William IV – as well as rehanging pictures and changing rugs and brocades. Bearing in mind that the palace was a not particularly well-designed home of six hundred rooms, many of which were uninhabitable and hardly suited for any purpose, this was no mean task. For the first time in her married life Queen Mary was given the opportunity to put her house in order. She could not wait to do so. When she was a child her parents had had no home of their own, and when she married Prince George York Cottage was furnished by Princess Alexandra, aided and abetted by Prince George.

King George was looking forward to the Coronation which would confirm him and Queen Mary officially in a role that had been ceremonially proclaimed but not yet publicly acclaimed by his peers and his eagerly awaiting subjects. The Dowager Queen was dreading the royal rite of passage, a reminder that less than ten years earlier her own regal status at the side of her husband had been confirmed. Queen Mary, more than anyone, sensed the anguish her mother-in-law was suffering and feared that some incident would trigger a breakdown and ruin the day for them all. Aware that the Dowager Queen and her daughter, Princess Victoria, had never liked her, she feared that they might well conspire out of jealousy to undermine the role she was creating for herself and behind which she was to shelter for the remainder of her life. Queen Alexandra was becoming seriously depressed. Her inability to give up her past – revealed by her reluctance to prepare herself for the move to her 'new' home – was due as much to depression as it was to a more or less unconscious wish to sabotage her daughter-in-law's Coronation. She was tearful, dwelt on the past and felt 'hopeless' and 'helpless'. She became preoccupied again with the death of her beloved son Eddy nineteen years earlier and reminded her family that following the death of his father Eddy should rightfully have been King. She had conveniently 'forgotten' that her eldest son was ill-educated and virtually illiterate, vague and unintelligent and the subject of a homosexual scandal of which his younger brother seemed to be ignorant. Prince George's abhorrence of same-sex relationships had caused him once to comment that he thought people like that shot themselves.

The country had been spared a homosexual King and seemed not displeased that a brother whose homophobic views seemed unnecessarily vehement was to take his place. The family breathed a sigh of relief when the Dowager Queen declared she was too ill to attend the Coronation service.

Queen Mary was relieved that she would not have to cope with her mother-in-law on a day she saw as 'hers'. She had still to contend with interference from another source. King George's conservatism, which had developed into a controlling urge to preserve the *status quo,* made clear his views about contemporary dress. The fashions of the late Victorian era, which were good enough for his parents, were not only good enough for him but also for his wife. His insistence that Queen Mary dress in the same *passé* style as Queen Alexandra set a new vogue. Following a state visit to France just before the outbreak of war in 1914 a newspaper reported that 'the Queen had a wonderful success, the Paris mob went mad about her, and it was rumoured that her out-of-date hats and early Victorian gowns would become next year's fashions'. This prediction may have been made tongue in cheek but, had it not been for the war, what was intended as satire might well have come about.

The socially anxious and self-conscious hide beneath uniforms and uniformity. George V convinced himself that it was his knock-knees which no tailor was able to disguise that had made him emotionally vulnerable since childhood rather than his pathological attachment to his mother. To his chagrin his son Bertie also suffered from knock-knees. The effort which he had made to cure his son's defect – notwithstanding the pain caused by keeping a child in leg braces day and night and the tears which resulted – was as much a reflection of his anxiety about his own appearance as it was for the well-being of his son.

The Coronation of King George V and Queen Mary, which took place on 22 June 1911, was on a grand scale. Eight thousand people attended the ceremony in Westminster Abbey and many thousands more lined the streets of London to cheer first the Queen's procession and then the King's procession as they entered the Abbey. Thousands more well-wishers stood outside Buckingham Palace as, after the ceremony, the newly crowned King and Queen appeared repeatedly on the balcony before their subjects. The seventeen-year-old David, shortly to be invested as Prince of Wales in Caernarvon Castle and now heir to the throne, summed up in his diary, in terms all the more revealing for what was omitted, the events of the day.

> Buckingham Palace, London June 22 1911. Papa and Mama's Coronation day. Papa rated me a midshipman – I breakfasted early & saw Mama & Papa at 9.00 & then dressed in my Garter clothes and robe, & left in a state carriage at 10.00 with Mary & the brothers. We arrived in the Abbey at 10.30 & then walked up the Nave & Choir to my seat in front of the peers. All the relatives & people were most civil & bowed to me as they passed. Then Mama & Papa came in & the ceremony commenced. There was the recognition, the anointing and then the crowning of Papa, and then I put on my coronet with the peers. Then I had to go & do homage to Papa at his throne, & I was very nervous . . .

This is an account of the most eventful day in the lives of two people, one who had not wanted to be King and the other who wanted nothing more than to be Queen.

The entry in the King's diary was even less emotional than his son's:

> We left Westminster Abbey at 2.15 (having arrived there before 11.0) with our Crowns on and our sceptres in our hands. This time we drove by the Mall, St James' Street & Piccadilly, crowds enormous & decorations very pretty. On reaching B.P. [Buckingham Palace] just before 3.0 May & I went out on the balcony to show ourselves to the people. Downey photographed us in our robes with Crowns on. Had some lunch with guests here. Worked all afternoon with Bigge & others answering telegrams & letters of which I have had hundreds. Such a large crowd collected in front of the Palace that I went out on the balcony again. Our guests dined with us at 8.30. May and I showed ourselves again to the people. Wrote & read. Rather tired. Bed at 11.45. Beautiful illuminations everywhere.

And so with comments reminiscent of an entry in a ship's log, the couple's longest day came to an end.

Barely had the Coronation been concluded than preparations began for the ceremony to be repeated in India. This was not so much for the benefit of the people of India as for King George, who, now no stranger to pageantry, was looking forward to a Durbar at which he could crown himself Emperor of India. His fascination with India had begun during his first visit in the winter of 1905–6. With his overwhelming self-consciousness temporarily assuaged by the success of the events of 22 June, he was encouraged to seek further reassurance from the people of India that he was their Emperor in fact as well as in name. He convinced himself that his visit to a country in the midst of nationalist fervour would somehow 'allay unrest', as he put it to Lord Morley, the Secretary of State for India, in a letter dated 8 September 1910. 'I am sorry to say [the] seditious spirit unfortunately exists in some parts of India.' Perhaps he recalled a similar optimism on his part when, following his visit to Ireland in 1897, he had convinced himself that the friendly accord between its people and the Crown which he had fostered would somehow resolve the political issues of the day.

Lord Morley was understandably reluctant to give consent to such a financially, and perhaps politically, costly venture. Four days later, in a letter to the King, the Secretary of State tactfully pointed out that the cost of the visit would have to be borne by the Indian tax-payer and that the absence of the Sovereign might cause some embarrassment to business at home. He went on to congratulate the King on his strong sense of 'Imperial duty' and the 'sympathetic, almost passionate, interest taken in the people of India that inspire[s] the present proposal in Your Majesty's mind'. Two months later the Cabinet reluctantly agreed to the visit but only after it had closely considered the cost of its many implications. Since it was forbidden for the crown worn at the Coronation to be taken out of the country, this necessitated the making of a special Imperial Crown, which was undertaken by Garrard, the Crown Jeweller. The second Coronation, however, to which the King had been looking forward, was not possible. The Archbishop of Canterbury pointed out that because many of the guests at the ceremony would be Muslims and Hindus the Christian service of consecration, deemed essential by the Archbishop, would be inappropriate. It was therefore decided that the King should appear at the Durbar already wearing the new crown. The so-called 'boons' expected – which usually took the form of remissions of prison sentences or reductions in taxes, together with a proposed cash gift to further academic research – were considered too costly by the Cabinet. It was decided, again reluctantly, that it would be less expensive for the King's visit to mark the remove of the capital of British India from Calcutta to Delhi, thus reversing the controversial partition of Bengal introduced by Lord Curzon in 1905 which provoked the enmity of the Bengalis and was described as Lord Curzon's 'unintentional but grievous mistake'.

On 11 November 1911 the King and Queen left for India on the recently launched 13,000-ton P&O ship *Medina*. They were accompanied by a large suite including, among others, Lord Crewe, the Secretary of State for India, the Duke of Teck, the King's personal ADC, the King's Private Secretary, Sir Arthur Bigge (Lord Stamfordham), the Chief of the Metropolitan Police, the ADC General, as well as five equerries all personally known to the King. The ship carried 210 marines, 360 petty officers and ratings and thirty-two officers. The *Medina* was escorted throughout the journey by four cruisers under the command of Admiral Sir Colin Keppel. Queen Alexandra and the King's and Queen's two older boys, Prince Edward (David) and Prince Albert (Bertie), came to Portsmouth to see them off. David expressed disappointment at once again being separated from his parents. His father, being reminded of earlier sad farewells ('as horrible as ever'), probably felt the same. David wrote immediately to his mother: 'I shall never forget that moment when I saw you waving from the window of the railway carriage as we slowly steamed away from you in the wind & rain.'

On 2 December 1911, after the month-long voyage, the last part of which was in the sweltering heat of the Indian Ocean, the *Medina* dropped anchor at Bombay, the 'gateway' to India, The royal party disembarked on 5 December, a week before the Durbar ceremony, and were met by the Viceroy Lord Hardinge. Passing through streets lined by cheering crowds, they made for Government House. A triumphal Muslim-style arch on the Apollo Bundar was officially opened in 1924 in honour of King George's visit and today is a popular meeting place.

The magnificent Delhi Durbar was described at the time as the most splendid spectacle in the history of India. Forty thousand tents to house 250,000 people had been erected over an area covering forty-five square miles on the plains alongside the Jumna River. The King, who was enthroned beneath a golden dome, towered over his subjects who came to pay homage to him. *The Times* summed up the day's events in a style appropriate to the occasion. 'The ceremony at its culminating point exactly typified the Oriental conception of the ultimate responsibilities of Imperial power. The Monarchs sat alone, remote but beneficent, raised far above the multitude but visible to all, clad in rich vestments, flanked by radiant emblems of authority, guarded by a glittering array of troops, the cynosure of the proudest Princes of India, the central figures in what was surely the most majestic assemblage ever seen in the East.'

At 12 noon on 12 December 1911, beneath the heat of the Indian sun, King George and Queen Mary felt that a moment had occurred in their lives that elevated them from the sphere of ordinary mortals. If they believed that the Coronation at Westminster Abbey was the climax of their lives, the Indian Durbar not only reinforced but enhanced this climax. No one at the Durbar could have failed to be moved by the pageantry of colour, the symbols of Empire and the fervour of a people who waited for a divine messenger to rescue them from a life they accepted because of the promise of happiness in the world to come. Had they imagined that they had been transported from squalor and poverty to the gates of Paradise by the spectacle before them it would have been understandable. King George himself was so moved by the ceremony that in a letter to his mother he wrote that 'the Durbar yesterday was the most wonderful & beautiful sight I have ever seen & one I shall remember all my life. We wore our robes & I the new crown made for the occasion. May had her best tiara on . . . I can only say it was most magnificent, the clothes & colours were marvellous . . . I had six pages & May had four to carry our robes, they were either young Maharajahs or sons of Maharajahs & all wore beautiful clothes of white & gold with gold turbans & they did look nice.'

King George was not only reliving a childhood fairy-tale but was acting it out. When the Durbar ended he removed his 'dressing-up clothes' to play another game. While Queen Mary travelled to Agra to visit the Taj Mahal he went shooting in Nepal. The Maharajah of Nepal provided 14,000 beaters and 600 elephants to facilitate the King's favourite pastime in which thirty-nine tigers, eighteen rhino and one bear were shot, a record the King considered would be 'hard to beat'. Although he and Queen Mary were apart for Christmas, they rejoined one another in Bombay to board the *Medina* for the voyage back to England. Overwhelmed by the events of the past few weeks, the King delivered his farewell speech and wept. When the *Medina* put into Malta he wrote to his mother: 'What joy there are only 9 days before we meet. I shall then feel proud that our historical visit to India had been accomplished successfully I hope and that I have done my duty before God & this great Empire, & last but not least that I have gained the approval of my beloved Motherdear.'

·17·

We shall try all we can to keep out of this

T HE YEARS THAT led up to 'the war to end all wars' brought King George into conflict with a number of issues since the turn-of-the-century struggle had been developing between women demanding equal rights with men and a society intent on denying them these rights. The King's views differed little from those of other Englishmen of the time, namely that women fell into two categories, those whom one married and who bore one's children and those who inhabited the *demi-monde.* He soon became aware that a third category, representing all women, was vociferously demanding recognition.

The move towards women's suffrage had begun in the second half of the nineteenth century. By 1913 it had gained considerable momentum when it was announced that a Reform Bill, launched by the Liberal Prime Minister H.H. Asquith, would be open to amendments relating to women's suffrage. The speaker of the House of Commons vetoed the amendments on the grounds that they would alter the character of the original Bill too profoundly for it to proceed. This setback infuriated the militants in the suffrage movement. The suffragettes, under the leadership of Emmeline Pankhurst, had already invited Queen Mary's disapproval by smashing plate-glass windows with hammers carried in their muffs, as well as by other acts of violence. King George's attention was dramatically drawn to the cause when, on Derby Day 1913, a young militant, Emily Wilding Davidson, threw herself under the hooves of the King's horse at Tattenham Corner and was killed. Queen Mary's immediate reaction was that the jockey, 'poor Jones', had been 'much knocked about'. The King, an opponent of every form of organized violence, must also have disapproved.

Five days before the Coronation about 40,000 supporters of the suffragette movement, mostly women, held a four-mile-long procession extending from Westminster to the Albert Hall. The purpose of the demonstration was to draw attention to their cause and to raise money to support it. Having already targeted the Royal Family on Derby Day, the militants in the movement had hoped that Queen Mary at least would understand the justice of their demands. They were disappointed. While the Queen had always been well aware of her own rights as a woman, she was now satisfied with her status and as the First Lady of the British Empire could feel only embarrassment at the importunity of her sisters. She had left far behind her the time when, as Princess May, she had considered herself less equal than other members of her family and clearly did not wish to be reminded of a struggle she had fought and won. Having overcome what she had experienced as 'social discrimination' in her upbringing, Queen Mary managed to delude herself that she was 'to the manner born'. Uncertain of her past she resented the struggle of those less secure than herself, and she did not support the efforts of the suffragettes to right social wrongs. Her comments on the miners who were striking for an improvement in underground working conditions, and on the disruptive transport strike, applied equally to the suffragette movement. 'Now we have a transport strike which may become very serious – really we have no luck, one tiresome thing after another.' This echoed a similarly deprecatory comment, this time in a letter to her Aunt Augusta, following the burning down of the 'little tea house' in Kew Gardens by militants. Other protests by 'unruly' women to draw attention to their rights included shouting at the King at a performance at His Majesty's Theatre and creating an explosion in Westminster Abbey, which slightly damaged the Coronation Chair and the Stone of Destiny. 'There seems no end to their iniquities,' wrote the Queen.

If social success and recognition of her regal status by a public almost unaware of her existence fifteen years earlier had been Queen Mary's goal, she had achieved it. King George had other goals. Ever since he had been obliged to confront his social phobias at the State Opening of

Parliament on 6 February, at the Coronation on 22 June and at the Durbar in Delhi soon afterwards, he had discovered a new confidence in himself that had encouraged him to take a closer interest in political issues. The fears that he had confided to his diary on 6 February : 'we walked in procession hand in hand to the House of Lords, it was indeed a terrible ordeal, as the House was crowded in every part & I felt horribly shy & nervous' – a touching reminder of the frightened child still present in the adult King – were slowly beginning to fade.

Unlike Queen Mary, who was concerned only with the behaviour of women in so far as she considered they would bring her own status into disrepute, the King began to feel passionately about the women's suffrage movement only when he feared it might blur the boundaries between the genders. When he was told of the forced feeding of women on hunger strike in Pentonville Prison, who had been charged with, and found guilty of, assault and damage, he was shocked. Having been brought up to idealize women and to put them on a pedestal in the belief that they could do no wrong, he was sufficiently distressed to order his Private Secretary, Lord Stamfordham (formerly Sir Arthur Bigge), to make his views known to the Home Secretary. The Home Secretary had already drafted his Prisoners (Temporary Discharge for Health) Bill 1913, which allowed for the temporary discharge of prisoners who were on the point of death and for rearresting them when they had recovered their health. Since most of the women rearrested resumed their hunger strikes on their return to prison, the Bill became known as the 'Cat and Mouse Act'. 'The King desires me to write to you on the question of "forcible feeding",' wrote Lord Stamfordham. 'His Majesty cannot help feeling that there is something shocking, if not almost cruel, in the operation to which these insensate women are subjected through their refusal to take necessary nourishment. His Majesty concludes that Miss Pankhurst's description of what she endured when forcibly fed is more or less true. If so her story will horrify people otherwise not in sympathy with the Militant Suffragettes. The King asks whether, in your "Temporary Discharge of Prisoners Bill" it would not be possible to abolish forcible feeding.'

The concept of women behaving and being treated like men was repugnant to the King. If a woman was not a woman his sexual anxieties would not allow him to relate to her. His insistence that Queen Mary exaggerate her femininity by wearing a bustle and emphasizing her hair allowed him to set aside any idea of same-sex closeness, acceptable to him only in brotherly love as between comrades-in-arms.

The Queen needed little encouragement to wear the jewels for which she had acquired a reputation. A year after the King's accession she was photographed adorned with the most dazzling of them, and she was never happier than when she was complimented on her appearance. In a photograph taken in 1912, among other self-appointed badges of rank she wore the massive Koh-i-noor diamond, the Star of Africa, a diamond crown, a collar of rows of diamonds, a diamond stomacher, the Garter and several other Stars and Orders. Her hair-style remained as it was when she was a young woman. The King is said to have insisted that his wife did not alter her coiffure (said by her critics to make her look like a poodle), his rationalization being that he wanted her to grow old looking as she had when he had asked her to marry him. Despite all the tiaras, all the crowns and all the coronets that she favoured, it was Queen Mary's hair that remained her 'crowning glory' and as if she was aware of its sexual significance she rarely uncovered her head other than in the privacy of her home. As far as King George was concerned, failure to emphasize her hair would deprive his wife of her femininity, and a defeminized woman was perhaps too close to masculinity for comfort. Having shut his eyes to same-sex involvements while in the Navy, nothing had horrified him more than the revelation of his brother's homosexuality at the time of the Cleveland Street scandal. His comment 'Homosexuals shoot themselves, don't they?' reflected his fear that he might turn out to be like his brother: a fear so absolute that were he to be 'contaminated' by this 'evil' he would kill himself. There is no evidence to suggest that King George himself had homosexual tendencies, only that his interest in women was one of respectful admiration and filial love. As a married man with children it is more likely that King George was asexual rather than homosexual. In adolescence his developing sexual interest was blunted by his ever-watchful guardians who forbade him appropriate sexual experimentation, and as an adult he put respectable women in a category similar to that of his mother, which encouraged feelings of exaggerated respect rather than sexual disinhibition.

In addition to the reverberations of the movement for the rights of women, other more violent events were developing in Europe. King George did his best to dissuade his ministers from involving Britain in any one of several conflicts – later described as the sparks that would sooner or later ignite the powder keg – which signalled the war of 1914.

Another issue threatened a civil war within the British Isles itself. The question of Home Rule for Ireland and the divisions within Britain may have given comfort to a Germany looking for an opportunity to break out of the 'encirclement' about which she had become increasingly concerned. Asquith's Liberal government, under pressure from Irish Nationalist MPs, had introduced a Home Rule Bill intended to devolve limited powers from Westminster to Dublin. The Bill, not surprisingly, failed to gain the approval of the Conservative-dominated House of Lords which threw it out first in 1912 and again a year later. Since the delaying power of the House of Lords was limited to two years, by 1914 all that was required for the Bill to become law was the royal assent. King George, readily identifying with Conservative prejudice and aristocratic grandiosity, refused this on the grounds that to assent to the Bill would be to inflame the Protestants in Ulster who might violently resist any attempt to force them into a union with the rest of Ireland.

The King was supported in his decision by his favourite author, the imperialist Rudyard Kipling, Edward Elgar who wrote 'Land of Hope and Glory' and Sir Edward Carson, a barrister and the leader of the Unionists who had won the King's approval for his prosecution of Oscar Wilde. King George was not supported by the Prime Minister, who tried to allay his fear that the Army would mutiny if it were asked to force Ulster into a union with the rest of Ireland. When the Home Rule Bill was introduced for its third and last time in March 1914 the King's refusal to assent to it led to a compromise. Asquith proposed that Ulster be excluded for six years from the provisions of Home Rule to allow for a testing of national opinion on the issue and that the nine counties be allowed to ballot independently on whether they wished to be excluded from it. The Irish Nationalists reluctantly agreed, but the Ulster Unionists, led by Carson, vehemently disagreed. He told the House of Commons that 'We do not want sentence of death with a stay of execution for six years.' Arms began to pour into Ulster encouraged by a very few officers in the Cavalry Brigade, who did not in fact threaten mutiny but merely said that they would resign their commissions if called on to fight against the Unionists.

King George had been thrown into the deep end of a political situation which he had not only made worse but which was now virtually set in stone. Had he assented to the Home Rule Bill on the eve of the Great War (during which many other issues, including the women's suffrage movement, were forced into abeyance for four years), the men of Ulster and the Catholic patriots might conceivably have achieved a *modus vivendi*. The two factions might perhaps have been able to coexist during peacetime, as had done those of them who fought alongside each other in British regiments in wartime. Had the King supported the Bill one more religious war might have been avoided.

The sense of power that King George brought back with him from India, the satisfaction of knowing that his visit was the first by a reigning British monarch and that millions of people had seen him as a God who could answer their prayers, soon started to wane. He began to realize that however powerful his status among his subjects in India his power to influence matters at home was almost non-existent. He was disappointed that his efforts to resolve the sectarian difficulties of the Irish had come to nothing. On 8 May 1914 he saw what he hoped might be an opportunity to avert problems in a different area of conflict.

Prince Henry of Prussia, the younger brother of Kaiser Wilhelm, had breakfasted at Buckingham Palace to discuss with the King the increasing rivalry between Austria and Russia. The discussions were amicable. King George's strong sense of family encouraged him to believe that his closeness to Prince Henry and the high regard the two cousins had for each other might allow them to rise above the rhetoric of politicians for whom the King had little regard. When Prince Henry came briefly to Buckingham Palace on 26 July 1914 to say goodbye before returning home, the King made it clear to him that England would not allow Russia to be overthrown in the event of an attack upon it by Germany. Two days later, when the Prince reached Kiel, he wrote to the Kaiser quoting a statement he claimed was made by the King: 'We shall try all we can to keep out of this and shall remain neutral.' King George's alleged statement could not have come at a worse time. On 28 June Archduke Franz Ferdinand, heir to the Austrian throne, and his wife the Duchess of Hohenberg were assassinated at Sarejevo by a Serbian student. The assassination at first was thought to be another anarchist attack on the monarchy. Austria, however, took the view that its unfriendly neighbour Serbia was behind the affair and issued Serbia with an ultimatum so onerous that it would not have been possible for any government to comply with it. Two days later Austria declared war on the Serbs and the Emperor of Russia mobilized the Russian Army to defend its ally against the Austrian attack. The British Prime Minister Asquith insisted that a telegram be sent in the name of the King to his cousin Tsar Nicholas II urging restraint. It was too late. Within a few hours Germany, coming to the support of Austria, was at war with Russia and declared war on France, now Russia's ally. After Germany invaded Belgium Great Britain, too, entered the war.

The year 1914 saw the values of Victorian England vanish for ever, the British class system begin to crumble and a misguided belief develop that the war would be over by Christmas. King George V, who had been trained to be of service to his country and to do his duty, had done his best to help resolve the major problems of the day. He had not been trained in diplomacy or the arts and was unable to engage in small talk, but before his retirement from the Navy he had been briefly given his own command. He had learned how to handle a warship in a time of peace. He knew that he had no idea how to handle the ship of state in a time of war, and after the failure of his efforts in Ireland and Europe he did not, to his credit, pretend otherwise.

As the German armies advanced through Belgium and northern France on the way to the Channel ports the King, who hitherto had been only able to cope with his underlying violence through sublimating it, had now to confront it. He found himself becoming increasingly distressed by the vast number of British soldiers who died in their efforts to halt the German advance. With his self-importance deflated by the horrors of a war that, despite his best efforts, he had failed to abort, he felt restless and anxious. His pessimistic mood echoed the gloomy prognostication of the Foreign Secretary Sir Edward Gray, as he watched the gaslights dim in Whitehall: 'The lights are going out all over Europe. We shall not see them lit again in our lifetime.' Years later, in September 1935, just three months before his death, the King, when informed of Mussolini's invasion of Abyssinia, replied: 'I've been through one war and I can't stand another one.'

The King's two eldest sons were already in the Services. Prince Edward (David) had been gazetted to the 1st Battalion Grenadier Guards and as a special honour had been detailed to the King's Company. At five feet seven inches he described himself as 'a pygmy among giants'. He was, however, prevented from taking an active role at the front by Lord Kitchener. The Secretary of State for War had told him that 'If I were sure you would be killed, I do not know if I should be right to restrain you. But I cannot take the chance, which always exists until we have a settled line, of the enemy taking you prisoner' (Windsor, 1951). His younger brother Prince Albert (Bertie), a midshipman on HMS *Collingwood,* was on sick leave soon after war broke out owing to what had been put down to complications following surgery for appendicitis. Bertie had complained of severe abdominal pain and sickness in September 1914 while at sea. His pain persisted long after the operation, leading to the eventual realization that his symptoms were due not to the increasingly popular diagnosis of appendicitis but to the peptic ulceration to which he had been prone since childhood. Bertie was ill for more than a year, recovering just in time to take part in the Battle of Jutland in 1916.

The King's opportunity for more personal involvement came in

November 1914 when he paid his first visit to the Western Front. He and the Queen were parted for the first time. In a letter dated 29 November 1914, interesting principally for demonstrating how much his wife had taken over the role of his mother, Queen Mary wrote: 'My own darling Georgie dear, I felt very sad at seeing you go today on your important mission, without me, for all these years I have thank God been able to accompany you on all important journeys during our married life, so I feel it rather having to stay at home.' She went on to warn her husband to take care and avoid becoming overtired and hoped the weather would not be too cold. She ended her letter with: 'God bless & protect you my own darling Georgie dear ever your very loving wife — May.'

The war was slow to strike home and most people – other than the families of sons who had been killed or wounded – did their best to carry on as if nothing had happened. This state of denial, understandable in the face of a danger no one wished to acknowledge, was shared by the King and Queen. In the early days of the war King George, certain that his German family could wish him no harm, was slow to abandon friendships with their emissaries. Count Albert Mensdorff, the Austrian ambassador, was connected to the British Royal Family through his relationship to Queen Victoria's mother, the Duchess of Kent, and also to Prince Albert's father, the Duke of Saxe-Coburg-Gotha. The King wrote to the Count assuring him that he would be welcomed back to London after the war, ending his letter with 'ever your devoted friends and cousins George and Mary'.

It was some time before the King was able to accept that war was not merely a misunderstanding between members of his family but a fight to the death between European alliances. Hatred of all things German by most Britons extended even to the Royal Family. The First Sea Lord, Prince Louis of Battenberg (father of the late Lord Louis Mountbatten of Burma), had been a naturalized British subject since he was fourteen years old. Although he was married to a granddaughter of Queen Victoria, he had been born in Germany and was therefore obliged to resign his post. Others with even the vaguest of German connections shared the same fate. The Lord Chancellor, Lord Haldane, felt it incumbent upon him to resign because he had in the past expressed pro-German sentiments. Violence broke out in the streets and was directed at British citizens with German-sounding names. There was, understandably, an embargo on all German imports. Even those who drank German wine were suspected of disloyalty, although Winston Churchill refused to give up Hock, explaining that he was merely 'interning' it. For a while more anti-German activity seemed to be taking place at home than on the war fronts. British victories were few and far between, and by the end of 1915, with trench warfare showing no sign of achieving any result for either side, the British Commander-in-Chief, Sir John French, was forced to resign. He was replaced by Sir Douglas Haig (of the whisky family), a friend of King George.

Sir Douglas's first blunder was in October 1915. During the King's second visit to France he lent the King his charger, having reassured him that the horse was crowd trained. As King George inspected the First Wing of the Royal Flying Corps, the call for 'Three cheers for the King' frightened the horse which reared and threw him. He was pinned to the ground and suffered massive bruising and a fractured pelvis which kept him confined to bed for about a month. The King never completely recovered his health and Queen Mary's concern for her husband's welfare, so vividly described in her letter to him during his first visit to the front, was well justified. Sir Douglas Haig's second blunder was of a much greater magnitude and concerned his conduct of the war during the latter half of 1916. Between July and November 1916 Haig's massive Somme offensive, which was aimed at smashing through the German lines, resulted in 420,000 British losses, 76,000 of which were sustained on the first day. By the end of 1916 scarcely a mile had been conceded by either side and Haig's reputation was in shreds. The fact that these terrible losses had been suffered by soldiers, many of them mere boys, aroused less anger in the King than when civilians were targeted. While he had been informed that there could be some indiscriminate 'bomb throwing' by Zeppelins flying over London, he insisted on watching them from the balcony of Buckingham Palace. These acts of violence, this intrusion, this invasion of his 'space' taking place so near his home so enraged him that, following a visit to Charing Cross Hospital to comfort the casualities caused by the raids, he wrote in his diary 'the Germans are murderers and proud of it'.

The 74-year-old Admiral Lord Fisher, who had replaced Prince Louis of Battenberg as First Sea Lord, was so incensed that he suggested that batches of German prisoners be shot for every Zeppelin raid. The King was as horrified by Lord Fisher's suggestion as he was by the Cabinet's recommendation that captured German submarine crews should be executed as 'pirates'. This was despite his personal view that the submarine crews' behaviour in sinking unarmed merchant vessels at night was 'brutal and inhumane'. In a letter to his son Bertie the King wrote that 'It is simply disgusting that Naval Officers could do such things'.

Another act of violence against civilians, this time by British soldiers, aroused far less indignation. On Easter Monday 24 April 1916 the extremist Irish Volunteer Movement had, with the help of rifles and other weapons landed by the German ship *Aud*, seized the main Post Office in Dublin as well as other buildings in the surrounding area. British soldiers were murdered on the streets, and in the ensuing fighting over the four days which it took to restore order 100 British soldiers and 450 Irish civilians were killed. Fifteen ringleaders were executed and two thousand other rebels were brought to England and imprisoned. The Easter Rising, seen in England as a disgraceful act of wartime treason by the King's Irish subjects and in Ireland as a successful political statement by Catholic Ireland, signalled the end of debate and the beginning of a belief, principally by Catholic Ulstermen at first, that only violence would be listened to by the British. The King now realized that by having withheld his assent to the final reading of the Home Rule Bill he had missed an opportunity to reconcile the needs of the Irish nationalists with those of the minority Protestant unionists. He was saddened and confused. It was not only the hated Germans who had brought violence to his homeland but the Irish whom he loved.

King George V was no stranger to violence. He had lived with it as a child, been punished for it as a growing boy, taught to suppress it in the Navy and found a sociably acceptable outlet for it as an adult. Shooting animals was a passion. He neither wished to understand the nature of his passion nor saw any reason to relinquish it. The shooting now taking place in France was another matter. At first fascinated and compelled to visit the Western Front as often as possible, the King now became sickened by the violence, and echoes of his impotent rage as a child resonated with the death and destruction. As the war drew closer the King, at first 'protective' of his 'enemy' relations and friends, now found it more difficult to justify this stance. He rationalized his heavily defended identification with the killing by the use of patriotic phraseology: 'laying down one's life for one's country' and the emotive use of words like 'sacrifice' and 'valour' enabled violence to become acceptable both to society and, to a lesser extent, to the King.

Forbidden as monarch to take part in the fighting, King George was angered by reports of daily carnage brought about by the inadequacies of General Haig who by 1917 had not relinquished the idea that to win a war one had to throw more and more soldiers into battle, irrespective of the casualty rate. The King turned at last against his German family and disassociated himself from them. The Royal House of Saxe-Coburg-Gotha ceased to be. On 17 July 1917 the King proclaimed that his Royal House was henceforth to be known as the House of Windsor and that all German titles held by members of his own family were to be changed to English ones. The King's cousin, Prince Louis of Battenberg, became the Marquis of Milford Haven, his two brothers-in-law, the Prince of Teck and Prince Alexander of Teck, became respectively the Marquis of Cambridge and the Earl of Athlone. Even Queen Mary's German origins were suspect and were used by republicans to whip up anti-royal feeling. Kaiser Wilhelm, not previously known for his sense of humour, said that he was looking forward to the next performance of that well-known opera 'The Merry Wives of Saxe-Coburg-Gotha'. Having failed so far to defeat his enemies abroad, King George had turned on his relatives at home.

Three months later he failed to attempt a rescue of his beleaguered Russian cousins, all of whom, including his *doppelgänger* Tsar Nicholas II, were murdered by the Bolsheviks in St Petersburg. The turning of the King's anger on to his family (and in reality on to aspects of himself), together with the guilt which resulted from his abandonment of them, led him to become severely depressed. His low mood, never far from the surface, now erupted. Even the sudden change in fortune in 1917 brought about by the arrival of American troops under the command of General Pershing, and the formation of a new coalition government under the powerful leadership of Lloyd George, did little to improve his self-esteem. Throughout the trench warfare the King had supported the foolhardy policies of the blinkered General Haig and had loudly opposed the Liberal policies of 'that damned fellow' Lloyd George. When the war was over Lloyd George's bitter comment 'I owe him nothing. He owes his throne to me' was the first, but not the last, anti-monarchical blow dealt to the new House of Windsor. In a letter to *The Times* H.G. Wells referred to the King as a foreigner and the Court as 'alien and uninspiring', a Labour MP called him a 'German pork butcher', and Max Beerbohm wrote an offensive poem with a refrain that referred to the King and Queen as 'dull'.

By 1918 the German fleet had mutinied and there was a revolution in Berlin. Germany had lost the war and King George V some members of his family. This real and metaphorical bereavement revived the sense of loneliness present in the King from the moment his beloved mother, with her protestations of undying love and without protest, had bidden the twelve-year-old 'darling Georgie' goodbye for three long years.

· 18 ·

If any question why we died, tell them that our fathers lied

THE END OF the 1914–18 war coincided with a short-lived economic boom. Although food rationing had been introduced in February 1918 and there were shortages of consumer goods, because of the demands of the war unemployment was at an all-time low. More than 750,000 men were mourned by their bereaved families and those servicemen who had survived the war were angered by the slow rate of demobilization. The 1918 Reform Act gave the vote to all men over twenty-one and, as a result of the militant suffrage movement, to women over the age of thirty-five. There was a sense of relief throughout the country that with the signing of the armistice, on 11 November 1918, the war with Germany was finally over. Those who had lost loved ones were in sombre mood as they prepared to celebrate the first post-war Christmas, four years after they had confidently predicted that it would all be over by Christmas 1914.

In 1919 the Treaty of Versailles, signed on behalf of Britain by Lloyd George, brought the war officially to an end. The treaty decreed that peace was to be made on the basis of President Woodrow Wilson's Fourteen Points. The frontiers of most of the countries of Europe were redrawn; the victors gained land from the losers; republics were created where Kings and Emperors had once ruled, and the foreign affairs of the Dominions (Canada, Australia, New Zealand and South Africa) ceased to be managed from Whitehall. Above all, a League of Nations was set up 'in order to promote international cooperation and to achieve international peace and security by the acceptance of obligations not to resort to war'. Every party to the treaty agreed these terms, an agreement which within a few years was to become not worth the paper it was written on.

Not one of the major participants of the 1914 war had gained by the conflict. Poverty had begun to replace prosperity everywhere and a dangerous humiliation had been imposed on Germany and her allies. In every village and town in Britain 'Lest We Forget' memorials were erected, but twenty-one years later, as peace came of age, a new generation forgot and only remembered by repeating what it had forgotten. Changes in land frontiers provided the victors with territorial gains, but it was the overwhelming response by government and people alike to the slogan 'Let Germany pay' that created the economic depression in Germany which sowed the seeds of the Second World War.

Reparations demanded of Germany by the Allies, the return of massive unemployment owing to the closure of munitions factories and the repatriation of the troops began to cause social chaos not only in Germany but throughout Europe. The stresses of the previous four years had so compromised the collective immune system that outbreaks of virulent influenza occurred, causing almost as many casualities as in the worst days of the fighting. Lloyd George's promise to the men who had survived the conflict, that Britain would be a land 'fit for heroes', was only briefly fulfilled, as the immediate but short-lived post-war economic boom came to an abrupt end.

King George V found himself in an alien world. In 1918 Lloyd George and his Coalition had been returned to power with a majority of 249 over the opposition and Asquith had not only been defeated at East Fife but had, somewhat spitefully, been denied a seat at the Peace Conference by Lloyd George. The Irish problem the King had tried so hard to resolve had not gone away. The newly formed Sinn Fein party had been successful in the general election and was demanding independence from Britain. For two years violence returned to the British Isles until a new Home Rule Bill was passed in 1920 which divided Ireland into two. Ulster in the north would remain part of the United Kingdom, although it would have its own parliament, and the remainder of Ireland would become a Free State with its parliament in Dublin. King George looked around him for friends and allies. Most of them were dead.

The King could not bring himself to forgive his cousin the Kaiser for his dishonourable conduct during the war. Among other 'ungentlemanly' acts, the German navy had not only fired on unarmed merchant ships but on 7 May 1915 had sunk a passenger ship off the coast of Ireland, the British registered *Lusitania,* with the loss of 1,195 lives. King George did not go so far as to endorse the cries of 'Hang the Kaiser' which were heard on the streets of London, but his opinion of his cousin was radically changed from his pre-war view that he might in some way have avoided the disaster. Unlike the Kaiser, who had come to hate Britain, the King felt almost sorry for his cousin's lack of judgement. He was certainly relieved when, after the Kaiser's abdication less than two weeks before the end of hostilities, the Dutch government offered him asylum. He could not bring himself to speak to his cousin for five years.

King George V disliked music and the performing arts. As far as books were concerned he identified only with those that spoke of a world he had once known and loved, in which nothing changed, where everyone knew his or her place, in which heroes were admired and rewarded and battles (in particular naval ones) were fought with honour. It was a world that was gone for ever. John Buchan and Rudyard Kipling were the King's favourite authors. He not only shared Kipling's jingoism but his prejudices. Reminded of the two visits he had himself paid to India, he was fascinated by Kipling's depictions of Indian life which were based on his memories of Bombay, his birthplace, and later on his experiences as sub-editor of the Lahore *Civil and Military Gazette.* Kipling's views and opinions resonated with the King's. The two men, who were born in the same year, died within twenty-four hours of one another.

Kipling came not from an aristocratic but from an artistic background. His father had been a painter, and two of his sisters married artists. In 1907 he was awarded the Nobel Prize for Literature, and no stronger recommendation of his writing could have been made than that by Robert Bridges, the Poet Laureate: '[Kipling] is the greatest living genius that we have in literature.' Before he met Rudyard Kipling King George had decided that the man whose views so impressed him, but who, unlike himself, was able to articulate them in prose and poetry, was deserving of official recognition. He accordingly instructed that the poet be appointed a Companion of Honour in 1917, the year that the honour was introduced. Kipling believed himself unworthy of such recognition and wished to be recognized in no way other than through his poetry. Refusing the honour, he wrote to Bonar Law asking him how he would like it 'if you woke up one morning and found that they had made you Archbishop of Canterbury'.

Kipling claimed that his refusal was due to his wish not to be associated with any political party, but this does not explain why on three occasions he also declined the Order of Merit, the last time being in 1924 when it was personally offered to him by the King. At each refusal Kipling was careful to assure the King of his loyalty and his gratitude. It is likely that his sense of guilt, associated with the death of his only son in France in 1917, caused him to feel that he was undeserving. While he was glad that his son had been given the opportunity to serve his country, having encouraged him to enlist, he reproached himself for his untimely death. Kipling, like many other writers, was probably at his happiest when he was alone in his study. At Batemans, his Sussex home, with only his typewriter for company, he could, if only for a moment, distract himself from his grief. A lonely man, he was as shy and uncomfortable in social situations as King George himself had been, until his father's death endowed him with a status behind which he could hide his feelings of inadequacy.

King George's absolute belief in the monarchy gave him the illusion that he was always right, since few had the temerity to prove otherwise. Hiding behind the uniform of rank, those of lesser rank (almost everyone) seldom dared challenge him. Long after the war had ended 'uniforms' remained important. It reassured the King to know that his clothes served to remind his subjects of his rank and he retained his formal style of dress long after it had gone out of fashion. The curly-brimmed bowler-hat, the frock coat (a gardenia always in the buttonhole), his trousers pressed at the sides, the ceremonial attire, the kid gloves spoke for him when he found it difficult to speak for himself. Kipling also hid himself from the world but in his case behind his writing. While King George and his favourite author lived fantasy lives, Kipling's was an invention while King George's was bestowed upon him by a thousand years of privilege.

The King and Kipling were not actually to meet until 1922, although it would have been impossible for them to be unaware of one another. King George read Kipling's novels, which moved him emotionally, and Kipling admired his Emperor, the only person in a changing world whose attachment to what 'had been' matched his own. Appropriately enough, their meeting was in the war cemeteries of France in which the hopes and aspirations of both lay buried.

In the spring of 1922 King George and Queen Mary visited northern France. Although the visit was an official one it was probably more of a pilgrimage for them. Rudyard Kipling was also there to commemorate the death of his son, as was the King to commemorate the death of the many members of his own family. The construction of the seemingly endless war cemeteries had almost been completed, and the King had been called to inspect them on behalf of those whose sons were buried there. Kipling was officially present as a Commissioner for War Graves. In 1914, when war was declared, Kipling was forty-eight and too old for combat. His sense of patriotism and his desire to fight for his King and Country, however, was so intense that he encouraged his only son to volunteer in his place. John Kipling, born in August 1897, was barely seventeen and physically unfit. He was so short-sighted that he could scarcely see without glasses, but after leaving them at home he was passed as fit by an equally short-sighted medical officer. He was commissioned as a lieutenant in the Second Battalion of the Irish Guards and was believed to have been killed on 27 September 1915 at the Battle of Loos. His body was never found, and for a year Kipling, who had not accepted his son's death, begged the Army Council to keep John's name on the Army List.

His hopes were momentarily raised by a letter from an officer who thought it possible that his son might have been captured by the Germans. But by 1918 all hope had gone. Like Abraham before him Kipling had sacrificed his son for his god (King and country), but, while Abraham's God at the eleventh hour had relieved him of his obligation to demonstrate his faith, Kipling's god had not. As literary adviser to the Imperial War Graves Commission in 1919 Kipling composed a simple inscription to be used on gravestones wherever unidentified bodies had been buried: 'A soldier of the Great War known only to God.' He may have considered himself fortunate when in 1922 he was given the opportunity to meet his god – the King – in person.

Like Kipling, King George had also sent his sons to the front. Protected by those with the interests of the monarchy at heart, however, both of them had survived. The King's speech at the cemetery in which he said that 'there can be no more potent advocates of peace upon earth than this massed multitude of witnesses to the desolation of war' impressed Kipling. The King spoke to his wife Carrie, telling her how sorry he was that her son had died so young, and he also addressed a few words to Kipling. On King George's return to England he set the seal on their developing rapport by inviting the author to meet him again at a private house in London. It was to be the first of many meetings.

What Kipling did not know was that King George and Queen Mary had also experienced a personal loss. Their sixth and last son, Prince John, born with brain damage and mentally retarded, at the age of four had been diagnosed as suffering from epilepsy, a disorder not only virtually untreatable but which carried considerable social stigma. Neither King George nor Queen Mary coped well with illness, and in 1917 they decided that Prince John should be removed for ever from his home, from his family and from the public gaze to a remote farmhouse on the Sandringham estate. In 1919, at the age of fourteen, the boy died suddenly in his sleep. Sad though Queen Mary undoubtedly was, she was able to rationalize her son's death and commented in her diary: 'For the poor little boy's restless soul, death came as a great release.' After a quiet service Prince John was buried in the graveyard at Sandringham Church. He had been cared for in life by the royal nannie, Lala Bill, who coped with her charge's sudden death with the same loving concern that she had shown towards the older children while they were in her care. Queen Mary, who was good at concealing her feelings, was less overtly emotional. She had provided for her son to the best of her ability and during his brief life, marred as it had been by frequent and difficult-to-control epileptic seizures, he had been well looked after. His death, which occurred barely two months after the end of the war when so many, including two of Queen Mary's other sons, had been in mortal danger, came as an anticlimax.

One person, however, remained at the graveside when the other mourners had left. Queen Alexandra, Prince John's grandmother, wept for her youngest grandson. Since her own Prince John had lived for only a few hours, she alone of the immediate family knew what it was to have lost a child. The two Princes were buried next to one another in the church-yard. Both Kipling and King George felt guilty about the deaths of their respective sons. Although Prince John had died two years after John Kipling, as far as King George and Queen Mary were concerned he could as well have died in 1917, which was the last time his mother saw him and the same year in which Kipling's son was killed in action. The two fathers, neither of whom knew at the time of the other's grief, were destined to become friends during King George's sudden and near-fatal illness in 1928.

On 21 November 1928, while at Buckingham Palace, the 63-year-old King developed a fever and a cough and was in a state of near collapse. His doctor, Sir Stanley Hewitt, at once recognized the gravity of his condition and sent for Lord Dawson of Penn. Lord Dawson arranged for blood tests which showed the King to be suffering from streptococcal septicaemia. Following a portable chest X-ray (the first ever performed outside a hos-pital), the cause was found to be an abscess in the King's right lung. Before the advent of antibiotics the prognosis was poor. Within three weeks the King's physical condition had become so serious that, despite the best efforts of eleven doctors and five nurses, his death was considered immi-nent. On 5 December a bulletin that hardly reflected the seriousness of his condition was issued from Buckingham Palace. 'His Majesty the King passed a quiet morning. Though the temperature is now 100.2 the slight improvement in the general condition noted in the last bulletin is main-tained.' The bulletin was signed by all five of the King's consultants:

Stanley Hewitt, L.E.H.Whitby, E. Farquhar Buzzard, Humphry Rolleston and Dawson of Penn. One week later, on the afternoon of 12 December, the King slipped into a coma.The appropriate treatment would have been surgical drainage of the abscess, but X-rays had failed to reveal its exact location. It was now too late for an exploratory operation to be carried out, since the King would certainly have failed to survive the anaesthetic. On impulse, and certainly not before time, Lord Dawson inserted a needle into the chest. By a stroke of luck he found the abscess and aspirated some sixteen ounces of purulent fluid, with immediate improvement. A few hours later the King was well enough to be operated upon by Mr Hugh Rigby who removed a rib and inserted a drain into the abscess. It was not until the following March that the patient had recovered sufficiently to be allowed a cigarette! Two months later he developed an infection at the operation site and in July further surgery was needed to drain the original abscess, necessitating the removal of another rib. Full recovery did not take place until September 1929, ten months after the onset of illness.

There was inevitable criticism of Lord Dawson's management of His Majesty's illness, by both the uninformed and the informed. He was particularly blamed by certain members of the medical profession for not calling in Britain's leading chest surgeon Mr Arthur Tudor Edwards. King George convalesced at a house loaned to him by Sir Arthur du Cros at Aldwick overlooking the English Channel near Bognor. Not unnaturally, the King found convalescence boring. He discovered little to divert him. He had always relied on external sources of stimulation to distract him and to keep depression at bay and had developed few internal resources to fall back on. He had never been reflective or introspective. As a child he had discovered that the best way to survive the prolonged absences from home was to deny his feelings. As time passed he had become adept at this and as a result had more or less lost contact with the pain of loneliness, other than when an incident reminded him of the sadness of separation. Queen Mary, who was always by his side, protected him against these feelings simply by being there for him. Irritability, always easily provoked, was never 'denied' and was a feature of the King's convalescence. One visitor, however, never failed to raise his spirits; this was his three-year-old grand-daughter Princess Elizabeth. Her infectious enthusiasm and her obvious love for her grandfather dispelled his apathy. He asked her mother, Elizabeth Duchess of York, to bring the child to see him as often as she could.

During King George's convalescence he and Rudyard Kipling became better acquainted. Although few visitors were allowed, Kipling was always welcome. They had much to discuss in their love for India, for the mon-archy and for the country. Kipling kept King George well supplied with the few books he enjoyed reading, Edgar Wallace being one of the King's favourite writers at the time. It is likely that Kipling was also able to make some occasional contribution to the sovereign's speeches, as the author was later to do for his cousin, Stanley Baldwin, when he became Prime Minister. It was essentially the similarity of the two men, however, that allowed their friendship to prosper.

· 19 ·

The King is dead and has taken his trumpeter with him

DESPITE THE PROBLEMS that Britain had to face after the war, there were some indications that the British way of life, at least among the upper classes, had not been entirely eradicated. The return of tennis at Wimbledon, the Eton and Harrow match at Lords, racing at Epsom and, not least, the Trooping of the Colour on Horse Guard's Parade were seen by some as evidence that the good old days were back. Within the next twelve months other signs of 'normality' began to appear. The King attended the Derby at Epsom, sailed his old yacht *Britannia* at Cowes and later in the year received the new German Ambassador to the Court of St James, with his comment that it was 'the first time I have shaken hands with a German for six years'.

On 11 November 1920, when the second Remembrance Day after the war had ended, the Cenotaph in Whitehall was unveiled for the first time. After the two minutes' silence, ushered in by the firing of maroons, the King attended the burial service for the Unknown Soldier at Westminster Abbey.

With the pre-1914 days gone for ever, when divisions of class and gender were more clearly defined, the 1920s saw the emancipation both of the working man and of women. The industrial unrest, which began with rising unemployment figures, presaged an economic disaster. By 1925 coal mines were running at a loss and cheaper coal from European mines was being supplied to Britain's customers abroad. British mine owners were obliged to cut wages, and the miners were ordered to work longer hours to stave off their competitors. The mine workers and the mine owners were on a collision course from which neither side would budge. A Royal Commission was convened and nine months later agreed with the owners that wages must be reduced. The miners immediately came out on strike, whereupon the owners locked them out. Workers in other industries came out in support of the miners and at midnight on Tuesday 4 May 1926 a general strike, which divided the country, was declared. To the great relief of the King, who had been warned by Winston Churchill of the possibility of armed conflict, the strike lasted for nine days only and the miners were finally forced back to work having been in a state of near starvation for six months. A year later the Trades Disputes Act made all sympathetic strikes illegal.

On the political front, the Coalition Government had fallen owing to Lloyd George's resignation in 1922. Party politics returned under Arthur Bonar Law as Prime Minister, but when he was forced to resign for reasons of health he was soon replaced by Stanley Baldwin. A few months later Bonar Law died from throat cancer. If King George was secretly relieved to see the Conservatives back in office, he was to be disappointed the following year when the Baldwin government was defeated. On 22 January 1924 he 'entrusted Mr Ramsay Macdonald with the formation of a new government' which Mr Macdonald accepted. The King noted in his diary that 'Today [on 22 January 1901] dear Grandmama died. I wonder what she would have thought of a Labour government!' It was likely that his diary entry was more a reflection of his own opinion than speculation about Queen Victoria's. None the less, King George's attitude to Ramsay Macdonald was cordial and in fact no different from his attitude towards others who served him, whether personally or in government.

Against this background Edward Prince of Wales (David), the heir to the throne, began at last to assert himself. Having been in awe of his father for as long as he could remember, he took comfort from the fact that on his tours at home and abroad he had been enthusiastically received. By 1919 the 25-year-old Prince had become the darling of the gossip columnists. His slim build, pleasant smiling face and brilliant blue eyes were attractive to women everywhere. On a tour of North America in 1919 the American magazine *Vanity Fair* summarized in an eye-catching headline what American women thought of the Prince (Edwards, 1984). 'Hats off to the indestructible Dancing, Drinking, Tumbling, Kissing, Walking, Talking – but not Marrying – Idol of the British Empire.' It was rumoured that the Prince was involved with one or another of several women. In reality he had fallen in love with Freda Dudley Ward, mother of two children and the divorced wife of a Member of Parliament. He remained devoted to Mrs Ward for fourteen years, until another 'friend' – Thelma, Lady Furness, Lord Furness's American wife with whom he was also having an affair – introduced him at a dinner party in 1931 to another American, the twice divorced Mrs Wallis Simpson.

In his frequent need for reassurance from women the Prince of Wales was certainly not emulating his father, and neither did he emulate King George in his dress. The Prince dressed in a manner that his father considered unseemly. He wore plus-fours on the golf course, tied his tie in a double knot (the Windsor knot) and wore patterned sweaters and socks. When the King noticed that his son had turn-ups on his trousers, he asked David if it was raining. It was just as well perhaps that the King had not realized his son's fly-buttons had been replaced by a zip fastener. It was becoming increasingly apparent that the Prince of Wales's role model, as far as his behaviour was concerned, was not his father King George but his grandfather King Edward VII. Both the Prince and King Edward had rebelled against an upbringing that had deprived them of hands-on mothering. They both sought admiration from motherly women, they were both intent on being noticed and both had addictive personalities. King Edward sought gratification through eating, drinking, smoking, gambling and womanizing, whereas Prince Edward (David) sought similar gratification partly with alcohol but mainly through sex.

King George and Queen Mary had a more relaxed relationship with their two younger sons. They were less demanding of Prince Henry and Prince George, probably because they were far removed from the accession. If David or Bertie had been asked when they were growing up whether the family was a close one they would have probably said that it was. It was a closeness at best often heavily paternalistic. Attention was focused primarily on David, as his parents sought to prepare him for the role ordained for him. The King's view – perhaps not unreasonable since his subjects had been so impressed with his wartime leadership – was that if David modelled himself on his father he would not go far wrong. David admired his father and throughout the 1920s was content to follow his example by undertaking one tour after another, both at home and abroad. He was, however, unable to adopt the 'regality', the other-worldliness, the detachment of his parents as they carried out their duties. He found it impossible to follow the advice of courtiers who told him that only by allowing himself to be put on a pedestal and remain more detached from the public would he ensure the continuation of the royal mystique. His highly publicized indiscretions in London society, and to a lesser extent in politics, met with chilly disapproval from his parents.

Of the two, the Queen, essentially a private person, was possibly the more disapproving. Seldom, if ever, did she reveal her true feelings which she hid behind her upright posture, her armour-like clothing, her aggressive jewellery and her daunting toques. Her success in not giving anything of herself away enabled those who did not know her to form whatever opinion of her they chose. She exuded a regal otherness which was to be disrupted two generations later by her great-grandchildren with their 'let it all hang out' attitude. Giving nothing of herself away, Queen Mary was all things to all people and, chameleon-like, took on the colour of her surroundings. To some she epitomised a mother or a sister, to others a daughter or a wife. She seemed to belong to every family and because of this was much loved. It distressed her greatly to see her elder son bring the monarchy she loved into disrepute.

One of King George's great strengths, which was valued highly by his subjects in the rapidly changing post-war years, was his stability. His constancy of manner, his unaltered mode of dress, his insistence on punctuality, the predictable unpredictability of his mood, his keen sense of duty, his insistence on the preservation of social values were reminders not only of what once was but of what he hoped in vain still might be. His dependable appearance reassured those who mourned the loss of a past in which life, for the privileged classes at least, appeared to have been rosy and in which the senseless slaughter of young men on the horrendous scale of the 1914–18 war was as yet unknown.

The King's disapproval of David did not extend to his brother Prince Albert (Bertie) whom on 5 June 1920 he created Duke of York, Earl of Inverness, Baron Killarney. In thanking his father for so honouring him Bertie told him that he hoped he would be able to live up to the title that once had been his father's. The King wrote to his son, in headmasterish tones, to tell him to think of his father as his 'best friend'. He did not add 'because I'm your father and I know what's best for you', but the implication was there and Bertie, far from disagreeing with his father, believed him to be correct. The fact that his son was so compliant endeared him to the King. Obedience to a 'commanding officer' had been so instilled into him that he valued it highly in others. Bertie had always tried to please his father but often with a singular lack of success. His need for his father's approval was so intense that when it was withheld the recurring bouts of depression that were a feature of his adult life were exacerbated.

Although David and Bertie were fond of one another, the two brothers were very different in temperament. David had asserted himself somewhat late in the day and as a young adult, prone to adolescent behaviour, had rebelled against the *modus vivendi* to which his father was so committed. Bertie, on the other hand, was more timid. Far from rebelling, he had long ago realized that King George's love for him was conditional on his obedience to his wishes, and he did whatever he could to please his father. When, despite his best efforts, he failed to do so, he experienced feelings of bereavement. Since King George had left his children for long periods so often during their childhood, it was hardly surprising that Bertie grew up to believe that if he were to disobey his father he might abandon him for good.

After his near-fatal illness in 1928 King George never fully recovered his strength. Although his recovery had been slow, it was welcomed by his subjects who over the years had grown to appreciate him. The King's courage, his attention to detail, his insistence on correctness, his self-discipline, his regard for his subjects both at home and overseas and his genuine concern for the health and vigour of a nation in turmoil in the immediate post-war years all endeared him to them.

The 'all for one and one for all' spirit that typified the war years had dissipated. While many supported the growing concern for the welfare of the working man, many others were still wedded to the idea that the past, with its archaic class structure, should be preserved at all costs. Conservatives blamed the King for not playing a more active role in stemming 'the swelling Socialist tide', and Socialists complained that the monarchy was spending too much money on ceremonial state visits abroad. While the King was certainly unimpressed with socialism since the murder of his Russian relatives in the revolution of 1917, he could not see what, if anything, could be done about it.

The King had barely recovered from his illness when a new General Election was fought in 1929. The government elected in 1924 had almost come to the end of its statutory term and when the King received Ramsay Macdonald and invited him to form a government he was not yet well enough to leave his bedroom at Windsor. The new Labour government lasted for only two years. The Great Depression of October 1929, the massive increase in unemployment and the collapse of American credit were eventually to lead to its fall. In 1931, at a time when the economy had all but collapsed, Ramsay Macdonald, no longer having an overall majority, was persuaded by the King to form a Coalition government. The Labour Party turned against the Prime Minister on the grounds that by forming an alliance with the old enemies of the party he had become a traitor to the socialist cause. Macdonald had to face a run on sterling, the suspension of the gold standard, a 25 per cent devaluation of the pound, a 10 per cent cut in the salaries of the civil service, as well as a reduction in unemployment benefit. This last was a particularly hard decision at a time when unemployment was running at around the five million mark. With the support of the King, Macdonald managed to survive until 1935, despite Labour's dislike of his policies. With the Prime Minister's great oratorical powers gone, his memory failing and his speech inarticulate, he continued in office until increasing signs of dementia put an end to his career. He was then succeeded by Stanley Baldwin.

The King began once more to take a keen interest in both home and foreign affairs. Having been made conscious of his mortality by his illness, it was as if he wanted to make his mark in politics while there was still time. His long association with India, where the Raj reigned supreme, and his love for the country which had in 1911 had so warmly welcomed him, led to feelings of sadness as India moved inexorably towards independence. His great wish was for India to remain within the British Empire and he thought back to the time when after his departure from Bombay work had begun on the triumphal arch on the waterfront. The monument had been built not only to commemorate his visit but – as he saw it – to welcome through it both him and his descendants as Emperors. Indian nationalism had, however, found a powerful voice in Mahatma Gandhi who was achieving remarkable success in the non-cooperation movement, a form of passive resistance in which no one would be hurt.

The King's nostalgia for the Indian subcontinent and his wish to return to it in the role of favourite son was in naïve contrast to Gandhi's more intellectual approach to the apparently insoluble problem of Indian independence. In no way was India calling her surrogate son home from across the seas, as the King would like to have believed. She was calling rather to her own sons to grow up and take responsibility for themselves. Gandhi was in touch with the teachings of the psychoanalytic movement, and his concept of independence was very different from that of King George V who saw it as an abrupt and painful divorce, with little hope of reconciliation and with both parties going their separate ways. His own separations (from his biological mother) had been abrupt and had been caused by long journeys overseas. They were, as a consequence, painful. In 1925 Gandhi's search for independence through peaceful coexistence took him to a meeting of the Calcutta psychoanalytic society where a solution to the ever-present problems of Hindu–Muslim cooperation was discussed (Kakar, 1997).

Unlike Gandhi, King George sought not a coexistence between equals but, as always, the perpetuation of a parent–child dependency between Mother India and 'darling Georgie'. In 1935, at a conference in London which echoed the verbal violence that the King had been used to, both in the school room and as a naval cadet, he warned Gandhi that he would not tolerate any form of terrorism. He showed no understanding of Gandhi's well-known insistence on non-violent forms of protest.

Other than the slow disintegration of the British Empire, more sinister events were gradually becoming apparent, not least of which was the erosion in the fabric of the League of Nations. Following the election of Adolf Hitler as Chancellor of Germany in 1933, Germany had withdrawn from the League of Nations when the Disarmaments Committee had refused their demands for military parity with France. In 1932 Japan had already done likewise after she had illegally seized possession of Manchuria. The King's interest in what was going on around him allowed for some forthright although undiplomatic responses. Never one for small talk, and occasionally at a loss with big talk, he was, however, familiar with the bluntness of the ward room. At a meeting with the German Ambassador in 1934 he told him that Germany was the peril of the world and that if she went on at her present rate, there could be a war within ten years. King George knew how to deal with bullies. He had had plenty of experience. The King took an immediate dislike to Hitler. Unlike some of his ministers who believed that it might be possible for an accommodation to be reached with the German dictator in the interests of avoiding conflict, King George, no more prescient than they, saw in Adolf Hitler a reminder of the tyrant that he had discovered his cousin the Kaiser to be, another German hate object which allowed him to focus all the violently angry feelings that less than twenty years earlier he had had to suppress in the interests of family unity. The cold politics of appeasement were not for him. In the last two or three years of his life he had found in Adolf Hitler an appropriate outlet for the bottled-up rage of his over-controlled upbringing.

Despite the occasional feeling that gloom and despair were once again on the move over Europe, Britain was pleased to be diverted by the kind of ceremonial distraction that had so pleased the nation when King George and Queen Mary had married twenty-five years earlier and with which as a child the King had been familiar when separation had been in the air. A military band at the quayside, however, was not going to heal the rifts in Europe any more than it had healed the rifts when Prince George's personal world was falling apart. Neither the King nor the Queen could have known that four years after their accession in 1910 the First World War was to break out: neither could they then have predicted that twenty-five years later and four years after the celebration of their Silver Jubilee another world war would be initiated by Germany, involving more or less the same protagonists.

The Silver Jubilee of King George and Queen Mary was celebrated on 6 May 1935, a warm summer's day. On his return from the Jubilee Thanksgiving Service at St Paul's Cathedral the King, together with the Queen, stood on the balcony of the palace. Looking down at the welcoming crowds with amazement, he said: '[This is] the greatest number of people in the streets that I have ever seen in my life.' In the evening the King spoke to his people on the wireless. Many of his listeners stood in silence and to attention while he spoke. For a man who normally eschewed public emotion he was unusually outspoken. As if he was aware that within seven months he would be dead, he thanked the people of Britain for the love they had shown him, a love he probably thought he deserved but which none the less he was touchingly gratified to receive.

The King may have had greatness thrust upon him, but on his sometimes faltering journey through life he had made his way without recourse to psychotherapeutic help to enable him to unravel his dysfunctional upbringing. It would have occurred to him neither to disclaim accountability for his own shortcomings nor to blame his parents for their haphazard attention to his emotional needs. Familiar with the name of Freud, but probably not with the significance of his discoveries, he would have been intolerant of any intrusion into the privacy of his thoughts or of any suggestion that others might have been to blame for his adult behaviour. The King had risen through the ranks from cadet to commander, from child to adult. In the end he was a better commander than he had been a cadet. He had inherited an image. His subjects recognized before he did that, as with all icons, the more one looks at them the more of their hidden treasure they reveal.

Less than three months before his death the King, although already frail, had one last pleasant duty to attend to. On 6 November 1935 his third son, Prince Henry the Duke of Gloucester, married Lady Alice Christabel Montagu-Douglas-Scott. The ceremony was a private one, not only because of King George's failing health but also because of the recent death of Lady Alice's father, the Duke of Buccleuch and Queensbury. The ceremony took place in the chapel at Buckingham Palace. In possibly the last letter the King wrote, he informed his new daughter-in-law that he 'would try to take [her father's place] & would do anything to try to help her'. Although he had done his best during his lifetime, he had not shone as a father. He tried to make up for this both as a grandfather and as a surrogate 'father' to anyone who needed him.

King George V died at his home at Sandringham on 20 January 1936 with his children dutifully gathered around the bedside. For two days crowds of well-wishers had been gathering outside Buckingham Palace to read the bulletins posted on the gates. The first hint of imminent disaster came at 3.30 p.m. on 18 January. A bulletin signed by Sir Frederic Willans, Sir Stanley Hewett, Lord Dawson of Penn and the cardiologist Sir Maurice Cassidy stated that 'His Majesty the King had had some hours of restful sleep. The cardiac weakness and the embarrassment of the circulation have slightly increased and give cause for anxiety.' Lord Dawson of Penn's final bulletin was broadcast at midnight. 'Death came peacefully to the King at 11.55 p.m.'

Fate had it that the nation would mourn not only the King but the poet Rudyard Kipling whose love for one another was a brotherly one and continued until the end. 'The King is dead,' the newspapers declared, 'and has taken his trumpeter with him'. The two men who met in 1922 among the war graves in the presence of death and whose friendship flourished through the sadness of their mutual loss were parted in death fourteen years later.

It is said that Dawson hastened to end the King's suffering by injecting his jugular vein with morphine and cocaine (he was already in a coma) so that his patient's death would occur before midnight. Thus it would be first reported in the morning rather than in the less prestigious evening papers (Watson, 1986). The King had never been overimpressed with Lord Dawson since his handling of his near-fatal illness in 1928. He would most probably have been amused by the acid wit of Margot Asquith – the widow of his first Prime Minister and a woman addicted to outrageous flights of fancy – who commented in old age: 'The King told me he would never have died if it had not been for that fool Dawson of Penn' (Longford,1989).

· 20 ·

And it all goes into the laundry, but it never comes out in the wash

KING GEORGE V'S death was peaceful. His family were at his bedside. Queen Mary turned to her eldest son and, bowing, took his hand and kissed it. In a clear voice she uttered 'God save the King', words that had ensured the continuity of the monarchy for a thousand years. The following day the Prince of Wales acceded to the throne and the day after that he was officially proclaimed King Edward VIII. On 24 January the coffin of the late King George V was taken by train from Sandringham to London. From there it was carried on a gun-carriage to Westminster Hall for the four-day lying in state before the burial in the chapel of the Knights of the Garter at Windsor Castle. The Imperial Crown, made especially for King George V for the Coronation Durbar in India, had been secured to the lid of the coffin, but as the cortège turned into New Palace Yard the jewelled Maltese Cross which was attached to the coffin fell to the ground. It was quickly retrieved by one of the escorting guardsmen, but King Edward VIII, who had seen the incident, gloomily, and in the event presciently, declared it a 'most terrible omen'. Whether the new King thought of the omen as foretelling the fall of the Empire or his own downfall is a matter for speculation.

In the five generations that have passed since the reign of Queen Victoria it is highly possible that in at least four of them the failure of male heirs to the throne to have bonded with the parent of the opposite sex has been in part responsible for the emotional crises that have befallen the Royal Family. This failure to bond causes boys to seek often inappropriate compensation for the absence of this love from other women in later life. Because it has long been the custom for those born to royal parents to be cared for from birth by attendants other than their mothers, such children grow up feeling not only excluded from the family circle but also excluded from what they believe to be their parents' love for them. The essential love affair with the opposite-sex parent, for both boys and girls, in early childhood is often ignored by parents who confuse the physical needs of their children with their emotional needs. 'It is the fate of all of us, perhaps, to direct our first sexual impulse towards our mother and our first hatred and our first murderous wish against our father' (Freud, 1900). Royal heirs may even have 'denied' this oedipal wish to kill their fathers and marry their mothers, because their 'god-like' fathers were essentially too remote. Their patricidal impulses may instead have been turned inwards upon themselves or unwittingly directed at other 'fathers', like the husbands of the married women with whom they sometimes seek out affairs. Such 'fathers' are also to be found in religion ('our Father which art in heaven'), in respected tutors and advisers (in the case of King George V) or in same-sex encounters (as in the case of Prince Eddy).

The reign of King George V, midway between that of Queen Victoria and Queen Elizabeth II, played a pivotal role in reinforcing this mode of behaviour. Changes in royal child-rearing methods, however – such as can be observed in the case of Prince William and Prince Harry – could bring the faulty pattern to an end.

Queen Victoria's life may have been a model of sexual propriety, but it was marred by her unfulfilled dependent needs which she handed on to her children. Brought up without a father (the Duke of Kent had died from pneumonia when Princess Victoria was a baby of nine months), as a young woman the Princess had suffered from long periods of depression. An ageing uncle, King Leopold, and a Prime Minister, Lord Melbourne, did what they could with their advice and support to help her, but it was not until as Queen she met and married her cousin Prince Albert that her loss was assuaged. Eager to have the comfort and compensation of a large family the Queen bore nine children over the course of seventeen years. For much of her life a 'child' in search of a father, Queen Victoria had little time for other children, including her own. She pronounced her heir

Prince Edward unattractive from the moment of his birth, handed him over to a wet nurse at the earliest possible moment and did not set eyes on him again for six weeks. Her consort Prince Albert was the only male in her life. Believing that she had found in her husband the father she had lost, she was inconsolable when Prince Albert died from typhoid fever in 1861, and she unjustly blamed Prince Edward's 'scandalous' behaviour with the actress Nellie Clifden and the aftermath of it for his father's death.

Disapproved of by both his parents, but particularly by his mother, Prince Edward grew up insistent upon righting the wrongs of his childhood. He sought illusory compensations for the absence of his mother's love in food, drink, gambling and sex. Not having a father to whom he could direct his murderous rage, King Edward VII forced the cuckolded husbands of his mistresses into the role. His continuing urge to satisfy his own need for love and attention allowed him little time to satisfy similar needs in his children.

King Edward VII's heir, Prince Eddy, and his younger son, Prince George, were apparently happy and carefree in their early days on the Sandringham estate. Their idyllic childhood came to an abrupt end at the ages of eight and six with the arrival of their new tutor, Mr Dalton. Prince George, the brighter and more intelligent of the two boys, was frustrated by being taught at the slow pace of his intellectually slow older brother. Five years later he was shocked once again by his banishment from home to the draconian Naval Academy at Dartmouth where he was told by his father that 'a man would be made of him'.

Boys generally metamorphose into men through emulating the behaviour of their fathers. Since for much of his childhood Prince George's male role model was unavailable to him (which in view of King Edward VII's philandering may have been all to the good), he was forced to seek alternatives in authoritarian men, while his brother Eddy found father substitutes in sexually promiscuous ones. King George V consequently grew up to be as rigid and unbending as the senior naval officers on whom he modelled himself.

As a cadet, Prince George soon realized that once again he would not be allowed to develop at a pace suited to his temperament but one that suited the officers in the institution in which he had been incarcerated. While it is true that many of the other cadets came from a similar background, few, if any, would have stepped straight from the sheltered environment of a school with only two pupils to a far stricter school in which they were surrounded not only by fellow cadets but also by midshipmen, officers and crew older and bigger than them. It is unlikely that any would have been brought up to believe himself so special that his overwhelmingly doting mother would want to keep him by her side for ever. Prince George never became reconciled to the pain of parting. The once good-natured and sensitive boy eventually became so indoctrinated by the life-style into which he had been forced – believing it to be for the best, otherwise his loving mother would not have permitted it – that in the course of time he insisted upon a similar life-style for his children.

Satisfied with the love that his mother had impressed upon him, the Prince, unlike his father, was not forced to seek compensatory love from women. Because of his mother's many absences he sought compensatory love instead, first from his dreamy and effeminate brother and later from his spouse who neglected her children in order to attend to his dependent needs. Prince George's adolescence was spent in a claustrophobic, all-male institution in which he was indoctrinated with the importance of obedience and duty. In company with other graduates from the naval college, he offloaded on to other victims, including his children, the violent practices he had been taught.

King George's personality was well suited to the rigid training he received. From the age of six his upbringing had been over-structured and over-disciplined. He had sensed his mother's persistent unhappiness, owing both to her ill health and the indifferent attitude of her husband. Prince George tried to comfort her, but because she often left him for prolonged periods it must have appeared to 'darling Georgie' that his efforts to please her had failed. He became angry both with his mother and with himself; angry with his mother because of her unavailability and the fact that she had allowed him to be sent away from home, and angry with himself because he had not pleased her sufficiently. Like other children in the same predicament he was unable to express his anger because he feared that one day his mother might leave him for ever.

Prince George was trained to perform for his instructors, but his ambivalence towards them led him to join in with the practical 'jokes' which allowed for a respectable acting-out of hostility to authority. Prone to angry outbursts, he later learned to control his feelings lest he damaged those he loved. His bullying tactics towards his sons, who were unable to leave him, turned one of them against him and the other into a timid and depressed adult.

When he was well into his career as a naval officer and had begun to settle into the passive role of gentleman landowner, with only his guns to reflect his slowly awakening sexuality, the 25-year-old Prince George was plunged once again into a role for which he was unprepared when, on Eddy's death, he unexpectedly found himself heir to the throne. While King Edward VII and Queen Alexandra mourned their son, Prince George grieved for the loss of his big brother.

A generation later, against a background of the social changes of the inter-war years, King George V's eldest son Prince Edward (David) rebelled against the blind obedience to orders demanded of him by a father who, when he was a child, had come between him and his mother. Had King George been able to find it in him to exercise tolerance during his son's prolonged adolescence, the course of royal history might have been changed. In the event, he came down heavily against David's insubordination and found scapegoats for the anger which should have been directed at his neglectful but affable father, King Edward VII, in his sons. David and Bertie may not have been rivals for the love of the King's doting mother Queen Alexandra but they were certainly rivals for the love of his wife Queen Mary.

Disapproving of almost every aspect of David's life, from his dress to his choice of friends, King George converted a foolish, fun-loving 'child' into an angry and ultimately subversive adult. He only became a more caring father when, after a lifetime of service to the mother country his people gave him the unconditional love that he had lacked as a child. He may have had shortcomings as a father but as a son to his people he was without fault.

David, King George V's heir, resembled his self-indulgent grandfather. He had a better relationship with King Edward VII than with his father who appeared to him to be not only bigoted but constantly disapproving. David's naturally ebullient feelings were suppressed by his parents in the interests of training him for kingship. As a young adult, like his grandfather and much to his parents' disgust, he formed liaisons with a number of women. Although unable to admit it, he admired his father's genuine patriotism, but as King Edward VIII he directed this admiration towards the distorted nationalistic 'patriotism' of Nazi Germany. In the shadow of the Second World War the British establishment became increasingly suspicious of his fascination with Nazi ideology and particularly with his relationship with Joachim von Ribbentrop, the German envoy in Britain.

King Edward VIII reigned for only 326 days after the death of his father. Forced out of the country by the leaders of both Church and state, he was secretly suspected of becoming a security risk. The stratagem of banning his marriage to the American divorcée Mrs Wallis Simpson was used to banish him. The King had refused to end his relationship with Mrs Simpson after his proclamation. When she was granted a decree nisi at Ipswich Assizes on 27 October 1936 he announced to Stanley Baldwin, the Prime Minister, that he intended marrying Mrs Simpson as soon as her divorce was made absolute. The Church, Queen Mary and the Cabinet (the latter invoking various precedents) refused to consider a marriage which would result in Mrs Simpson becoming Queen Consort. The King insisted that he was unable to live without the woman he loved, and on 10 December 1936 he was forced to sign the Instrument of Abdication, leaving the throne to his brother Bertie, the Duke of York. Kept in the dark about King Edward VIII's enchantment with the enemy, the British people were sorry to see him go.

Like his father before him, Bertie, Duke of York, was second choice for

King. Like his father, he was anxious, inarticulate and unprepared for the role. He had greatness thrust upon him by a war that gave him a status he had never sought. He and his wife Lady Elizabeth Bowes-Lyon, crowned King George VI and Queen Elizabeth in May 1937, helped to restore to the monarchy a popularity not seen since the reign of King George V and Queen Mary.

By the time of her death in 1953, the Dowager Queen Mary had lost her parents, her brother Prince Frank, her husband, her sons Prince John, Prince George, Duke of Kent (in an air crash in 1942) and Bertie (from cancer in 1952). She had thus lost most of the 'jewels' in her crown but not the monarchical role that she had craved. Her attachment to the monarchy remained firm and she neither condemned nor criticized it. She had known that Prince Eddy was unsuited to be King, but she had agreed to marry him. She had accepted Prince George's hand in marriage despite her realization that she would be marrying her intellectual inferior. She had even supported her son David whose morality she deplored. She would certainly support her son Bertie, knowing his weaknesses but appreciating his strengths. She accepted the psychological difficulties of Bertie's younger brother Prince Henry, later the Duke of Gloucester, and the homosexuality and drug abuse of the youngest of all, Prince George, later the Duke of Kent. As far as she was concerned her heirs were free to behave as badly as they wished as long as such behaviour was in private and did not bring the monarchy into disrepute. Queen Mary lived long enough to see the new King and Queen, in their wartime role, bring fresh honours to the House of Windsor.

In the immediate post-war years, despite the financial hardship and unemployment that resulted, the British people knew that King George VI and Queen Elizabeth, who had gone through the war with them, had shared their hopes and fears. Now that the war was over they found that the Royal Family was still by their side as the Festival of Britain celebrated the birth of the post-war era.

With the abdication of King Edward VIII, the legacy of sexual need posing as love (ironically passed on by the seemingly asexual King

George V) seemed to have come to an end. King Edward VIII's brother King George VI showed no interest in sexual philandering. He had no sons to bully, as his father had bullied him, and when the reins of monarchy were handed over to his daughter Princess Elizabeth, on her father's death in 1952, it seemed reasonable to assume that the pattern of promiscuity introduced by King Edward VII had now ended.

Queen Elizabeth II carries on the tradition emulated by her revered grandfather King George V. Living as he did in the monarchical past, she wears the clothes of an earlier time and, like her grandmother Queen Mary, has not changed her hair-style since her accession. Not for her 'the more things change the more they stay the same'. She abhors change but, as Princess Elizabeth, had married a man whose fractured upbringing was not dissimilar to that of her father. The Duke of Edinburgh's father, Prince Andrew of Greece, had abandoned his wife shortly after the family had been helped to escape to France from a revolution in Greece by King George V. The young Prince Philip was brought up by his deaf mother and his four elder sisters. With no father on whom to model himself, Prince Philip relied on naval discipline to bring up his son Prince Charles. Determined, true to form, to 'make a man of him' he sent Prince Charles away to a school whose harsh discipline was quite unsuited to his son's timid personality. The combination of absentee parents (constitutional duties following the death of King George VI took Queen Elizabeth and Prince Philip away for months at a time) and a martinet of a father set Prince Charles on a well-trodden royal road.

Encouraged to marry the unhappy, love-seeking Lady Diana Spencer, but refusing to give up his long-standing relationship with a married woman, Prince Charles once again provoked a royal scandal, which was this time brought to the public eye by an intrusive press. When Prince Charles's wife, by then Princess Diana, publicly retaliated against her husband's self-declared adultery the monarchy seemed to be in danger of being replaced by a republic. Ironically, it was Princess Diana's tragic death at the age of thirty-six that made the British people realize that Royalty was a role model for other families only if their indiscretions were kept well hidden. Having been blamed for hounding the Princess to her death, and now bound to silence, the press called a moratorium and finally allowed the monarchy if not to mend its ways at least to keep quiet about them.

King George V had bestowed upon the House of Windsor a status that was almost destroyed by his son King Edward VIII and later by his great-grandson Prince Charles. Despite having grown up in a broken home and being sent away to boarding schools, Prince William and Prince Harry were dearly and manifestly loved by both their mother and Prince Charles. If left in peace by the media, they might yet inherit the mantle of nobility and dignity left to them by their great-great-grandfather King George V.

Select Bibliography

Alice, Princess of Athlone (1966) *Some Reminiscences for My Grandchildren*, London: Evans Brothers.

Arthur, Sir George (1929) *King George V*, London: Jonathan Cape.

Battiscombe, Georgina (1969) *Queen Alexandra*, London: Constable.

Belloc, M.A. (1902) *TRH the Prince and Princess of Wales* London: George Newnes.

Buchan, John (1935) *The King's Grace 1910–1935*, London: Hodder and Stoughton.

Cowles, Virginia (1956) *Edward VII and His Circle*, London: Hamish Hamilton.

Dalton, John (1886) *The Cruise of HMS Bacchante 1879–1882*, London: Macmillan.

Edwards, Anne (1984) *Matriarch*, London: Hodder and Stoughton.

Friedman, Dennis (1993) *Inheritance: A Psychological History of the Royal Family*, London: Sidgwick and Jackson.

Freud, Sigmund (1900) *The Interpretation of Dreams*, London: Allen and Unwin, 1955.

Gibb, Sir Philip (1936) *George the Faithful: George V*, London: Hutchinson.

Gore, John (1941) *King George V*, London: John Murray.

Hibbert, Christopher (1976) *Edward VII*, London: Allen Lane.

Howarth, Peter (1987) *George VI*, London: Hutchinson.

Judd, Dennis (1973) *The Life and Times of George V*, London: Weidenfeld and Nicolson.

Kakar, Sudhir (1997) *Culture and Psyche*, Delhi: Oxford University Press.

Kelley, Kitty (1997) *The Royals*, New York: Warner Books.

Lacey, Robert (1977) *Majesty*, London: Hutchinson.

Lee, Sir Sydney (1925–7) *King Edward VII: A Biography* (two volumes), London: Macmillan.

Longford, Elizabeth (ed.) (1989) *The Oxford Book of Royal Anecdotes*, Oxford: Oxford University Press.

Lutyens, Mary (1980) *Edwin Lutyens*, London: John Murray.

Magnus, Sir Philip (1964) *King Edward the Seventh*, London: John Murray.

Menkes, Suzy (1987) *The Royal Jewels*, London: Grafton Books.

Nicolson, Harold (1952) *King George V*, London: Constable.

Pope-Hennessy James (1959) *Queen Mary*, London: George Allen and Unwin.

Rose, Kenneth (1983) *King George V*, London: Macmillan.

Rutherford, Andrew (ed.) (1994) *The Sayings of Rudyard Kipling*, London: Duckworth.

Smith, A.A. (1932) *Our Sailor King*, London: Shaw.

Souhami, Diana (1997) *Mrs Keppel and Her Daughter*, London: Flamingo.

Thompson, F.M.L. (1988) *The Rise of the Subordinate Society*, London: Fontana.

The Times (1935) *King and People*, London: The Times.

Victoria, Queen (1908) *Letters, Vols 1–3*, London: John Murray.

Walvin, James (1987) *Victorian Values*, London: André Deutsch.

Watson, Francis (1986) 'The Death of George V', *History Today*, Vol. 36, No. 12.

Wheeler-Bennett, John (1958) *King George VI: His Life and Reign*, London, Macmillan.

Windsor, Duke of (1951) *A King's Story*, London: Cassell.

Wortham, H.E. (1931) *Delightful Profession: Edward VII*, London: Jonathan Cape.

Index

231

Family of Queen Alexandra

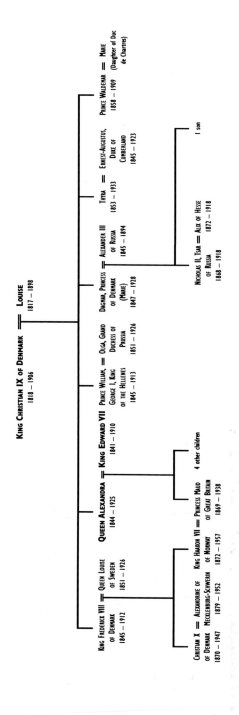